Soft Computing Principles and Integration for Real-Time Service-Oriented Computing

In recent years, soft computing techniques have emerged as a successful tool to understand and analyze the collective behavior of service-oriented computing software. Algorithms and mechanisms of self-organization of complex natural systems have been used to solve problems, particularly in complex systems, which are adaptive, ever-evolving, and distributed in nature across the globe. What fits more perfectly into this scenario other than the rapidly developing era of Fog, IoT, and Edge computing environment? Service-oriented computing can be enhanced with soft computing techniques embedded inside the Cloud, Fog, and IoT systems.

Soft Computing Principles and Integration for Real-Time Service-Oriented Computing explores soft computing techniques that have wide application in interdisciplinary areas. These soft computing techniques provide an optimal solution to the optimization problem using single or multiple objectives. The book focuses on basic design principles and analysis of soft computing techniques. It discusses how soft computing techniques can be used to improve quality-of-service in service-oriented architectures. The book also covers applications and integration of soft computing techniques with a service-oriented computing paradigm. Highlights of the book include:

- A general introduction to soft computing
- An extensive literature study of soft computing techniques and emerging trends
- Soft computing techniques based on the principles of artificial intelligence, fuzzy logic, and neural networks
- The implementation of service-oriented computing with a focus on service composition and orchestration, quality of service considerations, security and privacy concerns, governance challenges, and the integration of legacy systems
- The applications of soft computing in adaptive service composition, intelligent service recommendation, fault detection and diagnosis, service level agreement management, and security
- Such principles underlying service-oriented computing as loose coupling, reusability, interoperability, and abstraction
- An IoT-based framework for real-time data collection and analysis using soft computing

Soft Computing Principles and Integration for Real-Time Service-Oriented Computing

Edited by
Punit Gupta, Dinesh Kumar Saini, and Kashif Zia

CRC Press
Taylor & Francis Group
Boca Raton London New York

CRC Press is an imprint of the
Taylor & Francis Group, an **informa** business

First edition published 2024
2385 NW Executive Center Drive, Suite 320, Boca Raton FL 33431

and by CRC Press
4 Park Square, Milton Park, Abingdon, Oxon, OX14 4RN

CRC Press is an imprint of Taylor & Francis Group, LLC

ISBN: 9781032551883 (hbk)
ISBN: 9781032716701 (pbk)
ISBN: 9781032716718 (ebk)

DOI: 10.1201/9781032716718

Typeset in Garamond
by Newgen Publishing UK

Contents

Preface

In recent years, soft computing techniques have emerged as successful tools to understand/analyze the collective behavior of the service-oriented computing paradigm. Algorithms and mechanisms of self-organization of complex natural systems have been used to solve the problems, particularly in complex systems, which are adaptive, ever-evolving, and distributed in nature across the globe. What fits more perfectly into this scenario other than the rapidly developing era of Fog, IoT, and Edge computing environment? The service-oriented computing (SOC) paradigm performance enhances with soft computing techniques embedded inside the Cloud, Fog, and IoT base computing.

A new era of complexity science is emerging in which motivation for collective problem-solving is coming from soft computing integration with the Cloud, IoT, and Fog computing principles. At the same time, the complexities of the systems are increasing. A manifestation of how demanding the nature of problems would be evident in the upcoming era of the Internet of Things (IoT) and Fog computing. Will Complexity Science residing on the principles of nature be able to tackle this challenge? The real-time usages of the service-oriented computing paradigm with user-define applications depend on a hybrid approach that includes Cloud, Fog, and IoT-based computing with soft computing methodologies.

The chapters proposed for the book include soft computing techniques that have wide applications in interdisciplinary areas. The soft computing techniques provide an optimal solution to the optimization problem using single or multiple objectives. The book focuses on basic design principles and analysis of soft computing techniques. These techniques are used for quality of service (QoS) improvement of the service-oriented architecture-supported computing paradigm. The book will majorly focus on applications and interrogation of the soft computing techniques with a service-oriented computing paradigm.

Chapter 1 covers the general introduction to soft computing. Soft computing is considered the application of thinking and propositioning; it represents the psychological conduct of human intellect. Soft computing is the structure of reasoning insight into machines. Compared to rugged computing, soft computing is open-minded toward imprecision, vulnerability, fragmentary accuracy, and approximation. The foundation of soft computing is to exploit the power to take imprecision, vulnerability, and fractional accuracy to achieve manageability. Soft computing capabilities are now employed as a tool for solving real-life problems. Soft computing methods are adopted because of the uncertainty and vulnerability of the diversified processes. Some soft computing tools employed for this target are genetic algorithm, ant colony optimization, swarm intelligence, and particle swarm optimization. In this chapter, we want to introduce a segment of the methods for recognizing and using its application to lead intelligent practices.

Chapter 2 comprehends an extensive literature study of soft computing techniques and emerging trends recently surfaced through research. It is observed that genetic algorithms, fuzzy sets theory, neural nets, neuro-fuzzy systems, adaptive neuro-fuzzy inference systems (ANFIS), coactive neuro-fuzzy inference systems (CANFIS), evolutionary computing, probabilistic computing, deep learning, convolutional network and Computational Intelligence (CI) have been extensively deployed for various engineering problems individually or in hybrid forms.

Chapter 3 discusses how soft computing techniques are becoming increasingly popular in various fields of technology, from engineering to finance. These techniques are used to solve complex problems that are difficult to solve using traditional computing techniques. Soft computing techniques are based on the principles of artificial intelligence, fuzzy logic and neural networks. In recent years, the applications of soft computing techniques have grown significantly. These techniques are being used to solve a wide range of problems, including optimization, forecasting, pattern recognition, and decision-making. One of the most important emerging trends in the applications of soft computing techniques is the use of evolutionary algorithms.

Chapter 4 addresses the challenges organizations may encounter during the implementation of SOC, thoroughly examining intricate aspects such as service composition and orchestration, QoS considerations, security and privacy concerns, governance challenges, and the integration of legacy systems. To top it off, the chapter delves into emerging trends within SOC, including microservice architectures, serverless computing, cloud-native computing, containerization, orchestration, and the integration of artificial intelligence (AI). By providing valuable insights into future research avenues, this comprehensive chapter equips practitioners and researchers alike with the knowledge and tools to navigate the ever-evolving landscape of SOC and unlock its transformative potential in modern software architectures.

Chapter 5 explores the role of soft computing methodologies in service-oriented computing, focusing on their fundamentals, applications, and benefits. The applications of soft computing in adaptive service composition, intelligent service recommendation, fault detection and diagnosis, service level agreement (SLA) management, and security demonstrate the diverse and practical applications of these methodologies. Embracing soft computing techniques empowers organizations to create intelligent, adaptable, and secure service-oriented environments, ultimately leading to improved service quality, customer satisfaction, and business success.

Chapter 6 covers the five fundamental principles of service-oriented computing: modularity, loose coupling, abstraction, encapsulation, and reusability.

Modularity is the concept of breaking down a system into smaller, more manageable components. This allows for the system to be more easily maintained and updated, as well as to be more easily scaled up or down. In service-oriented computing, this principle is applied by breaking down a system into individual services that can be independently developed, deployed, and managed. Loose coupling is the concept of keeping components of a system independent of each other. This allows for the components to be more easily changed or replaced without affecting the other components.

Chapter 7 highlights the possibilities of tailored healthcare remedies, adaptable educational settings, evidence-based decision-making, and instantaneous data analysis. Subsequently, an analysis is conducted to examine the potential factors that are influencing the development of SOC with regard to its social advantages in these specific areas. The utilization of SOC has the capacity to transform the provision of services across multiple domains and yield considerable societal advantages by capitalizing on its capacity to augment service delivery, foster cooperation, and advance constructive social transformation.

Chapter 8 presents the key focus, which includes cloud computing and service-oriented architecture (SOA), overview of agricultural business management, cloud computing service models and a platform for agriculture business. The service-oriented architecture for agriculture business describes using case studies and success stories of cloud computing in agricultural business management.

Chapter 9 discusses in detail the introduction to principles underlining SOC, such as loose coupling, reusability, interoperability, and abstraction. Their impact on aspects such as business agility, operational efficiency, and the creation of flexible IT infrastructure is taken into account. Transitioning to SOC is not without challenges, and this chapter considers the technical and organizational complexity that can complicate this process. The chapter provides a careful look at strategies that can address these challenges, emphasizing the importance of strategic planning, meticulous execution, robust governance, and effective change management.

Chapter 10 covers an IoT-based framework for real-time data collection, analysis using soft computing. The data produced using a rainfall sensor, soil moisture sensor, soil PH sensor, and soil NPK sensor, respectively. The real time data is stored inside the IoT cloud platform for further analysis. The analysis of the data related to the soil health is analyzed using supervised machine learning methodologies. The presented framework will be helpful for farmers to decide the crop type's cultivation. The cultivation of crop classification relies on features of the sensor nodes, that is. acting as input parameter to machine learning approaches.

Chapter 11 presents the service-oriented architecture and usages of SaaS model in real time application of service-oriented computing using case studies followed with some real time cloud service providers services. The performance of the service-oriented computing paradigm can be improved using soft computing approaches. The soft computing approaches can be integrated with the cloud for better outcomes in terms of time, cost, and efficiency of the system. The integrated system provides the quality of service with performance metrics.

Chapter 12 covers the type of computing that uses techniques such as fuzzy logic, neural networks, and evolutionary algorithms to solve complex problems. By combining these techniques with Cloud, Fog, and IoT-based computing systems, system designers can create more efficient, reliable, and secure systems. For example, cloud computing can be used to store data and provide computing power for applications.

Chapter 13 covers a comprehensive review during 2000–2023 in applying intelligent techniques to solve soft-computing related problems. Soft computing also collaborates with various intelligent techniques used. (1) neural networks (NNs); (2) fuzzy logic; (3) genetic algorithm; (4) decision tree; (5) case base reasoning; (6) Probabilistic Reasoning (PR); and (7) Evolutionary Computation (EC) and other techniques of soft computing.

We hope that the works published in this Book will be able to serve the concerned communities of machine learning and healthcare society.

Acknowledgments

The editors are thankful to the authors and reviewers who contributed to this book with their scientific work and useful comments.

Editors

Punit Gupta

Dr. Punit Gupta is currently associate professor in the Department of Computer and Communication Engineering at Manipal University Jaipur, India. He received his PhD in Computer Science and Engineering from Jaypee University of Information Technology, Solan, India. He is a gold medalist in M.Tech from Jaypee Institute of Information Technology. He has research experience in Internet of Things, Cloud Computing, and Distributed Algorithms and authored more than eighty research papers in reputed journals and international conferences. He is guest editor in *Recent Patent in Computer Science Journal* and editorial manager of *Computer Standards and Interfaces*, and *Journal of Network and Computer Applications*.

He is currently serving as a member of Computer Society of India (CSI), a Member of IEEE, a professional member of ACM. He has organized a special session on Fault Tolerant and Reliable Computing in Cloud, ICIIP 2019, India. He has published more than fifty articles and book chapters in peer-reviewed journals and conferences. He has enthusiastically acted as an organizing committee member of numerous IEEE and other conferences.

Dinesh Kumar Saini

Prof. (Dr.) Dinesh Kumar Saini has a PhD in Computer Science, an M.E. in Software Systems, and an M.Sc. in Technology from one of the premier universities in India, BITS PILANI Rajasthan. Dr. Saini is full professor in the department of Computer and Communication Engineering, School of Computing and Information Technology, Manipal University, Jaipur India. Dr. Kumar Saini has vast experience in academics—as a professor, researcher, and administrator—in Indian universities such as BITS Pilani, and abroad, and a proven record of accomplishment of leadership skills in higher education and the tertiary education sector. He served as dean in the Faculty of Computing and Information Technology of Sohar University in Sultanate of Oman. He has been an associate professor at Sohar University, Oman, since 2008, and an adjunct associate and research fellow at the University of Queensland, Brisbane, Australia between 2010 and 2015. He also was the founder, program coordinator and head of Department for Business Information Technology at Sohal University, Sohar for more than 10 years. He won the Emerald Literati Award for 2018 for his article, "Modeling human factors influencing herding during evacuation," published in the *International Journal of Pervasive Computing and Communications*. His academic credentials are aptly measured by different quantifiable metrics (e.g. Research Gate score 36.36, and Google citation count 976, H-Index-13, i10 Index 22). Dr. Saini believes in the spirit of teamwork and therefore has constantly augmented and consolidated research capacity building of faculties by encouraging and supporting his fellow colleagues and junior faculty members to publish in journals and participate in conferences. This approach is evident in several publications that have been done in collaboration with his teammates in the faculty. He has visited the United States, UK, France, Germany, Austria, UAE, Australia, Russia, Bharin, and the KSA, for academic purposes and learned many good practices in the universities of these developed countries.

Kashif Zia

Dr. Kashif Zia is currently associate professor in the Faculty of Computing and Information Technology, Sohar University, Oman. He obtained his PhD in 2013 from the Institute for Pervasive Computing, Johannes Kepler University in Linz, Austria. Dr. Zia's research interests revolve around socio-technical systems, particularly focusing on crowd dynamics and simulation. His PhD work is related with large-scale, agent-based modeling and analysis of socio-technical systems utilizing parallel and distributed simulation. He has over 100 research publications out of which 21 were published by leading journals.

Contributors

Nameer N. El-Emam completed his PhD with honors in 1997 at Basra University. He is an associate professor in the computer science department, Philadelphia University, Amman, Jordan. He is chair of computer science department and deputy dean of the faculty of Information Technology. His research interest is focusing on Computer Simulation with Intelligent System, Parallel Algorithms, and Soft Computing and Steganography.

Pooja Gupta joined the School of Computing as an assistant professor in July 2019. She received her Masters in Computer Science and Engineering from Uttarakhand Technical University. She has 14 years of experience, including academics and research. Ms. Gupta has published in various journals, including *Inderscience* and *IGI Global,* and for Elsevier Publishers. Her research interest is in Machine Learning and Data Science. She is a strong believer in continuous learning, hence keeps upgrading her skills. She has completed various short-term courses such as three months SFRF from IIT Delhi.

Punit Gupta is a post-doctoral researcher at University College, Dublin. He received his B.Tech degree in Computer Science and Engineering from Rajiv Gandhi Proudyogiki Vishwavidyalaya, Madhya Pradesh, in 2010. He received an M.Tech degree in Computer Science and Engineering in 2012 from Jaypee Institute of Information Technology (Deemed University) in Trust Management in Cloud computing. He is a gold medalist in M.Tech. He received a doctoral degree from Jaypee Institute in 2017.

Shivani Jaswal is assistant professor in Computing at National College, Ireland.

Narendra Kumar completed his M.Tech in Computer Science from BIT Mesra Ranchi, and his PhD from D.D. U Gorakhpur University. Kumar has more than 14 years of experience in the Computer Science and Engineering field. He has been at DIT University as an assistant professor for the last 14 years. His research area includes image processing, optimization techniques and the Internet of Things and Deep Learning. Kumar is editor of two books by CRC Press, Taylor & Francis

Group and Springer Publications. He has published numerous research papers in international journals and conferences, including IEEE, Springer, and Elsevier.

Srabanti Maji is assistant professor in DIT University. She completed her PhD (CSE) in 2013. Her research interests include Bioinformatics, Machine Learning, Data Mining, and Healthcare Science.

Kefaya Qaddoum began teaching at DigiPen this spring in the Department of Computer Science. She earned her PhD in artificial intelligence from the University of Warwick, UK, and has worked internationally, publishing a large body of research—often involving Data Mining, Machine Learning, and more. As a computer scientist, Qaddoum has specialized in applying AI and predictive techniques towards a multitude of problems related to agriculture, cybersecurity, social networks, and other fields.

Dheeraj Rane is associate professor in the Department of CSE, IIST Indore, Madhya Pradesh, Rane received his PhD in computer science and engineering from IIT Indore, and B.Tech in Information Technology from IET (DAVV) Indore. His area of research lies in the fields of cloud computing and IoT.

Pradeep Singh Rawat joined the Department of Computer Science and Engineering as assistant professor in 2010. He received his PhD in Computer Science and Engineering from Uttarakhand Technical University, Dehradun. He received his M.Tech in Information Security and Management from Uttarakhand Technical University, Dehradun, India, and his BTech in Computer Science and Engineering from Kumaun University, Nainital. Pradeep's interests center upon Cloud Computing and its Application, Data Communication and Networking, Data Science Application in Cloud, and Soft Computing. He received the Research Excellence Award 2019–2020 at DITU and is a bronze medalist in his post-graduation (M.Tech) from Uttarakhand Technical University, Dehradun. He has published four papers in SCIE indexed journal with the highest impact factor (6.72). Rawat has more than 11 years of experience in academics. He has published and presented several research papers in various international journals and conferences. He is an active member of the Universal Association of Computer and Electronics Engineers.

Surendra Shukla is assistant professor at the Department of Computer Engineering, SVKM'S NMIMS, Shukla has a PhD (CSE) from DAVV Indore, an M.E. (C.E.) from IET DAVV, Indore, and a B.E. (C.E.) from SGSITS Indore, Diploma (CSE) in Computer Science from SATI, Vidisha.

Maanas Singal is a CSE graduate with interest in varied fields, especially Aerospace, Physics, and Applied Mathematics. In the field of Computer Science, he finds the most interesting branches are Cloud Computing, and DevOps along with an interest in cross-platform application development. He is proficient in Linux Automation using Ansible, and has a core knowledge of basic languages along with a passion for AI/ML. He aspires to be an astronaut, or a research scientist at space agencies such as ISRO, ESA, and NASA. His aim is to develop flight automation software programs for companies such as SPACEX, Blue Origin, Virgin Galactic, Boeing, and others.

Prateek Kumar Soni is a PhD scholar at ABV-Indian Institute of Information Technology and Management, Gwalior, India.

Garima Verma has been assistant professor in the School of Computing, DIT University since 2013. Garima received her PhD in Computer Science Engineering from DIT University in 2018, and M.Tech in Computer Science Engineering from Uttarakhand Technical University in 2011. Garima has Qualified UGC Net in Computer Science and received a gold medal (First Merit) in M.Tech from Uttarakhand Technical University. Garima's research interests includes Cloud Computing, Blockchain, and Machine Learning, particularly the security aspects of Cloud Computing. The techniques she is working on are Attribute-based Encryption, De-duplication, VM Migration, Identity-based encryption, and secret sharing encryption. She has over 17 years of industry and academic experience. Before DIT University, she has worked with CMC as a software developer and NIET Greater Noida as an assistant professor.

Rohit Verma is currently assistant professor and program director of the PG Dip in Cyber Security course at the School of Computing, National College of Ireland, Dublin. Previously, he was a postdoctoral researcher at Insight SFI Research Centre for Data Analytics, Dublin City University. I worked on the EU H2020 funded project TRACTION. He was part of the Performance Engineering Laboratory under the supervision of Prof. Gabriel-Miro Muntean. Verma also had a stint with Manipal Institute of Technology, MAHE, Manipal, India, as an assistant professor (NIRF Ranking #8). He received a PhD in Computer Science and Engineering from the Indian Institute of Technology, Indore. He was part of the Service Computing Lab under the supervision of Dr. Abhishek Srivastava, where he conducted and led research activities in service computing and mobile computing. His research was geared toward enabling the computing environment over the resource-constrained environment. Before pursuing a research career, he had a brief industrial stint at Marvell and VMware.

Chapter 1

Soft Computing Techniques Design and Analysis

Kefaya Qaddoum[1] and Nameer N. El-Emam[2]

[1]*The Department of Computer Science, Digipen Institute of Technology, Washington, United States*

[2]*Department of Computer Science, Philadelphia University, Jordan*

1.1 Introduction

Soft Computing Techniques have become increasingly popular in recent years due to their ability to solve complex problems that are difficult or impossible to solve with traditional approaches. This chapter will provide an overview of soft computing techniques, including their design and analysis. Next, we will explore the main principles behind soft computing techniques, such as fuzzy logic, neural networks, and evolutionary algorithms, and examine how they can be applied to different domains. Additionally, we will discuss the advantages and limitations of soft computing techniques and some recent developments in the field. By the end of this chapter, readers will better understand soft computing techniques and their potential applications.

1.1.1 Soft Computing Techniques Design and Analysis

This chapter is concerned with developing and applying computing techniques capable of handling uncertain, imprecise, and incomplete data. In addition, the chapter explores various soft computing techniques such as fuzzy logic, neural networks, genetic algorithms, and swarm intelligence.

DOI: 10.1201/9781032716718-1

The chapter aims to provide a detailed understanding of soft computing techniques and their applications. It also examines the advantages and disadvantages of these techniques and discusses their suitability for different types of problems. Additionally, the chapter focuses on analyzing soft computing techniques and explores various evaluation metrics for assessing their performance.

In this chapter, we delve into the fascinating realm of soft computing techniques, exploring their design principles and conducting a comprehensive analysis of their effectiveness. Soft computing, as a field, encompasses various computational paradigms inspired by biological systems, aiming to address complex problems that are difficult to solve using traditional methods. The chapter introduces readers to the fundamental concepts and principles underlying soft computing and provides insights into the design and analysis of these techniques.

Section 1.2: Introduction to Soft Computing The chapter begins with an overview of soft computing, highlighting its interdisciplinary nature and significance in tackling real-world challenges. Next, we discuss the motivation behind developing soft computing techniques, emphasizing their ability to handle uncertainty, imprecision, and incomplete information.

Section 1.3: Design Principles of Soft Computing Techniques This section explores the design principles that underpin soft computing techniques. We discuss the critical components of soft computing systems, such as fuzzy logic, neural networks, evolutionary computation, and probabilistic reasoning. Each component, including its theoretical foundations and practical applications, is explained in detail. Furthermore, we analyze how these components can be integrated to create hybrid soft computing systems, harnessing the strengths of each approach.

Section 1.4: This section discusses the application of soft computing in the healthcare sector, transportation, and much more.

Section 1.5: Analysis of Soft Computing Techniques In this section, we analyze soft computing techniques. We examine various evaluation metrics and methodologies used to assess the performance and robustness of these techniques. The chapter covers benchmarking, sensitivity analysis, and performance comparison against traditional computing approaches. Additionally, we discuss the interpretation and visualization of soft computing results, addressing the challenges of explaining complex models and making their outputs easier for humans to interpret.

Section 1.6: The importance of soft computing in big data problems and artificial intelligence is studied.

Section 1.7 and 1.8: These sections show parameters for analyzing soft computing techniques and how to interpret the results of soft computing models.

Section 1.9: This section discusses the future directions and challenges in soft computing research. We highlight emerging trends, such as deep learning and swarm intelligence and their potential impact on the field. Additionally, we address the ethical considerations and limitations associated with soft computing techniques, and issues of existing soft computing techniques.

Overall, this chapter aims to equip readers with a comprehensive understanding of the design and analysis of soft computing techniques. By delving into the theoretical foundations, practical applications, and evaluation methodologies, readers will gain the necessary knowledge to utilize these techniques effectively in their research or problem-solving endeavors.

1.2 Introduction to Soft Computing

Soft computing is an interdisciplinary field encompassing computational techniques inspired by biological systems, aiming to tackle complex problems that are difficult to solve using traditional methods. Unlike traditional computing, which relies on precise mathematical models and deterministic algorithms, soft computing embraces inherent uncertainty, imprecision, and incomplete information in real-world scenarios. Furthermore, by drawing inspiration from human-like intelligence and adaptive behavior, soft computing techniques offer powerful tools to address challenging problems across various domains.

1.2.1 Motivation for Soft Computing

The motivation behind developing soft computing techniques stems from recognizing that many real-world problems are characterized by ambiguity, vagueness, and uncertainty. Traditional computing approaches often struggle to handle these inherent complexities, as they rely on rigid and precise models. Soft computing, on the other hand, embraces the imperfections and approximations inherent in real-world data, enabling the development of robust and adaptive systems [1]. One of the primary motivations for soft computing is to address the pervasive presence of uncertainty and imprecision in real-world problems. Traditional computing techniques assume complete problem-domain knowledge and precise data inputs. However, data may be incomplete, noisy, or inherently uncertain in many practical scenarios. Soft computing techniques provide the means to handle and process such uncertain and imprecise information, allowing for more realistic and practical problem-solving.

When it comes to emulating human-like intelligence, soft computing draws inspiration from the remarkable ability of human intelligence to handle complex and uncertain situations. Human cognition exhibits adaptability, robustness, and the ability to make decisions based on incomplete or ambiguous information. Soft computing techniques attempt to replicate these qualities in computational systems, aiming to develop intelligent systems that can learn, adapt, and make decisions in a human-like manner. By mimicking human intelligence, soft computing techniques can tackle problems beyond traditional computing approaches' capabilities. Moreover, soft computing can address complex and non-linear relationships.

Many real-world problems involve complex and non-linear relationships that traditional mathematical models cannot easily capture. However, soft computing techniques like neural networks and fuzzy logic, excel at discovering and representing these complex relationships. Neural networks can learn intricate patterns and correlations from data, enabling them to model highly non-linear relationships effectively. Fuzzy logic provides a flexible framework for handling vague and imprecise concepts, allowing for more nuanced and human-like reasoning in complex problem domains [2].

Soft computing has the required robustness in the existence of noisy and incomplete data in real-world data, which is often plagued by noise, missing values, and outliers. Soft computing techniques are designed to be robust in such noisy and incomplete data. For example, neural networks can generalize from incomplete or noisy training samples, making accurate predictions even when faced with imperfect data. In addition, soft computing techniques' inherent adaptability and self-learning capabilities contribute to their robustness, as they can adapt their models and decisions based on the available data [3].

Soft computing scalability and flexibility allow a better way to handle problems of varying complexity and scale. Evolutionary computation, for instance, can efficiently explore large solution spaces to find optimal or near-optimal solutions [4], [5]. The ability of soft computing techniques to deal with high-dimensional data, handle real-time processing, and adapt to changing environments makes them well-suited for dynamic and complex problem domains. Another motivation to use soft computing techniques is that it is easy to find applications across various disciplines and industries. These techniques have been successfully employed in finance, healthcare, engineering, robotics, image and speech processing, and data analysis [6], [7]. By providing powerful tools to handle uncertainty and imprecision, soft computing enables the development of intelligent systems capable of addressing complex challenges in diverse domains.

1.3   Soft Computing Techniques

Soft computing comprises several key components, each contributing to the overall capability of the approach. These components include fuzzy logic, neural networks, evolutionary computation, and probabilistic reasoning.

1.3.1   Fuzzy Logic

Fuzzy logic provides a framework to handle imprecise and uncertain information by allowing degrees of truth or membership rather than binary values. It allows for a more nuanced representation and reasoning in situations where traditional logic falls short. Unlike traditional binary logic, which relies on crisp, precise values, fuzzy logic allows for gradual membership of truth values ranging from 0 to 1. Fuzzy logic is based on the concept of fuzzy sets, which capture the degree to which an element belongs to a particular set. This flexibility enables soft computing systems to model and reason with uncertain, imprecise, or incomplete information, making fuzzy logic a fundamental component of soft computing.

1.3.2   Neural Networks

Neural networks, inspired by the human brain's structure and function, can learn from data and extract patterns and relationships. As a result, these networks offer powerful tools for pattern recognition, data analysis, and decision-making. These networks consist of interconnected artificial neurons that process and transmit information. Neural networks learn from data, detect complex patterns, and make predictions or classifications. With their ability to model non-linear relationships and adapt their internal parameters through training, neural networks form a core component of soft computing, enabling intelligent analysis and decision-making in various domains. They excel in pattern recognition, classification, and prediction tasks and have been instrumental in various fields, including image and speech processing.

1.3.3   Evolutionary Computation

Evolutionary computation draws inspiration from Darwinian evolution to solve optimization and search problems. Through genetic algorithms, evolutionary strategies, and genetic programming, evolutionary computation explores a population of potential solutions, adapting and evolving them over generations to find optimal or near-optimal solutions. Evolutionary computation generates a population of candidate solutions and applies genetic operators like selection, crossover, and mutation to evolve and improve the solutions over generations. This component of soft computing enables efficient exploration of large solution spaces, leading to the discovery of near-optimal or optimal solutions.

1.3.4   Probabilistic Reasoning

Probabilistic reasoning forms the basis for handling uncertainty and making decisions under incomplete or noisy data conditions. This component involves representing and manipulating probabilities to model uncertainty and dependencies between variables. Techniques such as Bayesian networks and probabilistic graphical models enable the integration of prior knowledge and observed evidence to infer posterior probabilities and make informed decisions. Probabilistic reasoning provides a principled and mathematically rigorous framework for uncertainty modeling, making it a crucial component of soft computing.

1.3.5 Machine Learning

Machine learning encompasses algorithms and techniques that automatically enable systems to learn and improve from data without explicit programming. This component includes supervised learning, unsupervised learning, and reinforcement learning. Supervised learning involves training a model on labeled examples to make predictions or classifications. Unsupervised learning focuses on finding patterns and structures in unlabeled data. Reinforcement learning deals with learning optimal behaviors through interactions with an environment. Integrated into soft computing, machine learning techniques enhance a systems' ability to adapt, generalize, and improve performance based on data.

1.3.6 Hybrid Approaches

Hybrid approaches involve combining and integrating different soft computing techniques to leverage their strengths and address complex problems more effectively. By combining fuzzy logic with neural networks, evolutionary computation, or other components, hybrid approaches can handle diverse data types, model complex relationships, and make intelligent decisions in dynamic and uncertain environments. As a result, hybridization enables soft computing systems to overcome limitations and achieve higher performance, making hybridization an essential component of soft computing design and analysis.

While the components of soft computing are distinct, they often synergize and complement each other when combined in hybrid systems. The interplay between fuzzy logic, neural networks, evolutionary computation, and probabilistic reasoning allows for the creation powerful computational models capable of handling diverse challenges. Hybrid soft computing systems leverage the strengths of each component, providing enhanced problem-solving capabilities and increased flexibility.

1.4 Applications of Soft Computing

Soft computing techniques have found applications across a wide range of domains. They have been successfully employed in pattern recognition, data mining, optimization, control systems, decision support systems, and robotics. These techniques enable the development of intelligent systems that can learn from experience, adapt to changing environments, and make informed decisions in complex and uncertain scenarios [8], [9].

Soft computing techniques have been widely applied across various disciplines, demonstrating their versatility and effectiveness in addressing complex problems [10], [11]. This section explores the multidisciplinary nature of soft computing techniques, highlighting their applications in diverse fields and their ability to tackle challenging problems that span different domains.

1.4.1   Healthcare and Medical Diagnosis

Soft computing techniques have made significant contributions to healthcare and medical diagnosis. In this domain, soft computing is employed for disease diagnosis, prognosis, medical imaging analysis, and drug discovery. Neural networks, for instance, have been used to analyze medical images and detect abnormalities or tumors with high accuracy. Fuzzy logic-based systems assist in medical decision-making by handling uncertainties and imprecise information. Soft computing techniques enable healthcare professionals to make more accurate diagnoses, develop personalized treatment plans, and improve patient outcomes.

1.4.2   Finance and Investment Analysis

Soft computing techniques have proven valuable in the finance industry, particularly in investment analysis and decision-making. Neural networks and evolutionary computation are utilized to predict stock prices, model financial markets, and optimize investment portfolios. Fuzzy logic-based systems aid in risk assessment, fraud detection, and credit scoring. By leveraging soft computing techniques, financial institutions can analyze complex market data, make informed investment decisions, and manage risks effectively.

1.4.3   Transportation and Traffic Management

Soft computing techniques play a crucial role in transportation and traffic management systems. Neural networks and fuzzy logic-based systems are used for traffic prediction, congestion management, route optimization, and intelligent transportation systems. These techniques enable real-time traffic data analysis, adaptive signal control, and efficient traffic flow management. Soft computing helps alleviate congestion, reduce travel time, and enhance overall transportation efficiency, improving urban mobility.

1.4.4   Environmental Modeling and Management

Soft computing techniques find applications in environmental modeling and management. Fuzzy logic-based systems assist in air and water quality monitoring, ecological modeling, and environmental impact assessment. Neural networks are employed for climate modeling, weather prediction, and renewable energy forecasting. By utilizing soft computing techniques, environmental scientists and policymakers can analyze complex environmental data, make informed decisions, and develop sustainable management strategies.

1.4.5 Robotics and Automation

Soft computing techniques have significantly impacted the field of robotics and automation. Neural networks and evolutionary computation are employed for robot control, motion planning, object recognition, and autonomous decision-making. Fuzzy logic-based systems facilitate human–robot interaction and reasoning under uncertainty. Soft computing techniques enable robots to adapt to changing environments, learn from experience, and perform complex tasks in real-world settings.

1.4.6 Natural Language Processing and Sentiment Analysis

Soft computing techniques have revolutionized natural language processing and sentiment analysis. Neural networks, particularly deep learning models, have succeeded in language translation, text classification, sentiment analysis, and chatbot development. By leveraging soft computing techniques, natural language processing systems can understand and generate human-like language, extract meaning from textual data, and provide valuable insights for various applications, including social media analysis, customer feedback analysis, and information retrieval.

1.4.7 Engineering and Industrial Applications

Soft computing techniques find extensive applications in engineering and industrial domains. Neural networks, fuzzy logic-based systems, and evolutionary computation are utilized for process optimization, fault diagnosis, quality control, and predictive maintenance. These techniques enable efficient design optimization, adaptive control, and reliable operation of complex engineering systems. Soft computing techniques improve performance, reduce costs, and enhance reliability in diverse engineering and industrial applications.

1.5 Analysis of Soft Computing Techniques

In this section, we focus on analyzing soft computing techniques. We examine various evaluation metrics and methodologies used to assess the performance and robustness of these techniques [12]. The chapter covers benchmarking, sensitivity analysis, and performance comparison against traditional computing approaches. Additionally, we discuss the interpretation and visualization of soft computing results, addressing the challenges of explaining complex models and making their outputs more interpretable to humans [13].

1.5.1 Evaluation Metrics

Evaluation metrics play a crucial role in assessing the performance and effectiveness of soft computing techniques. These metrics provide quantitative measures that enable researchers and practitioners to compare different algorithms, validate their models, and make informed decisions regarding their applicability [14], [15]. This section explores various evaluation metrics commonly used in designing and analyzing soft computing techniques, highlighting their significance and considerations for practical evaluation [16], [17], [18], [19].

1.5.1.1 Accuracy

Accuracy is a fundamental evaluation metric used to assess the performance and effectiveness of soft computing techniques. It measures the degree of correctness or agreement between the predicted outputs of a model and the ground truth values. This section focuses on the concept of accuracy in soft computing techniques, discussing its significance, calculation, and considerations for accurate assessment.

- **Importance of Accuracy**

Accuracy is a crucial indicator of the reliability and capability of soft computing techniques. It quantifies the ability of a model to make correct predictions or classifications, reflecting its overall performance in capturing patterns and generalizing from the available data. Accurate predictions are crucial in various application domains, including healthcare, finance, image recognition, natural language processing, and so forth. Therefore, achieving high accuracy is a primary objective in designing and analyzing soft computing techniques.

- **Calculation of Accuracy**

Accuracy calculation depends on the specific task and the data type being analyzed. For example, in classification tasks, accuracy is typically computed as the ratio of correctly classified instances to the total number of instances in the dataset. For binary classification problems, it can be calculated using the formula:

$$\text{Accuracy} = (TP + TN) / (TP + TN + FP + FN) \qquad (1.1)$$

where TP represents the number of true positives (correctly predicted positive instances), TN represents the number of true negatives (correctly predicted negative instances), FP represents the number of false positives (incorrectly predicted positive instances), and FN represents the number of false negatives (incorrectly predicted negative instances).

In regression tasks, accuracy is often measured using metrics such as the coefficient of determination (R-squared) or mean squared error (MSE). R-squared indicates the proportion of variance in the dependent variable that the model explains, while MSE measures the average squared difference between the predicted and actual values.

- Considerations for Accurate Assessment

When evaluating the accuracy of soft computing techniques, several considerations should be taken into account:

- Dataset Quality: The quality and representativeness of the dataset used for evaluation directly impact the accuracy of the technique. A diverse and unbiased dataset, with sufficient instances and appropriate distribution across different classes or target values, enhances the reliability of accuracy assessment.
- Class Imbalance: In scenarios where the dataset exhibits imbalanced class distributions, accuracy alone may not provide a comprehensive evaluation. It is essential to consider additional metrics such as precision, Recall, or F1 score, which account for the costs associated with misclassifying instances from different classes.
- Overfitting and Generalization: Soft computing techniques may achieve high accuracy on the training data but fail to generalize well to unseen data. Overfitting occurs when the model excessively adapts to the training data, resulting in poor performance in new instances. Therefore, it is crucial to assess accuracy on separate validation or testing datasets to evaluate the generalization ability of the technique.
- Evaluation Protocol: Choosing appropriate evaluation protocols, such as cross-validation or holdout validation, affects the accuracy assessment. Cross-validation techniques, including k-fold cross-validation, provide a more robust estimation of accuracy by iterative training and testing the model on different subsets of the data.
- Interpretation and Domain Relevance: Accuracy should be interpreted in the context of the specific application domain and the consequences of misclassifications or inaccuracies. Considering the real-world implications of the soft computing technique's performance and how accuracy aligns with the intended goals and requirements is essential.

Accuracy is a vital evaluation metric for assessing the performance and effectiveness of soft computing techniques. Its calculation depends on the task and data type, and on considerations such as dataset quality, class imbalance, overfitting, evaluation protocols, and domain relevance should be considered for accurate assessment. Researchers and practitioners can make informed decisions and improve the design by understanding and appropriately interpreting accuracy.

1.5.1.2 Precision and Recall

Precision and Recall are essential evaluation metrics used to assess the performance and effectiveness of soft computing techniques, particularly in binary classification tasks. In addition, these metrics provide insights into the quality and completeness of predictions made by the model. In this section, we delve into the concepts of precision and recall in soft computing techniques, discussing their significance, calculation, and considerations for accurate evaluation.

- **Precision**

Precision measures the proportion of correctly predicted positive instances among all predicted positive instances. It focuses on the quality of optimistic predictions, indicating the ability of the soft computing technique to avoid false positives. High precision indicates a low rate of false optimistic predictions, reflecting the model's reliability in correctly identifying positive instances.
Precision is calculated using the formula:

$$\text{Precision} = TP / (TP + FP) \tag{1.2}$$

where TP represents the number of true positives (correctly predicted positive instances) and FP represents the number of false positives (incorrectly predicted positive instances).

- **Recall**

Recall measures the proportion of correctly predicted positive instances among all positive instances. It emphasizes the completeness of optimistic predictions, indicating the ability of the soft computing technique to avoid false negatives. High Recall indicates a low rate of false pessimistic predictions, reflecting the ability of the model to capture the majority of positive instances.
The Recall is calculated using the formula:

$$\text{Recall} = TP / (TP + FN) \tag{1.3}$$

where TP represents the number of true positives (correctly predicted positive instances) and FN represents the number of false negatives (incorrectly predicted negative instances).

- **Significance of Precision and Recall**

Precision and Recall provide complementary insights into the performance of soft computing techniques, especially when dealing with imbalanced datasets or situations where the costs of misclassifications differ across classes. By considering both precision and Recall, we gain a comprehensive understanding of the strengths and weaknesses of the model.

Precision helps us evaluate the extent to which optimistic predictions are accurate. It is beneficial in applications where false positives have severe consequences or when we want to ensure high confidence in optimistic predictions.

Recall helps us assess the ability of the model to capture all positive instances. It is essential in scenarios where missing positive instances (false negatives) can have significant consequences, such as in medical diagnosis or anomaly detection.

- **Precision-Recall Trade-off**

Precision and Recall are often in tension with each other. Increasing one metric may lead to a decrease in the other. This trade-off stems from the decision threshold used for classification. Adjusting the threshold can impact the balance between precision and Recall. A more conservative threshold leads to higher precision but lower Recall, while a more lenient threshold leads to higher Recall but lower precision.

Understanding the precision-recall trade-off is crucial in selecting an appropriate operating point for the soft computing technique, depending on the application's specific requirements. In addition, domain knowledge and the consequences of false positives and negatives should guide the choice of the desired balance between precision and Recall.

1.5.1.3 F1 Score

The F1 score is a single metric that combines precision and Recall into a balanced measure. It is the harmonic mean of precision and Recall and provides a single value to evaluate the overall performance of the soft computing technique.
The F1 score is calculated using the formula:

$$F1 \text{ Score} = 2 * (\text{Precision} * \text{Recall}) / (\text{Precision} + \text{Recall}) \tag{1.4}$$

The F1 score is instrumental when precision and Recall must be considered together, providing a summary measure that balances their contributions.

- **Considerations for Accurate Evaluation**

When using precision and recall for evaluating soft computing techniques, it is essential to consider the following:

> **Imbalanced Datasets**: If the dataset has imbalanced class distributions, precision and recall offer valuable insights beyond accuracy, as accuracy alone may be misleading.
> **Evaluation Protocol**: The choice of appropriate evaluation protocols.

1.5.1.4 Mean Squared Error (MSE)

Mean Squared Error (MSE) is a commonly used evaluation metric in soft computing techniques, especially in regression tasks. It quantifies the average squared difference between the predicted and actual values, providing a measure of the model's accuracy in estimating continuous or numerical outputs. This section focuses on the concept of MSE in soft computing techniques, discussing its significance, calculation, and considerations for accurate evaluation.

- **Importance of MSE**

MSE is a fundamental metric that enables assessing the predictive performance and precision of soft computing techniques in regression tasks. It allows researchers and practitioners to evaluate how well the model approximates the actual values and quantifies the magnitude of errors made by the model. Minimizing MSE is often a primary objective in the design and analysis of soft computing techniques.

- **Calculation of MSE**

The calculation of MSE involves computing the squared difference between the predicted values and the corresponding actual values and then taking the average of these squared differences. Mathematically, MSE is calculated as follows:

$$MSE = (1/n) * \Sigma(y - \hat{y})^2 \tag{1.5}$$

where n represents the number of instances, y represents the actual values, and $\hat{y}$ represents the predicted values.

- **Interpreting MSE**

MSE quantitatively measures the average squared deviation between the predicted and actual values. A lower MSE indicates better performance, reflecting a minor average error made by the soft computing technique. By squaring the differences, MSE penalizes more significant errors more than more minor errors, which can provide insights into the variability and dispersion of errors.

- **Considerations for Accurate Evaluation**

When using MSE to evaluate soft computing techniques, the following considerations should be taken into account:

- The scale of the Target Variable: The target variable's scale affects the MSE's magnitude. It is essential to interpret the MSE in the context of the scale of the problem. For example, if the target variable has an extensive range, the resulting MSE may also have a significant value, which should be considered relative to the problem's scale.
- Outliers: MSE is sensitive to outliers, as the squared differences amplify their impact on the overall error. Outliers can disproportionately affect the MSE and potentially skew the evaluation. Therefore, it is essential to identify and handle outliers appropriately to ensure accurate evaluation.
- Comparison with Baseline Models: MSE becomes more meaningful when compared with the MSE of baseline models or alternative techniques. Comparing the MSE of different models or algorithms helps determine the relative improvement or superiority of a particular soft computing technique.
- Generalization: MSE should be evaluated on the training data and separate validation or testing datasets. The model's ability to generalize its predictions to unseen data is crucial. For example, a low MSE on the training data may not guarantee good performance on new instances, indicating potential overfitting.
- Other Variants of MSE: Depending on the specific problem and domain, alternative variants of MSE may be used. For example, Root Mean Squared Error (RMSE) is the square root of MSE and measures the average absolute error between the predicted and actual values. RMSE is often used for better interpretability of the evaluation metric.

MSE is a widely used evaluation metric in soft computing techniques for regression tasks. It quantifies the average squared difference between predicted and actual values, providing insights into the accuracy and precision of the model. Considering the scale of the target variable, handling outliers, comparing with baselines, assessing generalization, and exploring alternative variants of MSE contribute to an accurate evaluation of soft computing techniques.

1.5.1.5 AUC

Area Under the Curve (AUC) is a widely used evaluation metric in soft computing techniques, particularly in binary classification tasks. It quantifies a model's overall performance and discriminative power by measuring the area under the Receiver Operating Characteristic (ROC) curve. This section focuses on the concept of AUC in soft computing techniques, discussing its significance, calculation, and considerations for accurate evaluation.

- Importance of AUC

AUC provides a comprehensive evaluation of the discrimination ability of a soft computing technique in binary classification tasks. It captures the trade-off between the valid positive rate (sensitivity) and the false positive rate (1 – specificity), allowing researchers and practitioners to assess the model's ability to correctly distinguish between positive and negative instances across different classification thresholds. In addition, a higher AUC indicates better discrimination performance, making it a valuable metric for model selection and comparison.

- Calculation of AUC

The calculation of AUC involves constructing the ROC curve and computing the area under it. First, the ROC curve is created by plotting the true positive rate (sensitivity) against the false positive rate (1 – specificity) at various classification thresholds. The AUC is then calculated by integrating the area under this curve.

- Interpreting AUC

AUC ranges from 0 to 1, where a higher value indicates better discrimination performance. For example, an AUC of 0.5 suggests that the model performs no better than random guessing. At the same time, an AUC of 1 represents a perfect classifier that can perfectly distinguish between positive and negative instances. AUC provides a holistic measure of the model's ability to rank instances correctly and is insensitive to the classification threshold, making it a robust evaluation metric.

- Considerations for Accurate Evaluation

When using AUC to evaluate soft computing techniques, the following considerations should be taken into account:

Imbalanced Datasets: AUC is less affected by imbalanced class distributions compared to accuracy. It provides a reliable evaluation even when the dataset has a significant class imbalance, where the number of instances from one class significantly exceeds the other. This makes AUC particularly useful in real-world applications where class imbalances are common.

Threshold Selection: AUC is not directly tied to a specific classification threshold. It assesses the overall discrimination performance of the model across all possible thresholds. However, depending on the application's specific requirements, it may be necessary to select an appropriate threshold to achieve the desired balance between true positive and false favorable rates.

Comparison with Baseline Models: AUC becomes more meaningful when compared with the AUC of baseline models or alternative techniques. Comparing AUC values helps determine the relative improvement or superiority of a particular soft computing technique.

Interpretation: The interpretation of AUC depends on the specific context and application. It is essential to consider the consequences of false positives and false negatives and the domain-specific costs associated with classification errors.

Confidence Intervals: When reporting AUC, it is beneficial to provide confidence intervals to capture the uncertainty in the estimated AUC value. This provides a complete understanding of the model's performance and enables robust comparisons between different techniques.

AUC is a practical evaluation metric in soft computing techniques for binary classification tasks. It provides a comprehensive assessment of the discrimination performance of a model, regardless of the classification threshold. Considering class imbalances, threshold selection, comparison with baselines, interpretation, and reporting confidence intervals contribute to accurately evaluating soft computing techniques using AUC.

1.6   Importance of Soft Computing in the Era of Big Data and Artificial Intelligence

1.6.1   *Soft Computing Methodologies Benchmarking*

Benchmarking is a crucial aspect of the design and analysis of soft computing techniques. It involves systematically evaluating and comparing different algorithms or models against well-defined datasets and evaluation metrics [20], [21]. This section focuses on benchmarking in soft computing techniques, discussing its significance, key considerations, and best practices for effective benchmarking.

1.6.2   *Significance of Benchmarking*

Benchmarking plays a vital role in assessing soft computing techniques' performance, strengths, and weaknesses. It enables researchers and practitioners to objectively compare the performance of different algorithms or models on standardized datasets, fostering advancements in the field.. Furthermore, by establishing a common ground for evaluation, benchmarking provides valuable insights into state-of-the-art techniques, promotes fair comparisons, and facilitates the identification of novel approaches.

1.6.3   Key Considerations for Benchmarking

To ensure reliable and meaningful benchmarking in soft computing techniques, the following considerations should be taken into account:

- Datasets: The choice of datasets is crucial for benchmarking. Selecting representative datasets that cover a wide range of scenarios and challenges relevant to the problem domain is essential. In addition, datasets should be diverse, balanced, and appropriately labeled to evaluate different techniques fairly.
- Evaluation Metrics: Appropriate evaluation metrics are essential for fair and comprehensive benchmarking. The choice of metrics should align with the specific task and objectives of the soft computing technique. Typical metrics include accuracy, precision, Recall, F1 score, AUC, and mean squared error (MSE). It is also essential to consider additional domain-specific metrics if applicable.
- Baseline Models: Establishing baseline models is crucial for comparative analysis. Baselines serve as reference points and provide a context for evaluating the performance of new or advanced techniques. Baseline models can include traditional machine learning algorithms, well-established soft computing techniques, or previous state-of-the-art approaches.
- Experimental Setup: Consistency in the experimental setup is essential for reliable benchmarking. Factors such as preprocessing techniques, feature selection or extraction methods, hyperparameter tuning, and cross-validation protocols should be clearly defined and standardized across different techniques. This ensures fair comparisons and reproducibility of results.
- Statistical Significance: It is crucial to determine the statistical significance of observed differences between techniques. Statistical tests such as t-tests or paired t-tests can be used to assess whether observed performance differences are statistically significant or simply due to random chance.

1.6.3.1   Best Practices for Effective Benchmarking

To ensure the effective benchmarking in soft computing techniques, the following best practices are recommended:

Reproducibility: Document and share the experimental setup, code, and parameters used in benchmarking to enable reproducibility and promote transparency. This allows other researchers to validate and build upon the results.

Open Datasets and Platforms: Utilize open datasets and benchmarking platforms that encourage collaboration and standardization. This fosters a community-driven approach and allows for broader participation, resulting in more robust evaluations.

Continual Updating: Benchmarking is an ongoing process, and it is crucial to keep up with the advancements in the field. Regularly update the benchmark datasets, evaluation metrics, and baseline models to reflect the current state of the art.

Community Engagement: Engage with the research community to gather feedback, incorporate suggestions, and promote collaboration. Participate in benchmarking competitions or challenges to evaluate the performance of soft computing techniques against others and foster innovation.

Reporting Guidelines: To ensure clear and comprehensive reporting of benchmarking results, follow established reporting guidelines, such as the STARD (Standards for Reporting Diagnostic Accuracy) or CARE (CAse REport) guidelines. This facilitates understanding, reproducibility, and comparability across different studies.

1.7 Sensitivity Analysis

Sensitivity analysis is a critical component of the design and analysis of soft computing techniques. It involves studying the sensitivity of a model's output or performance to changes in input variables or parameters. This section focuses on sensitivity analysis in soft computing techniques, discussing its significance, methods, and considerations for practical analysis.

Significance of Sensitivity Analysis
Sensitivity analysis plays a crucial role in understanding the behavior and robustness of soft computing techniques. It helps researchers and practitioners gain insights into the impact of input variables or parameters on the model's output, performance, or decision-making. In addition, sensitivity analysis provides valuable information for model optimization, parameter tuning, feature selection, and understanding the reliability and stability of the technique [22].

Methods for Sensitivity Analysis
Several methods can be employed for conducting sensitivity analysis in soft computing techniques. Some common approaches include:

One-variable-at-a-time (OVAT) Analysis: In this method, individual input variables or parameters are varied while keeping others fixed. The model's output or performance is observed in response to these variations to independently assess the model's sensitivity to each input variable or parameter.

Partial Derivatives: For models that can be differentiated, partial derivatives can be calculated to measure the sensitivity of the model's output concerning each input variable or parameter. This provides information on the magnitude and direction of the sensitivity.

Sobol's Indices: Based on variance decomposition, Sobol's indices are widely used in sensitivity analysis. They quantify the contribution of each input variable or parameter and their interactions with the overall variance of the model's output. Sobol's indices provide a comprehensive understanding of the relative importance and interactions of input variables or parameters.

Global Sensitivity Analysis: Global sensitivity analysis methods, such as Monte Carlo sampling, Latin hypercube sampling, or variance-based methods, explore the entire input parameter space to assess the sensitivity of the model's output to different combinations of input variables or parameters. These methods provide insights into the overall sensitivity patterns and interactions among variables.

Considerations for Effective Sensitivity Analysis

To ensure practical sensitivity analysis in soft computing techniques, the following considerations should be taken into account:

Input Variable or Parameter Selection: It is essential to carefully select the input variables or parameters to include in the analysis. Focus on variables or parameters that significantly impact the model's output or performance, as studying irrelevant or less influential variables may not yield meaningful insights.

Range of Variation: Define appropriate ranges or distributions for varying the input variables or parameters during sensitivity analysis. Consider both practical constraints and theoretical considerations to ensure a comprehensive exploration of the sensitivity space.

Model Complexity: The complexity of the soft computing technique and the relationship between input variables and the model's output should be considered during sensitivity analysis. More complex models may require sophisticated methods or approximations to analyze sensitivity effectively.

Uncertainty and Noise: Soft computing techniques often operate in environments with uncertainty and noise. Sensitivity analysis should account for these factors to assess the robustness and stability of the model's output or performance in realistic conditions.

Interpretation and Visualization: Sensitivity analysis results should be interpreted and visualized appropriately to facilitate understanding and decision-making. Visual representations such as sensitivity plots, tornado diagrams, or heatmaps can help identify important variables or parameters and their impact on the model's output.

Applications of Sensitivity Analysis
Sensitivity analysis in soft computing techniques finds application in various areas, including:

Model Optimization: Sensitivity analysis helps identify critical input variables or parameters that significantly influence the model's performance. This information can guide the optimization process by focusing on important factors.

Feature Selection: Sensitivity analysis can assist in feature selection by identifying relevant features that contribute significantly to the model's output or performance.

1.8 Soft Computing Results Interpreting and Visualizing

Interpreting and visualizing the results of soft computing techniques pose several challenges due to their complex nature and underlying algorithms [23]. This section focuses on the challenges associated with interpreting and visualizing soft computing results, discussing the limitations, considerations, and potential solutions for adequate understanding and communication.

■ **Complexity of Models**
   Soft computing techniques often employ complex models with numerous hidden layers, non-linear activation functions, or ensemble methods. The inherent complexity of these models makes it challenging to interpret the underlying decision-making process. As a result, extracting meaningful insights from complex models and understanding how input variables or parameters influence the output becomes a non-trivial task.

■ **Black Box Nature**
   Soft computing models are often considered "black box" models, meaning that the internal workings and decision rules are not easily understandable by humans. The lack of transparency poses challenges in interpreting the results and explaining the reasoning behind specific predictions or classifications. This hinders the trust and acceptance of soft computing techniques in critical domains where interpretability is essential.

■ **High-Dimensional Data**
   Soft computing techniques are frequently applied to high-dimensional data, such as images, text, or genomic data. Interpreting and visualizing results in high-dimensional spaces pose challenges due to human perception

and comprehension limitations. Traditional visualization techniques may not be suitable for representing complex relationships or patterns in high-dimensional data.

■ **Uncertainty and Confidence Estimation**
Soft computing techniques often encounter uncertainty due to noise in the data or inherent randomness in the algorithms. Interpreting and visualizing uncertainty estimates, confidence intervals, or probabilistic outputs can be challenging. Communicating the uncertainty associated with predictions or classifications becomes crucial for decision-making and trust in the results.

■ **Bias and Fairness**
Understanding and mitigating bias in soft computing results is a significant challenge. Biases can arise from biased training data or inherent biases in the algorithms themselves. Interpreting and visualizing biases, identifying their sources, and ensuring fairness and equity in the results require careful analysis and consideration.

■ **Context and Domain Knowledge**
Interpreting soft computing results often requires domain expertise and contextual understanding. Without proper domain knowledge, it can be challenging to interpret the significance of specific patterns or relationships discovered by the model. Incorporating domain experts in the interpretation process becomes essential to derive meaningful insights and actionable recommendations.

■ **Visualization of High-Dimensional Results**
Visualizing high-dimensional results is a challenging task. Traditional 2D or 3D visualizations may not capture the complexity and richness of the data. Techniques such as dimensionality reduction, clustering, or interactive visualization tools can aid in representing high-dimensional results effectively. However, selecting the appropriate visualization technique and ensuring its accuracy and interpretability remain challenging.

■ **Overfitting and Generalization**
Interpreting and visualizing results in the context of overfitting and generalization is crucial. For example, soft computing models may exhibit high performance on the training data but fail to generalize well to unseen data. Understanding the limitations of the model's generalization capabilities and conveying this information through interpretation and visualization is essential for proper decision-making.

Probabilistic graphical models, such as Bayesian networks or Gaussian processes, can model uncertainty and provide probabilistic outputs. Visualization techniques, such as error bars or density plots, can help convey the uncertainty associated with predictions or classifications. Additionally, techniques like Monte Carlo sampling can be used to explore the uncertainty space and visualize its impact on the results.

■ **Bias and Fairness challenges**

Challenge: Understanding and mitigating bias in soft computing results is significant. Biases can arise from biased training data or inherent biases in the algorithms themselves.

Interpretation and visualization techniques that highlight potential biases in the model's predictions can aid in understanding and addressing bias issues. For example, fairness-aware models and techniques, such as fairness constraints or fairness metrics, can ensure fairness and equity in the results. In addition, visualizations like fairness dashboards or disparity maps can help identify and communicate biases to stakeholders.

■ **Context and Domain Knowledge challenges**

Challenge: Interpreting soft computing results often requires domain expertise and contextual understanding.

Researchers have developed various techniques for interpreting and visualizing Soft Computing results to overcome these challenges. Some of these techniques include:

■ **Feature Importance**

This technique identifies the most essential features contributing to the model's results. This can help to understand which features are most relevant to the problem.

■ **Partial Dependence Plots**

This technique plots the relationship between a feature and the model's output while holding all other features constant. This can help to understand the relationship between individual features and the model's output.

■ **Visualization Techniques**

Various visualization techniques, such as heat maps, scatter plots, and parallel coordinates, can be used to visualize soft computing results. In addition, these techniques can help to identify patterns and relationships in the data.

■ **Model Transparency**

Researchers have developed various techniques for improving the transparency of soft computing models, such as sensitivity analysis and model compression. These techniques can help to understand how the model arrived at its results. Incorporating domain experts in the interpretation process is crucial to derive meaningful insights and providing contextual understanding. Collaborative efforts between domain experts and data scientists can help bridge the gap between technical analysis and domain-specific knowledge, enabling practical interpretation and decision-making.

1.9   Conclusion

Soft computing techniques play a crucial role in designing and analyzing complex systems, offering flexible and robust solutions to a wide range of problems. This chapter has explored various aspects of soft computing techniques, including their design, analysis, benchmarking, sensitivity analysis, and interpretation and visualization of results.

Designing effective soft computing techniques requires a deep understanding of the problem domain, careful selection of algorithms, and appropriate tuning of parameters. The use of hybrid approaches, combining multiple soft computing techniques or integrating them with traditional methods, can lead to improved performance and versatility. However, algorithm complexity, interpretability, and generalization must be carefully addressed.

Analyzing soft computing techniques involves evaluating their performance, robustness, and reliability. Benchmarking provides a standardized framework for comparing different algorithms or models, facilitating advancements in the field. In addition, sensitivity analysis helps understand the impact of input variables or parameters on the model's output or performance, aiding in optimization, feature selection, and model validation.

Interpreting and visualizing the results of soft computing techniques can be challenging due to their complex nature and black-box characteristics. However, solutions such as model simplification, rule extraction, post hoc explanation methods, dimensionality reduction, and uncertainty estimation techniques can enhance interpretability and facilitate the communication of results to stakeholders. Additionally, considerations for addressing bias, incorporating domain knowledge, and ensuring fairness are essential for the responsible and reliable application of soft computing techniques.

In conclusion, soft computing techniques provide powerful tools for solving complex problems in various domains. Their design, analysis, and interpretation involve several challenges. However, by carefully considering these challenges and applying appropriate solutions, we can harness the full potential of soft computing techniques. As soft computing continues to evolve, staying updated with advancements is crucial, as engaging in collaborative research and maintaining a strong focus on responsible and ethical use. With these principles in mind, soft computing techniques will continue to drive innovation and contribute to advancing science and technology. By introducing readers to the motivation, key components, hybridization, and application domains of soft computing, this chapter sets the stage for a comprehensive exploration of the design and analysis of these techniques. It establishes the foundation for understanding the unique capabilities of this field.

References

[1] Salim Idris Malami, Faiz Habib Anwar, Suleiman Abdulrahman, S.I. Haruna, Shaban Ismael Albrka Ali, S.I. Abba (2021), Implementation of hybrid neuro-fuzzy and self-turning predictive model for the prediction of concrete carbonation depth: A soft computing technique, *Results in Engineering*, Volume 10, 100228. ISSN 2590-1230. https://doi.org/10.1016/j.rineng.2021.100228

[2] Boudy Bilal, Kondo Hloindo Adjallah, Alexandre Sava, Kaan Yetilmezsoy, Mohammed Ouassaid (2023), Wind turbine output power prediction and optimization based on a novel adaptive neuro-fuzzy inference system with the moving window, *Energy*, Volume 263, 126159. ISSN 0360-5442, https://doi.org/10.1016/j.energy.2022.126159

[3] Bo Jin, Fazlullah Khan, Ryan Alturki, Mohammed Abdulaziz Ikram (2023), Computational intelligence-enabled prediction and communication mechanism for IoT-based autonomous systems, *ISA Transactions*, Volume 132, Pages 146–154. ISSN 0019-0578, https://doi.org/10.1016/j.isatra.2022.06.007

[4] Lis Arufe, Riccardo Rasconi, Angelo Oddi, Ramiro Varela, Miguel A. González (2023), New coding scheme to compile circuits for quantum approximate optimization algorithm by genetic evolution, *Applied Soft Computing*, Volume 144, 110456. ISSN 1568-4946, https://doi.org/10.1016/j.asoc.2023.110456

[5] Walter Leal Filho, Tony Wall, Serafino Afonso Rui Mucova, Gustavo J. Nagy, Abdul-Lateef Balogun, Johannes M. Luetz, Artie W. Ng, Marina Kovaleva, Fardous Mohammad Safiul Azam, Fátima Alves, Zeus Guevara, Newton R Matandirotya, Antonis Skouloudis, Asaf Tzachor, Krishna Malakar, Odhiambo Gandhi (2022), Deploying artificial intelligence for climate change adaptation, *Technological Forecasting and Social Change*, Volume 180, 121662. ISSN 0040-1625, https://doi.org/10.1016/j.techfore.2022.121662

[6] Xianyu He, Guanqiu Qi, Zhiqin Zhu, Yuanyuan Li, Baisen Cong, Litao Bai (2023), Medical image segmentation method based on multi-feature interaction and fusion over cloud computing, *Simulation Modelling Practice and Theory*, Volume 126, 102769. ISSN 1569-190X, https://doi.org/10.1016/j.simpat.2023.102769

[7] Dipak Kumar Jana, Prajna Bhunia, Sirsendu Das Adhikary, Anjan Mishra (2023), Analyzing of salient features and classification of wine type based on quality through various neural network and support vector machine classifiers, *Results in Control and Optimization*, Volume 11, 100219. ISSN 2666-7207, https://doi.org/10.1016/j.rico.2023.100219

[8] Albert Salim, Juliandry, Louis Raymond, Jurike V Moniaga (2023), General pattern recognition using machine learning in the cloud, *Procedia Computer Science*, Volume 216, Pages 565–570. ISSN 1877-0509, https://doi.org/10.1016/j.procs.2022.12.170

[9] Simon Kamm, Sushma Sri Veekati, Timo Müller, Nasser Jazdi, Michael Weyrich (2023), A survey on machine learning based analysis of heterogeneous data in industrial automation, *Computers in Industry*, Volume 149, 103930. ISSN 0166-3615, https://doi.org/10.1016/j.compind.2023.103930

[10] Samuel Omar Tovias-Alanis, Humberto Sossa, Wilfrido Gómez-Flores (2023), Learning smooth dendrite morphological neurons for pattern classification using linkage trees and evolutionary-based hyperparameter tuning, *Pattern Recognition Letters*, ISSN 0167-8655, https://doi.org/10.1016/j.patrec.2023.05.024

[11] Hossien Ali Ghiassirad, Faezeh Farivar, Mahdi Aliyari Shoorehdeli, Mohammad Sayad Haghighi (2023), Building Robust Neural Networks under Adversarial Machine Learning Attacks by using Biologically-inspired Neurons, *Information Sciences*, 119190. ISSN 0020-0255, https://doi.org/10.1016/j.ins.2023.119190

[12] José María Guerrero (2023), Chapter 5 – The history of modern artificial intelligence, in Mind Mapping and Artificial Intelligence, Academic Press, Pages 129–158. ISBN 9780128201190, https://doi.org/10.1016/B978-0-12-820119-0.00007-8

[13] Majid Mirbod, Hamidreza Dehghani (2023), Smart trip prediction model for metro traffic control using data mining techniques, *Procedia Computer Science*, Volume 217, Pages 72–81. ISSN 1877-0509, https://doi.org/10.1016/j.procs.2022.12.203

[14] Felipe Colombelli, Thayne Woycinck Kowalski, Mariana Recamonde-Mendoza (2022), A hybrid ensemble feature selection design for candidate biomarkers discovery from transcriptome profiles, *Knowledge-Based Systems*, Volume 254, 109655. ISSN 0950-7051, https://doi.org/10.1016/j.knosys.109655

[15] Chongchong Qi, Mengting Wu, Hui Liu, Yanjie Liang, Xueming Liu, Zhang Lin (2023), Machine learning exploration of the mobility and environmental assessment of toxic elements in mining-associated solid wastes, *Journal of Cleaner Production*, Volume 401, 136771. ISSN 0959-6526, https://doi.org/10.1016/j.jclepro.2023.136771

[16] Krishnan Balasubramanian (2022), 2.26 – Computational and artificial intelligence techniques for drug discovery and administration, Editors: Terry Kenakin, *Comprehensive Pharmacology*, Elsevier, Pages 553–616. ISBN 9780128208762, https://doi.org/10.1016/B978-0-12-820472-6.00015-3

[17] Tao Tan, Tao Zhao (2023), A data-driven fuzzy system for the automatic determination of fuzzy set type based on fuzziness, *Information Sciences*, Volume 642, 119173. ISSN 0020-0255, https://doi.org/10.1016/j.ins.2023.119173

[18] Moa Lee, Jeehye Lee, Joon-Hyuk Chang (2019), Ensemble of jointly trained deep neural network-based acoustic models for reverberant speech recognition, *Digital Signal Processing*, Volume 85, Pages 1–9. ISSN 1051-2004, https://doi.org/10.1016/j.dsp.2018.11.005

[19] Nicholas Baker, James H. Elder (2022), Deep learning models fail to capture the configural nature of human shape perception, *iScience*, Volume 25, 9, 104913. ISSN 2589-0042, https://doi.org/10.1016/j.isci.2022.104913

[20] Ana Cláudia Teixeira, Raul Morais, Joaquim J. Sousa, Emanuel Peres, António Cunha (2023), Using deep learning for automatic detection of insects in traps, *Procedia Computer Science*, Volume 219, Pages 153–160. ISSN 1877-0509, https://doi.org/10.1016/j.procs.2023.01.276

[21] Tao Zhang, Jiawei Yuan, Yeh-Cheng Chen, Wenjing Jia (2021), Self-learning soft computing algorithms for prediction machines of estimating crowd density, *Applied Soft Computing*, Volume 105, 107240. ISSN 1568-4946, https://doi.org/10.1016/j.asoc.2021.107240

[22] Benbu Liang, C. Natalie van der Wal, Kefan Xie, Yun Chen, Frances M.T. Brazier, Maxim A. Dulebenets, Zimei Liu (2023), Mapping the knowledge domain of soft computing applications for emergency evacuation studies: A scientometric analysis and critical review, *Safety Science*, Volume 158, 105955. ISSN 0925-7535, https://doi.org/10.1016/j.ssci.2022.105955

[23] Murad Ali Khan, Naeem Iqbal, Imran, Harun Jamil, Do-Hyeun Kim (2023), An optimized ensemble prediction model using AutoML based on soft voting classifier for network intrusion detection, *Journal of Network and Computer Applications*, Volume 212, 103560. ISSN 1084-8045, https://doi.org/10.1016/j.jnca.2022.103560

Chapter 2

Trends in the Applications of Soft Computing Techniques for IoT

Kefaya Qaddoum[1] and Nameer N. El-Emam[2]

[1]The Department of Computer Science, Digipen Institute
of Technology, Washington, United States

[2]Department of Computer Science, Philadelphia University, Jordan

2.1 Introduction

Soft computing techniques have revolutionized how we approach complex problems by providing flexible and adaptive solutions in the face of uncertainty, imprecision, and nonlinearity. As technology advances at an unprecedented pace, new and emerging trends in applying soft computing techniques are shaping the landscape of various domains. In this chapter, we delve into these emerging trends and explore their potential impact on the design and analysis of complex systems [1].

The application of soft computing techniques has expanded beyond traditional domains, such as control systems and pattern recognition, and now encompasses a wide range of fields. These emerging trends are driven by the increasing need to address real-world challenges that demand intelligent, adaptable, and robust solutions. Soft computing techniques offer unique capabilities to tackle such challenges by integrating fuzzy logic, neural networks, evolutionary algorithms, and other computational intelligence methods.

One prominent trend is the application of soft computing techniques in the Internet of Things (IoT). With the proliferation of IoT devices and the exponential

DOI: 10.1201/9781032716718-2

growth of data generated, soft computing techniques provide efficient means to analyze and make sense of the vast heterogeneous data streams. In addition, they enable intelligent decision-making, anomaly detection, and energy optimization in IoT systems, ultimately enhancing performance and efficiency.

Smart cities represent another domain where soft computing techniques are gaining significant traction. As cities become more interconnected and data-driven, the complexity of managing urban environments increases. As a result, soft computing techniques play a vital role in developing intelligent systems for traffic management, energy optimization, waste management, and resource allocation. By leveraging the power of soft computing, smart cities can enhance sustainability, improve quality of life, and optimize resource utilization.

The healthcare and medical systems domain also benefits from applying soft computing techniques. Soft computing techniques excel in personalized diagnosis, treatment optimization, and disease prediction. By analyzing large-scale medical datasets and leveraging machine learning algorithms, soft computing techniques enable healthcare professionals to make informed decisions, improve patient outcomes, and optimize healthcare delivery.

Financial and economic forecasting is another area where soft computing techniques have made significant contributions. These techniques enable accurate prediction of stock market trends, portfolio optimization, risk assessment, and fraud detection. By considering complex relationships and handling uncertainty, soft computing techniques enhance the accuracy and robustness of financial predictions, enabling better investment decisions and risk management.

Natural Language Processing (NLP) has witnessed tremendous advancements in soft computing techniques. Fuzzy logic-based models and neural networks have revolutionized sentiment analysis, machine translation, and text generation tasks. These techniques enable a more accurate and nuanced understanding of human language, facilitating effective communication and information retrieval in various applications.

The domain of robotics and autonomous systems has also experienced remarkable progress due to soft computing techniques. These techniques enable robust control, path planning, swarm robotics, and perception in dynamic and uncertain environments. Furthermore, by integrating soft computing techniques, robots, and autonomous systems become more adaptable and capable of learning and making intelligent decisions in complex scenarios.

Environmental monitoring and sustainability represent an area where soft computing techniques contribute to developing intelligent and eco-friendly solutions. By analyzing environmental data and optimizing resource utilization, soft computing techniques aid in air quality monitoring, water resource management, energy optimization, and other sustainability initiatives. This enables informed decision-making and promotes sustainable practices for a greener future [2].

The emerging trends in applying soft computing techniques present exciting opportunities for solving complex problems in diverse domains. Integrating fuzzy logic, neural networks, evolutionary algorithms, and other soft computing techniques enables intelligent, adaptive, and robust systems to address uncertainty, nonlinearity, and large-scale data challenges. This chapter explores these emerging trends in depth, shedding light on their potential impact and paving the way for innovative applications and advancements in soft computing.

2.2   Soft Computing and the Internet of Things (IoT)

The combination of soft computing and IoT has brought new opportunities for data analytics and predictive modeling. IoT devices generate a massive amount of data that can be analyzed using soft computing techniques to gain valuable insights and make accurate predictions [3], [4], [5], [6].

2.2.1   Soft Computing and IoT for Data Analytics and Predictive Modeling

The convergence of soft computing techniques and the Internet of Things (IoT) has opened new avenues for data analytics and predictive modeling. With the proliferation of IoT devices and the exponential growth of data generated, intelligent analysis and decision-making capabilities have become crucial. This section explores how integrating soft computing, and IoT facilitates data analytics and predictive modeling, enabling valuable insights and informed decision-making [7], [8].

- **Fuzzy Logic for Handling Uncertainty and Imprecision**

Fuzzy logic, a key component of soft computing, provides a robust framework for dealing with uncertainty and imprecision in IoT data analytics. Due to sensor limitations and environmental factors, IoT data often exhibit varying noise levels, incompleteness, and imprecision. Fuzzy logic allows for representing and manipulating imprecise and uncertain information, enabling more accurate modeling and inference. Furthermore, IoT data can be processed effectively using fuzzy logic, even with uncertain or incomplete information.

- **Neural Networks for Learning and Pattern Recognition**

Neural networks, a well-known soft computing technique, are crucial in IoT data analytics and predictive modeling. With their ability to learn from data and recognize complex patterns, neural networks excel in capturing the inherent nonlinear relationships present in IoT data. By training neural networks on historical IoT data, predictive models can be built to forecast future trends, detect anomalies, and make informed decisions. In addition, neural network's ability to adapt and generalize from data makes them well-suited for handling IoT datasets' diverse and dynamic nature.

- Integration of IoT Data Streams for Comprehensive Analysis

One of the unique features of IoT is the availability of diverse data streams from multiple sources. Soft computing techniques enable integrating and analyzing these heterogeneous data streams, allowing for a comprehensive understanding of the IoT ecosystem. Furthermore, leveraging fuzzy logic and neural networks allows IoT data streams from various sensors and devices to be fused and processed together. This integration facilitates a holistic view of the IoT system, identifying complex relationships and patterns that would be difficult to uncover using traditional analytical approaches [4].

- Real-Time Analysis and Decision-Making

Soft computing techniques enable real-time analysis and decision-making in IoT applications. As IoT systems generate massive amounts of data in real-time, processing and analyzing this data on time is crucial. Soft computing techniques, such as fuzzy logic-based controllers and neural networks with low-latency architectures, allow for the real-time processing of IoT data streams. This capability enables the timely detection of anomalies, prediction of events, and dynamic decision-making based on the evolving IoT environment.

- Adaptive and Self-Learning Models

Soft computing techniques, particularly neural networks, can develop adaptive and self-learning models for IoT data analytics and predictive modeling. Neural networks can continually update their parameters and adapt to changing conditions based on new data inputs. This adaptability allows predictive models to evolve and improve over time, capturing the evolving dynamics of IoT systems. In addition, the self-learning capability of soft computing models enables continuous improvement and fine-tuning of predictions, resulting in more accurate and reliable outcomes.

Integrating soft computing techniques with IoT data analytics and predictive modeling offers significant advantages in handling uncertainty, capturing complex relationships, and enabling real-time decision-making. Fuzzy logic provides a robust framework for handling imprecision and uncertainty in IoT data, while neural networks excel in learning patterns and capturing nonlinear relationships. By leveraging soft computing techniques, IoT systems can extract valuable insights, make accurate predictions, and facilitate informed decision-making, leading to improved efficiency, enhanced performance, and transformative applications across various domains [9].

2.2.2 Soft Computing and IoT for Anomaly Detection and Fault Diagnosis

Anomaly detection and fault diagnosis are critical aspects of maintaining the reliability and efficiency of IoT systems. Integrating soft computing techniques with the Internet of Things (IoT) presents unique opportunities for effectively detecting anomalies and diagnosing faults. This section delves into how soft computing and IoT work together to enable robust anomaly detection and fault diagnosis in IoT environments.

- Fuzzy Logic for Modeling and Detection

Fuzzy logic, a fundamental component of soft computing, provides a robust framework for modeling and detecting anomalies in IoT systems. Fuzzy logic enables the representation and reasoning of imprecise and uncertain information, which is common in IoT data streams. By defining fuzzy sets and fuzzy rules, IoT data can be processed to identify deviations from normal behavior. As a result, fuzzy logic-based anomaly detection systems can effectively capture and interpret IoT data's imprecise and uncertain nature, enabling timely identification of anomalous patterns or events.

- Neural Networks for Pattern Recognition

Neural networks, a critical soft computing technique, are crucial in anomaly detection and fault diagnosis in IoT systems. By leveraging their ability to learn from historical data, neural networks excel in recognizing complex patterns and identifying deviations from normal behavior. Training neural networks on a large volume of IoT data allows them to learn the system's normal operating conditions and detect anomalies when presented with new data. Additionally, recurrent neural networks are particularly effective in capturing temporal dependencies and detecting anomalies in time series IoT data.

- Integration of Heterogeneous Data Sources

IoT systems generate data from various sensors and devices, often resulting in heterogeneous and high-dimensional datasets. Soft computing techniques enable integrating and analyzing these diverse data sources, facilitating comprehensive anomaly detection and fault diagnosis. By combining fuzzy logic and neural networks, IoT data streams from different sources can be processed together, enabling a holistic view of the system. This integration identifies complex relationships and patterns that may indicate anomalies or potential faults.

- **Proactive Fault Diagnosis and Predictive Maintenance**

When combined with IoT data, soft computing techniques enable proactive fault diagnosis and predictive maintenance in IoT systems. By continuously monitoring IoT data streams and analyzing them using soft computing techniques, early signs of potential faults or anomalies can be detected. Soft computing models can predict equipment failures or system malfunctions, allowing for timely maintenance and minimizing the impact of faults on system performance. Proactive fault diagnosis and predictive maintenance increase system reliability, reduce downtime, and improve operational efficiency.

- **Real-Time Anomaly Detection and Decision-Making**

Soft computing techniques, such as fuzzy logic-based controllers and neural networks with low-latency architectures, enable real-time anomaly detection and decision-making in IoT systems. Processing and analyzing IoT data streams in real time is crucial for timely identification and response to anomalies. Soft computing techniques allow for rapid data analysis, enabling quick detection and classification of anomalies or faults. Real-time anomaly detection and decision-making enhance system resilience, reduce risks, and improve overall performance.

Integrating soft computing techniques with IoT systems presents significant anomaly detection and fault diagnosis advantages. Fuzzy logic and neural networks provide powerful tools for modeling, recognizing patterns, and identifying deviations from normal behavior. By leveraging soft computing techniques, IoT systems can proactively detect anomalies, diagnose faults, and enable timely maintenance action, improving system reliability, reducing downtime, and enhancing operational efficiency in diverse IoT applications [10], [11].

2.2.3 Soft Computing and IoT for Energy Optimization and Resource Management

In conjunction with the Internet of Things (IoT), soft computing techniques offer promising energy optimization and resource management solutions in various domains. Integrating soft computing algorithms and IoT technologies enables intelligent decision-making and efficient utilization of resources [12], [13]. This section explores how soft computing and IoT are utilized for energy optimization and resource management, resulting in improved sustainability, cost-effectiveness, and operational efficiency [14], [15].

- **Fuzzy Logic for Energy Demand Prediction and Optimization**

Fuzzy logic, a key component of soft computing, plays a vital role in energy optimization and resource management. Fuzzy logic-based models can accurately predict future energy demands using historical energy consumption data from IoT-enabled devices. These predictions enable proactive energy management and optimization strategies, such as load balancing, demand response, and peak shaving. Fuzzy logic also allows for optimizing energy distribution and resource allocation, ensuring efficient utilization and minimizing wastage.

- **Neural Networks for Load Forecasting and Adaptive Control**

Neural networks, a well-known soft computing technique, are extensively used for load forecasting and adaptive control in IoT-based energy systems. By analyzing historical energy consumption patterns and considering external factors such as weather conditions and occupancy data, neural networks can accurately forecast energy loads. These load forecasts enable proactive energy management, such as demand-side management and load scheduling, leading to optimized resource utilization and reduced energy costs. In addition, neural networks support adaptive control strategies, allowing energy systems to dynamically adjust parameters based on real-time data, leading to efficient resource allocation and energy optimization.

- **Optimization Algorithms for Energy-Efficient Routing and Resource Allocation**

Soft computing techniques and optimization algorithms are employed for energy-efficient routing and resource allocation in IoT networks. With the many connected devices in IoT systems, routing, and resource allocation decisions significantly impact energy consumption. Soft computing algorithms, such as genetic algorithms, particle swarm optimization, and ant colony optimization, can be used to find optimal routes for data transmission and allocate resources efficiently. These algorithms consider various factors, including energy consumption, network congestion, and quality of service requirements, to achieve energy-efficient and reliable communication in IoT systems.

- **Intelligent Energy Management Systems**

When integrated with IoT infrastructure, soft computing techniques enable the development of intelligent energy management systems. These systems leverage real-time data from IoT devices – such as smart meters, sensors, and actuators – to monitor energy consumption patterns and optimize resource allocation. Intelligent energy management systems can dynamically adjust energy usage, prioritize energy allocation, and automate energy-saving actions by employing fuzzy logic-based controllers and neural networks. These systems also facilitate demand response programs, enabling effective load balancing and energy conservation during peak demand periods.

- **Data Analytics for Energy Analytics and Optimization**

In combination with advanced data analytics, soft computing techniques empower energy analytics and optimization in IoT environments. By leveraging machine learning algorithms, data mining techniques, and big data analytics, soft computing enables the extraction of valuable insights from massive amounts of energy-related data. These insights can be used to identify energy inefficiencies, detect anomalies, and optimize energy consumption patterns. Furthermore, by continuously analyzing and learning from energy data, soft computing techniques contribute to long-term energy optimization, sustainable resource management, and improved energy efficiency in IoT systems.

We can see how the integration of soft computing techniques with IoT for energy optimization and resource management offers significant advantages in sustainability, cost-effectiveness, and operational efficiency. Fuzzy logic and neural networks provide potent tools for energy demand prediction, load forecasting, and adaptive control. Optimization algorithms enable energy-efficient routing and resource allocation, while intelligent energy management systems facilitate real-time decision-making and automation. The combination of soft computing and IoT technologies empowers organizations to optimize energy usage, reduce costs, and minimize environmental impact, leading to a greener and more sustainable future [16], [17], [18].

2.2.4 Soft Computing and IoT for Decision-Making and Intelligent IoT Systems

When combined with the capabilities of the Internet of Things (IoT), soft computing techniques enable the development of intelligent IoT systems that can make informed decisions in complex and dynamic environments. These systems leverage the power of soft computing algorithms to analyze vast amounts of IoT data, extract meaningful insights, and make intelligent decisions in real time [19], [20], [21]. This section explores how soft computing and IoT are utilized for decision-making and developing intelligent IoT systems.

- **Fuzzy Logic-Based Decision-Making**

Fuzzy logic, a core component of soft computing, provides a framework for handling imprecise and uncertain information. In the context of IoT, fuzzy logic enables intelligent decision-making by capturing and reasoning with the inherent vagueness and uncertainty present in IoT data. IoT systems can make decisions based on fuzzy inputs and linguistic variables by defining fuzzy sets, fuzzy rules, and fuzzy inference systems. Fuzzy logic-based decision-making allows for flexible and adaptive reasoning, facilitating effective decision-making in complex and uncertain IoT environments.

- Machine Learning for Predictive Analytics

Machine learning techniques, an essential aspect of soft computing, are extensively used in IoT systems to enable predictive analytics and decision-making. By training machine learning models on historical IoT data, these models can learn patterns, correlations, and relationships to make predictions and generate actionable insights. These predictions aid in decision-making processes, such as predictive maintenance, anomaly detection, and resource optimization. Machine learning algorithms, including neural networks, support decision-making by learning from data and adapting to real-time changing conditions.

- Expert Systems for Knowledge-Based Decision Support

Expert systems, a prominent soft computing approach, are employed in IoT systems to provide knowledge-based decision support. These systems utilize domain-specific knowledge and rule-based reasoning to make decisions and provide recommendations. In the context of IoT, expert systems leverage the knowledge of domain experts and combine it with data-driven insights from IoT devices. By incorporating expert knowledge into decision-making, intelligent IoT systems can handle complex scenarios, interpret complex data patterns, and offer context-aware recommendations.

- Intelligent Control Systems

Soft computing techniques are instrumental in developing intelligent control systems for IoT applications. These systems utilize fuzzy logic, neural networks, and adaptive control algorithms to adjust system parameters and optimize performance dynamically. Soft computing-based control systems can adapt to changing conditions, make real-time adjustments, and optimize energy consumption, resource allocation, and operational efficiency. By integrating feedback mechanisms and utilizing soft computing techniques, intelligent control systems enhance decision-making and enable autonomous operation in IoT environments.

- Cognitive Computing for Contextual Decision-Making

Cognitive computing, an emerging field within soft computing, enables IoT systems to understand and interpret contextual information for decision-making. Cognitive computing allows IoT systems to analyze unstructured data, understand user intent, and make context-aware decisions by incorporating natural language processing, machine learning, and knowledge representation techniques. These systems can interpret user preferences, environmental conditions, and contextual factors to deliver personalized services and optimize decision-making processes.

It is clear how integrating soft computing techniques with IoT enables the development of decision-making and intelligent IoT systems. Fuzzy logic, machine learning, expert systems, intelligent control, and cognitive computing techniques empower these systems to analyze IoT data, make informed decisions, and adapt to dynamic environments. The combination of soft computing and IoT technologies facilitates intelligent automation, enhances operational efficiency, and enables IoT systems to optimize resources, provide personalized services, and improve overall user experience. The emerging soft computing and IoT convergence trends hold immense potential for shaping the future of decision-making and intelligent IoT systems in a wide range of applications [22].

2.3 Soft Computing Techniques in Healthcare and Medical Systems

Soft computing techniques have revolutionized healthcare and medical systems by enabling intelligent analysis, decision-making, and patient-centric care. Integrating soft computing with healthcare and medical systems has paved the way for improved diagnostics, personalized treatment plans, efficient healthcare management, and better patient outcomes [23], [24], [25]. This section delves into the emerging trends and applications of soft computing techniques in healthcare and medical systems.

2.3.1 Medical Image Analysis and Diagnosis

Soft computing techniques, such as machine learning, deep learning, and fuzzy logic, have significantly advanced medical image analysis and diagnosis. These techniques enable the accurate and efficient analysis of medical images, including X-rays, MRIs, CT scans, and histopathological images. Machine learning algorithms can learn from large datasets to detect and classify abnormalities, tumors, and diseases in medical images. Deep learning techniques, such as convolutional neural networks, excel in feature extraction and segmentation tasks, aiding in precise diagnosis and treatment planning. Fuzzy logic-based systems assist in handling uncertainty and imprecision in medical image interpretation, improving diagnostic accuracy and reducing false positives/negatives.

2.3.2 Predictive Analytics and Early Disease Detection

Soft computing techniques are crucial in predictive analytics and early disease detection, empowering healthcare systems to identify potential health risks and intervene proactively. Machine learning models trained on diverse patient data can predict the likelihood of developing specific diseases or complications based on various factors, such as medical history, genetic information, lifestyle, and environmental factors.

These models enable early detection, timely intervention, and preventive measures, improving patient outcomes and reducing healthcare costs.

2.3.3 Clinical Decision Support Systems

Soft computing techniques contribute to developing clinical decision support systems that assist healthcare professionals in making informed decisions. These systems integrate patient data, medical knowledge, and machine learning algorithms to provide evidence-based diagnosis, treatment planning, and medication selection recommendations. By analyzing patient data and comparing it with relevant medical knowledge, clinical decision support systems can offer personalized treatment options, alert healthcare providers to potential risks, and improve overall care quality.

2.3.4 Health Monitoring and Personalized Medicine

Soft computing techniques combined with IoT devices and wearable sensors enable real-time health monitoring and personalized medicine. These technologies collect continuous data on vital signs, physical activity, sleep patterns, and other relevant health parameters. Soft computing algorithms process this data, analyze patterns, and provide personalized insights to individuals and healthcare providers. This information helps in the early detection of health issues, tracking treatment progress, and tailoring interventions based on an individual's specific needs, promoting preventive care and improving patient outcomes.

2.3.5 Healthcare Resource Management and Optimization

Soft computing techniques contribute to efficient healthcare resource management and optimization. By analyzing patient data, historical records, and operational data, machine learning algorithms can optimize resource allocation, such as hospital bed management, staff scheduling, and inventory management. Fuzzy logic-based systems aid in modeling and optimizing healthcare workflows, enabling efficient patient flow, reducing waiting times, and improving operational efficiency in healthcare facilities.

2.3.6 Intelligent Telemedicine and Remote Monitoring

In combination with telemedicine technologies, soft computing techniques enable remote patient monitoring and teleconsultation. Machine learning algorithms analyze patient data transmitted through IoT devices and provide real-time insights to healthcare professionals. This allows for remote diagnosis, monitoring of chronic conditions, and timely intervention. Soft computing techniques also support natural language processing and intelligent conversational agents, facilitating effective communication between patients and healthcare providers during teleconsultations.

2.4 Soft Computing Techniques in Natural Language Processing (NLP)

Natural Language Processing (NLP) is a field of study focusing on the interaction between computers and human language. Soft computing techniques have significantly contributed to NLP, enabling more accurate and sophisticated language processing tasks. This section explores the emerging trends and applications of soft computing techniques in NLP [26], [27], [28].

2.4.1 Sentiment Analysis and Opinion Mining

Soft computing techniques, particularly machine learning algorithms, have significantly advanced sentiment analysis and opinion mining. These techniques enable the automatic extraction of sentiment and opinions from textual data, allowing for the analysis of public sentiment toward products, services, or events. Machine learning models trained on large datasets can classify text as positive, negative, or neutral, aiding in understanding public perception, customer feedback, and market trends. By incorporating soft computing techniques, sentiment analysis algorithms can handle natural language's inherent ambiguity and variability, leading to more accurate sentiment classification.

2.4.2 Named Entity Recognition and Entity Linking

Named Entity Recognition (NER) is a fundamental task in NLP that involves identifying and classifying named entities such as person names, organization names, locations, and other proper nouns. Soft computing techniques, such as machine learning and deep learning algorithms, have significantly improved the accuracy of NER systems. By training models on annotated datasets, these techniques can recognize and classify named entities in text, enabling applications such as information extraction, knowledge graph construction, and entity linking. In addition, soft computing approaches excel in handling variations, context dependencies, and inherent uncertainties in named entity recognition.

- **Text Summarization and Automatic Document Processing**

Soft computing techniques are crucial in text summarization and automatic document processing. These techniques enable extracting critical information and generating concise summaries from large volumes of text. Machine learning algorithms, such as neural networks and reinforcement learning, can learn to identify essential sentences, extract key phrases, and generate coherent summaries. Fuzzy logic-based systems aid in handling linguistic uncertainties and making decisions about the relevance and salience of textual information. Soft computing techniques also support automatic document categorization, topic modeling, and document clustering, facilitating efficient document management and information retrieval.

2.4.3 Question Answering and Dialogue Systems

Soft computing techniques have advanced question-answering and dialogue systems, enabling more natural and interactive interactions between humans and machines. Machine learning models, including deep learning architectures such as recurrent neural networks and transformers, have significantly improved question-answering tasks. These models can understand and interpret user queries, retrieve relevant information from knowledge bases or documents, and generate accurate and context-aware responses. Soft computing techniques also support natural language understanding and dialogue management, enabling more conversational and intelligent dialogue systems.

2.4.4 Text Generation and Language Modeling

Soft computing techniques, particularly deep learning models such as recurrent neural networks and generative adversarial networks, have significantly advanced text generation and language modeling tasks. These models can learn the statistical properties of natural language and generate coherent and contextually relevant text. Applications of text generation include machine translation, automatic speech recognition, chatbots, and creative text generation in the fields of literature and art. In addition, soft computing techniques allow for more fluent, diverse, and realistic text generation, enhancing the quality and versatility of language models.

2.5 Soft Computing Techniques in Robotics and Autonomous Systems

Soft computing techniques have revolutionized the field of robotics and autonomous systems, enabling the development of intelligent machines capable of perceiving, reasoning, and making decisions in complex and dynamic environments. This section explores the emerging trends and applications of soft computing techniques in robotics and autonomous systems [29], [30].

2.5.1 Perception and Sensing

Soft computing techniques are crucial in perception and sensing tasks, allowing robots to gather and interpret information from their environment. For example, machine learning algorithms, such as deep neural networks, excel in object recognition, scene understanding, and image segmentation tasks. These techniques enable robots to perceive and interpret visual, auditory, and tactile information, enabling them to understand their surroundings and make informed decisions.

2.5.2 Localization and Mapping

Localization and mapping are essential for robots operating in unknown or dynamic environments. Soft computing techniques, including probabilistic methods like particle filters and fuzzy logic-based systems, contribute to accurate robot localization and mapping. By integrating sensor data with probabilistic models, these techniques enable robots to estimate their position, map the environment, and navigate effectively. In addition, soft computing approaches handle uncertainties, noise, and ambiguity in sensor measurements, improving the reliability and robustness of localization and mapping algorithms.

2.5.3 Motion Planning and Control

Soft computing techniques play a significant role in motion planning and control, allowing robots to navigate and interact with their environment autonomously. Evolutionary algorithms, reinforcement learning, and fuzzy control systems aid in generating optimal or near-optimal paths, selecting appropriate actions, and controlling robot movements. These techniques consider environmental constraints, optimize control parameters, and adapt to changing conditions, enabling robots to navigate complex terrain, avoid obstacles, and manipulate objects with dexterity.

2.5.4 Human-Robot Interaction

Soft computing techniques contribute to human-robot interaction, facilitating seamless and intuitive communication between humans and robots. Natural language processing, gesture recognition, and affective computing techniques enable robots to understand and respond to human commands, gestures, and emotional cues. In addition, soft computing approaches support the development of intelligent dialogue systems, emotion recognition algorithms, and social behavior modeling, enhancing the quality of human-robot interaction and collaboration.

2.5.5   Learning and Adaptation

Soft computing techniques, particularly machine learning, and reinforcement learning, enable robots to learn from data and adapt their behavior based on experience. These techniques allow robots to acquire new skills, refine their performance, and adapt to changing environments. Machine learning algorithms, including deep neural networks, enable robots to learn complex sensorimotor skills, object manipulation, and decision-making processes. Reinforcement learning techniques enable robots to learn optimal control policies through trial and error, allowing them to perform tasks efficiently and adapt to new situations.

2.5.6   Swarm Robotics and Collective Intelligence

Soft computing techniques contribute to swarm robotics and collective intelligence, where robots collaboratively perform tasks. Swarm algorithms inspired by natural systems, such as ant colonies and flocking birds, enable robots to coordinate their actions, distribute tasks, and achieve collective objectives. Soft computing approaches facilitate self-organization, the emergence of global behaviors, and robustness in swarm systems, allowing for decentralized decision-making and efficient task completion.

2.6   Soft Computing Techniques in Smart Cities

Smart cities aim to leverage technology and data to improve citizens' quality of life and enhance urban operations' efficiency. Soft computing techniques play a significant role in addressing the challenges faced by smart cities, enabling intelligent decision-making, optimization, and automation. This section explores the emerging trends and applications of soft computing techniques in smart cities [30].

2.6.1   Intelligent Transportation Systems

Soft computing techniques contribute to intelligent transportation systems, which enhance the efficiency, safety, and sustainability of urban transportation. Machine learning algorithms enable real-time traffic prediction, congestion detection, and route optimization. Fuzzy logic-based systems aid in traffic signal control, considering dynamic traffic conditions and optimizing signal timings for smooth traffic flow. Soft computing approaches also support intelligent parking systems, public transportation management, and autonomous vehicles, optimizing traffic management and reducing environmental impact.

2.6.2 Energy Management and Sustainability

Soft computing techniques are crucial in energy management and sustainability in smart cities. Machine learning algorithms help optimize energy consumption by analyzing historical data, weather patterns, and user behaviors. These techniques enable load forecasting, demand response, and energy-efficient scheduling of appliances. Fuzzy logic-based systems assist in intelligent energy distribution, balancing energy supply and demand, and optimizing energy storage. In addition, soft computing approaches support renewable energy integration, waste management, and smart grid operation, contributing to sustainable and environmentally friendly cities.

2.6.3 Infrastructure Monitoring and Maintenance

Soft computing techniques enable efficient monitoring and maintenance of critical infrastructure in smart cities. Machine learning algorithms can analyze sensor data to detect anomalies, predict equipment failures, and prioritize maintenance tasks. These techniques aid in predictive maintenance, reducing downtime, and improving reliability. In addition, fuzzy logic-based systems contribute to condition monitoring, enabling real-time assessment of infrastructure health and risk assessment. Soft computing approaches also support asset management, optimizing resource allocation for maintenance and minimizing costs.

2.6.4 Urban Planning and Governance

Soft computing techniques facilitate data-driven urban planning and governance in smart cities. Machine learning algorithms help analyze large-scale data, including demographic information, sensor data, and social media feeds, to inform urban planning decisions. These techniques aid in land use optimization, transportation network design, and emergency management. Fuzzy logic-based systems assist in decision support systems for urban planners, considering multiple criteria and uncertainties in decision-making. Soft computing approaches also support citizen engagement, sentiment analysis, and participatory urban planning, enhancing the transparency and inclusivity of governance processes.

2.6.5 Smart Grid and Energy Distribution

Soft computing techniques contribute to the efficient and reliable operation of smart grids and energy distribution systems. Machine learning algorithms enable load forecasting, demand response, and energy theft detection, optimizing energy distribution and improving grid stability. Fuzzy logic-based systems aid in voltage control, power flow optimization, and fault diagnosis. These techniques support real-time decision-making in energy distribution, enabling efficient utilization of resources and integration of renewable energy sources.

2.6.6 Public Safety and Security

Soft computing techniques are crucial in enhancing public safety and security in smart cities. Machine learning algorithms enable video surveillance, anomaly detection, and facial recognition for crime prevention and public safety. These techniques aid in the early detection of abnormal events and potential security threats. Fuzzy logic-based systems support intelligent alarm systems, risk assessment, and emergency response, enabling effective and timely interventions. Soft computing approaches contribute to cybersecurity, protecting critical infrastructure, and ensuring data privacy in smart city systems.

2.7 Soft Computing Applications in Engineering

Soft computing techniques have found extensive applications in various engineering fields, revolutionizing traditional approaches and enabling the development of intelligent systems that can handle complex problems. This section explores the emerging trends and applications of soft computing techniques in engineering [30].

2.7.1 Optimization and Design

Soft computing techniques, such as genetic algorithms, particle swarm optimization, and simulated annealing, have become powerful tools for optimization and design in engineering. These techniques can handle multi-objective optimization problems where multiple conflicting objectives must be considered. In addition, soft computing approaches enable efficient solution space exploration, finding optimal or near-optimal solutions for complex engineering problems. They are precious when the problem involves nonlinearity, uncertainty, and discrete or continuous variables.

2.7.2 Control Systems

Soft computing techniques have had a significant impact on control systems engineering. Fuzzy logic-based systems and neural networks allow for the development of intelligent controllers capable of handling complex and nonlinear dynamics. These techniques can learn from data, adapt to changing environments, and provide robust control solutions. Soft computing approaches are instrumental when precise mathematical models are difficult to obtain or when the system exhibits uncertainties and disturbances. They have been applied in various domains, including robotics, aerospace, manufacturing, and process control.

2.7.3 Prediction and Forecasting

Soft computing techniques, such as artificial neural networks, support prediction and forecasting tasks in engineering. They can model complex relationships between input and output variables, allowing for accurate predictions even in noisy or incomplete data. Soft computing approaches have been successfully applied in weather forecasting, energy demand prediction, stock market analysis, and structural health monitoring. By learning patterns and trends from historical data, these techniques enable engineers to make informed decisions and plan for the future.

2.7.4 Pattern Recognition and Image Processing

Soft computing techniques play a crucial role in pattern recognition and image processing tasks in engineering. Machine learning algorithms, including deep neural networks, excel in object detection, classification, and segmentation tasks. These techniques enable engineers to extract meaningful information from complex datasets, analyze images, and recognize patterns. Soft computing approaches have applications in fields such as medical imaging, quality control, surveillance systems, and autonomous vehicles, where accurate and efficient analysis of visual data is essential.

2.7.5 Simulation and Modeling

Soft computing techniques contribute to simulation and modeling tasks in engineering. Computational intelligence algorithms, such as genetic programming and fuzzy systems, enable engineers to develop accurate and efficient models of complex systems. These techniques can handle uncertainties, nonlinearities, and incomplete information, allowing for realistic simulations and predictive modeling. Soft computing approaches are widely used in engineering fields such as civil engineering, environmental engineering, transportation planning, and fluid dynamics, enabling engineers to understand system behavior better and make informed decisions.

2.7.6 Decision Support Systems

Soft computing techniques provide valuable support in decision-making processes in engineering. Soft computing approaches assist engineers in complex decision-making tasks by integrating multiple data sources, handling uncertainties, and considering multiple criteria. Fuzzy logic-based systems, genetic algorithms, and expert systems aid in decision support systems, risk assessment, and resource allocation. Soft computing techniques enable engineers to analyze complex situations, evaluate alternatives, and make optimal decisions in various engineering domains.

2.8 Challenges and Future Directions in Soft Computing

While soft computing techniques have made significant strides in various applications, there are still challenges and future directions to explore. This section discusses some of the challenges soft computing faces and highlights potential avenues for future advancements [30].

2.8.1 Interpretability and Explainability

One of the main challenges in soft computing techniques is the interpretability and explainability of the models generated. Many soft computing approaches, such as neural networks, are often considered black-box models, making it difficult to understand the underlying decision-making process. Future research should focus on developing techniques that provide more transparent and interpretable models, allowing users to understand and trust the results produced by soft computing systems.

2.8.2 Data Quality and Preprocessing

Soft computing techniques heavily rely on data, and the quality and preprocessing of data significantly impact the models' performance and reliability. Issues such as noisy, incomplete, or biased data can affect the accuracy and generalizability of soft computing systems. Therefore, future directions should focus on developing robust data preprocessing techniques, handling missing data, addressing the class imbalance, and incorporating domain knowledge to improve the quality of input data.

2.8.3 Scalability and Efficiency

As the volume of data continues to grow exponentially, soft computing techniques face scalability and efficiency challenges. Many algorithms require extensive computational resources and time to train and execute, hindering their applicability in real-time or large-scale applications. Future research should focus on developing scalable algorithms that can handle big data efficiently, enabling the application of soft computing techniques in resource-constrained environments.

2.8.4 Incorporating Prior Knowledge and Domain Expertise

Soft computing techniques often rely on data-driven approaches, which may overlook the importance of prior knowledge and domain expertise. Incorporating domain knowledge into the learning process can enhance the performance and interpretability of soft computing models. Future directions should explore methods to effectively integrate prior knowledge and expert insights into the learning process, enabling more informed and reliable decision-making.

2.8.5 Robustness and Security

Soft computing techniques must be robust against adversarial attacks and able to handle uncertain and dynamic environments. Ensuring the reliability and security of soft computing systems is crucial, particularly in applications such as autonomous vehicles, healthcare, and critical infrastructure. Future research should focus on developing techniques that enhance the robustness and security of soft computing models, making them resilient to adversarial manipulations and ensuring the safety and integrity of the systems.

2.8.6 Hybrid and Multimodal Approaches

Combining different soft computing techniques and integrating them with other technologies can unlock new possibilities and improve system performance. For example, hybrid approaches that combine different soft computing techniques, such as neural networks and fuzzy logic, can leverage their complementary strengths and overcome individual limitations. Additionally, integrating soft computing with other emerging technologies, such as blockchain, edge computing, and the Internet of Things (IoT), opens up new avenues for research and applications.

2.8.7 Ethical and Social Considerations

As soft computing techniques advance and become more pervasive, ethical and social considerations become paramount. Issues related to bias, fairness, accountability, and privacy must be addressed to ensure soft computing systems' responsible and ethical deployment. Future research should focus on developing frameworks and guidelines that promote transparency, fairness, and accountability in developing and deploying soft computing applications.

2.9 Conclusion

In this chapter, we have explored the emerging trends in the applications of soft computing techniques. As a multidisciplinary field, soft computing has made significant contributions to various domains by addressing complex problems that are challenging for traditional computational approaches. From healthcare and engineering to robotics and smart cities, soft computing techniques have revolutionized how we tackle real-world challenges.

Throughout the chapter, we have discussed the critical components of soft computing, including fuzzy logic, neural networks, genetic algorithms, and swarm intelligence. These techniques provide powerful tools for handling uncertainty, imprecision, and nonlinearity inherent in many real-world problems. Soft computing techniques have effectively addressed these challenges and opened new opportunities for advanced data analysis, modeling, decision-making, and optimization.

We have explored the diverse applications of soft computing techniques in various domains. For example, soft computing has contributed to diagnosis, treatment planning, and personalized medicine in healthcare and medical systems. In addition, soft computing techniques have enhanced communication and interaction capabilities in natural language processing and robotics, enabling more natural and intelligent human-machine interfaces. Soft computing has also been pivotal in developing smart cities, optimizing energy, anomaly detection, and diagnosing faults.

However, as with any evolving field, there are challenges and future directions to consider. The interpretability and explainability of soft computing models remain significant concerns. Researchers must strive to develop techniques that provide transparent and interpretable results, empowering users to trust and understand the decision-making process. Data quality and preprocessing also require attention, as robust and reliable models heavily rely on high-quality data. Scalability, efficiency, and incorporating prior knowledge are additional areas where advancements are necessary to unleash the full potential of soft computing techniques.

Addressing these challenges will lead us toward a future where soft computing techniques continue to shape our world. Hybrid approaches, multimodal integration, and the ethical and responsible deployment of soft computing systems should be at the forefront of research and development efforts. By integrating soft computing with emerging technologies and considering social and ethical implications, we can ensure the development of intelligent systems that are transparent, fair, secure, and aligned with human values.

In conclusion, soft computing techniques have emerged as powerful tools for handling complex and uncertain problems across various domains. Their multidisciplinary nature allows for innovative solutions and enables advancements in data analytics, predictive modeling, optimization, and decision-making. As we move forward, we must address the challenges and embark on future directions to further enhance soft computing techniques' interpretability, scalability, efficiency, and ethical aspects. By doing so, we can harness the full potential of soft computing and continue to drive transformative changes in our rapidly evolving world.

References

[1] Benbu Liang, C. Natalie van der Wal, Kefan Xie, Yun Chen, Frances M.T. Brazier, Maxim A. Dulebenets, Zimei Liu (2023), Mapping the knowledge domain of soft

computing applications for emergency evacuation studies: A scientometric analysis and critical review, *Safety Science*, Volume 158, pp 1-18. ISSN 0925-7535, https://doi.org/10.1016/j.ssci.2022.105955

[2] Decui Liang, Yiqi Wu, Weiyi Duan (2023), Multiple granularity user intention fairness recognition of intelligent government Q & A system via three-way decision, *Information Sciences*, Volume 631, 305–326. ISSN 0020-0255, https://doi.org/10.1016/j.ins.2023.02.070

[3] Gokmen Tayfur (2023), Chapter 10 – Application of fuzzy logic in water resources engineering, Editors: Saeid Eslamian, Faezeh Eslamian, *Handbook of Hydroinformatics*, Elsevier, 155–166. ISBN 9780128219621, https://doi.org/10.1016/B978-0-12-821962-1.00024-6

[4] Bo Jin, Fazlullah Khan, Ryan Alturki, Mohammed Abdulaziz Ikram (2023), Computational intelligence-enabled prediction and communication mechanism for IoT-based autonomous systems, *ISA Transactions*, Volume 132, 146–154. ISSN 0019-0578, https://doi.org/10.1016/j.isatra.2022.06.007

[5] Zuhal Y. Hamd, Huda I. Almohammed, Maha M.A. Lashin, Mohamed Yousef, Hanan Aljuaid, Sawsan M. Khawaji, Norah I. Alhussain, Alanoud H. Salami, Rand A. Alsowayan, Fatima A. Alshaik, Tahani K. Alshehri, Dalal M. Aldossari, Nouf F. Albogami, Mayeen Uddin Khandaker (2023), Artificial intelligence-based fuzzy logic systems for predicting radiation protection awareness levels among university population, *Radiation Physics and Chemistry*, Volume 208, pp. 1-36. ISSN 0969-806X, https://doi.org/10.1016/j.radphyschem.2023.110888

[6] Hongguang Wu, Yuelin Gao (2023), An ant colony optimization based on local search for the vehicle routing problem with simultaneous pickup–delivery and time window, *Applied Soft Computing*, Volume 139, 1-16. ISSN 1568-4946, https://doi.org/10.1016/j.asoc.2023.110203

[7] Michal Wieczorowski, Dawid Kucharski, Pawel Sniatala, Pawel Pawlus, Grzegorz Krolczyk, Bartosz Gapinski (2023), A novel approach to using artificial intelligence in coordinate metrology including nano scale, *Measurement*, Volume 217, 1-26. ISSN 0263-2241, https://doi.org/10.1016/j.measurement.2023.113051

[8] Giovanni Acampora, Angela Chiatto, Autilia Vitiello (2023), Genetic algorithms as classical optimizer for the quantum approximate optimization algorithm, *Applied Soft Computing*, Volume 142, 1-12. ISSN 1568-4946, https://doi.org/10.1016/j.asoc.2023.110296

[9] Barnali Brahma, Tusar Kanti Dash, Ganapati Panda, L.V. Narasimha Prasad, Rajesh Kulkarni (2023), Integrated swarm intelligence and IoT for early and accurate remote voice-based pathology detection and water sound quality estimation, *Healthcare Analytics*, 1-19. ISSN 2772-4425, https://doi.org/10.1016/j.health.2023.100200

[10] Mehdi Mabed, Lauri Salmela, Andrei Ermolaev, Christophe Finot, Goëry Genty, John M. Dudley (2023), Neural network analysis of unstable temporal intensity peaks in continuous wave modulation instability, *Optics Communications*, Volume 541, 8-1ISSN 0030-4018, https://doi.org/10.1016/j.optcom.2023.129570

[11] Abdollah Hatamizadeh, Behnam Sedaee (2023), Simulation of carbonate reservoirs acidizing using machine and meta-learning methods and its optimization by the genetic algorithm, *Geoenergy Science and Engineering*, Volume 223, 1-19. ISSN 2949-8910, https://doi.org/10.1016/j.geoen.2023.211509

[12] Nam Phuong Nguyen, Elham Maghsoudi, Scott N. Roberts, Beomjin Kwon (2023), Shape optimization of pin fin array in a cooling channel using genetic algorithm and machine learning, *International Journal of Heat and Mass Transfer*, Volume 202, 1-12. ISSN 0017-9310, https://doi.org/10.1016/j.ijheatmasstransfer.2022.123769

[13] Tao Tan, Tao Zhao (2023), A data-driven fuzzy system for the automatic determination of fuzzy set type based on fuzziness, *Information Sciences*, Volume 642, 1-16. ISSN 0020-0255, https://doi.org/10.1016/j.ins.2023.119173

[14] Luca Cagliero, Jacopo Fior, Paolo Garza (2023), Shortlisting machine learning-based stock trading recommendations using candlestick pattern recognition, *Expert Systems with Applications*, Volume 216, 1-15. ISSN 0957-4174, https://doi.org/10.1016/j.eswa.2022.119493

[15] Fizza Hussain, Yuefeng Li, Ashutosh Arun, Md. Mazharul Haque (2022), A hybrid modelling framework of machine learning and extreme value theory for crash risk estimation using traffic conflicts, *Analytic Methods in Accident Research*, Volume 36, 1-16. ISSN 2213-6657, https://doi.org/10.1016/j.amar.2022.100248

[16] Sunita M. Dol, Pradip M. Jawandhiya (2023), Classification technique and its combination with clustering and association rule mining in educational data mining – A survey, *Engineering Applications of Artificial Intelligence*, Volume 122, 1-19. ISSN 0952-1976, https://doi.org/10.1016/j.engappai.2023.106071

[17] Jianfei Yang, Yuecong Xu, Haozhi Cao, Han Zou, Lihua Xie (2022), Deep learning and transfer learning for device-free human activity recognition: A survey, *Journal of Automation and Intelligence*, Volume 1, Issue 1, 1-15. ISSN 2949-8554, https://doi.org/10.1016/j.jai.2022.100007

[18] Minghui Gu, Cheng Li, Li Chen, Shaobo Li, Naiyu Xiao, Dequan Zhang, Xiaochun Zheng (2023), Insight from untargeted metabolomics: Revealing the potential marker compounds changes in refrigerated pork based on random forests machine learning algorithm, *Food Chemistry*, Volume 424, 1-13. ISSN 0308-8146, https://doi.org/10.1016/j.foodchem.2023.136341

[19] Shahnaz Khademizadeh, Zahra Nematollahi, Farshid Danesh (2022), Analysis of book circulation data and a book recommendation system in academic libraries using data mining techniques, *Library & Information Science Research*, Volume 44, Issue 4, 1-18. ISSN 0740-8188, https://doi.org/10.1016/j.lisr.2022.101191

[20] Elizabeth Fernandes, Sérgio Moro, Paulo Cortez, Data Science (2023), Machine learning and big data in digital journalism: A survey of state-of-the-art, challenges and opportunities, *Expert Systems with Applications*, Volume 221, 1-23. ISSN 0957-4174, https://doi.org/10.1016/j.eswa.2023.119795

[21] Dilan Lasantha, Sugandima Vidanagamachchi, Sam Nallaperuma (2023), Deep learning and ensemble deep learning for circRNA-RBP interaction prediction in the last decade: A review, *Engineering Applications of Artificial Intelligence*, Volume 123, . ISSN 0952-1976, https://doi.org/10.1016/j.engappai.2023.106352

[22] Sunil Kumar Prabhakar, Seong-Whan Lee (2022), ENIC: Ensemble and nature inclined classification with sparse depiction based deep and transfer learning for biosignal classification, *Applied Soft Computing*, Volume 117, ISBN 1568-4946, https://doi.org/10.1016/j.asoc.2022.108416

[23] Hong-Yu Wang, Jie-Sheng Wang, Guan Wang (2022), A survey of fuzzy clustering validity evaluation methods, *Information Sciences*, Volume 618, 270–297. ISSN 0020-0255, https://doi.org/10.1016/j.ins.2022.11.010

[24] Xabier Sáez-de-Cámara, Jose Luis Flores, Cristóbal Arellano, Aitor Urbieta, Urko Zurutuza (2023), Clustered federated learning architecture for network anomaly detection in large scale heterogeneous IoT networks, *Computers & Security*, ISSN 0167-4048, https://doi.org/10.1016/j.cose.2023.103299

[25] Shahzeb Tariq, Jorge Loy-Benitez, KiJeon Nam, SangYoun Kim, MinJeong Kim, ChangKyoo Yoo (2023), Deep-AI soft sensor for sustainable health risk monitoring and control of fine particulate matter at sensor devoid underground spaces: A zero-shot transfer learning approach, *Tunnelling and Underground Space Technology*, Volume 131, 1-18. ISSN 0886-7798, https://doi.org/10.1016/j.tust.2022.104843

[26] Alberto Rey, Bernardino Arcay, Alfonso Castro (2021), A hybrid CAD system for lung nodule detection using CT studies based in soft computing, *Expert Systems with Applications*, Volume 168, 1-16. ISSN 0957-4174, https://doi.org/10.1016/j.eswa.2020.114259

[27] Ramjeet Singh Yadav (2021), Chapter 6 – Application of soft computing techniques to calculation of medicine dose during the treatment of patient: A fuzzy logic approach, Editors: Janmenjoy Nayak, Bighnaraj Naik, Danilo Pelusi, Asit Kumar Das, *Handbook of Computational Intelligence in Biomedical Engineering and Healthcare*, Academic Press, 151–178. ISBN 9780128222607, https://doi.org/10.1016/B978-0-12-822260-7.00003-0

[28] Xiaohan Jiang, Peng Hou, Hongbin Zhu, Bo Li, Zongshan Wang, Hongwei Ding (2023), Dynamic and intelligent edge server placement based on deep reinforcement learning in mobile edge computing, *Ad Hoc Networks*, Volume 145, 1-15. ISSN 1570-8705, https://doi.org/10.1016/j.adhoc.2023.103172

[29] Samriti Sharma, Gurvinder Singh, Manik Sharma (2021), A comprehensive review and analysis of supervised-learning and soft computing techniques for stress diagnosis in humans, *Computers in Biology and Medicine*, Volume 134, 1-19. ISSN 0010-4825, https://doi.org/10.1016/j.compbiomed.2021.104450

[30] Bechoo Lal, S. Ravichandran, R. Kavin, N. Anil Kumar, Dibyahash Bordoloi, R. Ganesh Kumar (2023), IOT-BASED cyber security identification model through machine learning technique, *Measurement: Sensors*, Volume 27, 1-18. ISSN 2665-9174, https://doi.org/10.1016/j.measen.2023.100791

Chapter 3

Emerging Trends in the Applications of Soft Computing Techniques

Narendra Kumar

School of Computing, DIT University Dehradun, Dehradun, Uttarakhand, India

3.1 Introduction

Applications of Soft Computing (SC) methods are becoming more popular in the realm of electromagnetic (EM) research. Because the exciting properties of metamaterials contribute to the efficiency of these electromagnetic applications, researchers have been encouraged to move forward in the direction of using soft computing techniques for the design and optimization of metamaterial structures. This is because the exciting properties of metamaterials add to the effectiveness of these electromagnetic applications.

Lotfi Zadeh is the one who came up with the phrase "soft computing" (1992). The term "soft computing" refers to a multidisciplinary system that incorporates neural networks (NN), fuzzy logic, and evolutionary computing techniques such as genetic algorithms (GA), particle swarm optimization (PSO) [20], genetic programming (GP), bacteria foraging optimization (BFO), simulated annealing (SA), and so on. The purpose of these soft computing technologies is to arrive at rapid answers that are analogous to the judgments that a person would make. These approaches to soft computing have applications in every discipline of engineering now in existence [22], [23], [24].

DOI: 10.1201/9781032716718-3

There are a lot of issues in the real world that we have to deal with on a daily basis and that we have attempted to address logically and theoretically, but we have not been able to solve them because they need a lot of resources and a lot of time to compute. When it comes to solving these difficulties, the naturally occurring technique is highly methodical and coherently effective; yet, in most practical cases, a solution that is close to optimum is sufficient. Hence, circumstances like this might be dealt with using techniques derived from biology and referred to as "soft computing" [17], [18], [19].

The areas of genetic algorithms, fuzzy logic, and artificial neural networks are the most extensively covered by soft computing. Alone or in combination with other methodologies, these fields of study are brought to bear on the issue at hand in Figure 3.1. The term "soft computing" refers to a group of computer approaches that fall under the umbrella of "computational intelligence." Soft computing and hard computing are both different technologies that may be used to solve problems. In hard computing, the focus is on the precise model, which allows for the generation of solutions that are both exact and accurate [2]. An approximation serves as the foundation for soft computing. Hard computing, also known as conventional computing, is not the same thing. Hard computing incorporates reasoning based on symbolic logic, but conventional computing completely ignores numerical modeling and search. Both approaches to problem-solving are shown in Figure 3.1 alongside type [3]. Soft computing, on the other hand, is entirely focused on building on the human mind. Tolerance for uncertainty, unpredictability, fuzziness approximation, cheap solution cost, and a stronger connection with reality are all characteristics of this trait. It is a collection of many different computing approaches, such as those

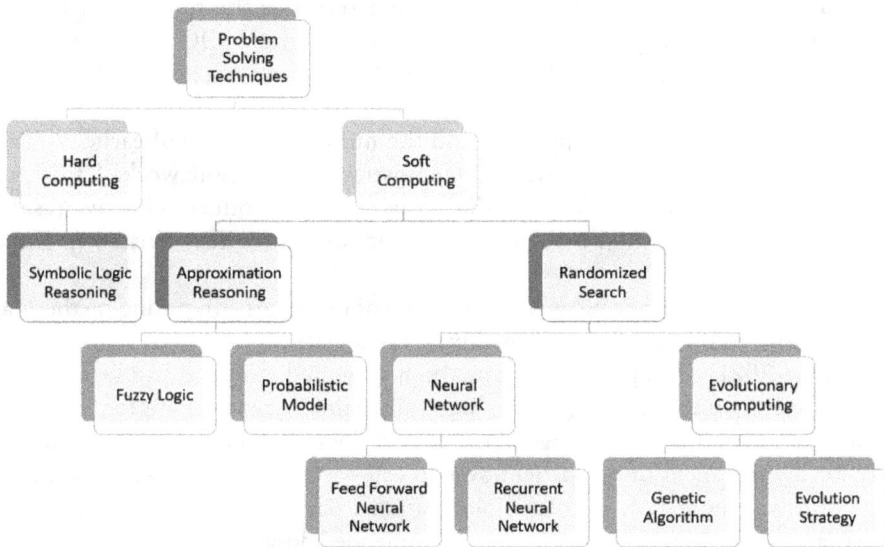

Figure 3.1 Overview of problem-solving techniques.

used in engineering fields including aircraft, mobile, robotics, cooling and heating, power electronics, and so on [4].

3.2 Related Work

(Liang et al., 2023) This research has suggested that future research should focus on investigating the possibilities of revolutionary soft-computing technologies for crowd modeling and allowing huge realistic evacuation simulations as well as optimization. This proposal is based on the review that was done [1].

(Esonye et al., 2021) This study provides a description of an optimum factor assessment for the maximum extraction of Dyacrodes edulis seed oil by using a central composite design that is based on an artificial neural network (ANN). [2].

(Kumar et al., 2021) The objective of this research is to find the dependability of the program by using soft computing approaches, which are the instruments that can assess its predictive potential with the greatest degree of effectiveness. It presents a novel comparison methodology in order to locate the artificial neural network that is the most appropriate and accurate, based on the software reliability model [3].

(Harirchian et al., 2021) The purpose of this article is to highlight the strengths, shed light on key factors, and apply each soft computing technique in the process of advancing the Rapid Visual Screening (RVS) field of study by presenting a thorough review of newly invented new methods and the most commonly used in Rapid Visual Screening using powerful soft computing techniques [4].

(Zafar & Iqbal, 2022) Word segmentation serves as the foundation for the proposed methodology, which also makes use of the HOG (Histogram-of-Oriented Gradient) and LBP (Local Binary Pattern) approaches for the extraction of feature data. As the study progresses, a comparison is made between the results of the proposed approach and the numerical results of earlier Arabic text-recognition systems in order to demonstrate the current work. Using the polynomial kernel of the SVM classifier, this strategy produces effective results with an accuracy of 97.05 percent when detecting Arabic text written in Kufic script [5].

(Ray et al., 2021) In this paper, the viability of using soft computing methods as an alternative to the deterministic method is investigated [6].

(Yadav, 2021) The approach that has been suggested is able to handle the computation of medication dosages for chronic intestinal sickness symptoms such as sedimentation and prostate antigen. The correct dosage of the medication is necessary for the treatment of any patient over an extended period of time. For the purpose of this investigation, I utilized observational data from 20 different patients. The trial outcome was compared to the recommended dosage of medication that was given by the physicians. In this regard, I have seen that the intelligent method that has been presented yields greater outcomes when compared to the dosage of medication that has been suggested by doctors or physicians [7].

(Dwarakish & Nithyapriya, 2016) This study discusses many approaches to soft computing as well as coastal remote sensing. The use of ANN for remote sensing is also covered in this research. The fundamentals of SVM have been discussed. The discourse is on the strengths of SVM in comparison to other methods [8].

(Dileep & Singh, 2017) This work provides a summary of the working principles of a number of different soft computing-based maximum power point tracking (SC-MPPT) techniques and compares them to one another based on a number of different parameters. Some of these parameters include accuracy, SPV (solar photovoltaic panel), complexity of algorithm, convergence time, tracking efficiency, array dependency, ability to handle PSCs (partial shading conditions), variables, and hardware implementation used. The material that has been acquired and analyzed in this work will be beneficial to researchers who want to conduct more studies in this field [9].

(Yue & Jia, 2013) The researchers define three negative ideal decisions that have the greatest amount of separation from the positive ideal decision. These negative ideal decisions are chosen in accordance with the TOPSIS technique, which combines an optimistic coefficient. Due to the fact that each negative ideal option may successfully eliminate a danger, this strategy is well-suited for cautious decision-making (decisions that minimize risk) [10], [11].

(Hiziroglu, 2013) The present uses of soft computing approaches in the segmentation issue are examined based on certain essential aspects in this article. These crucial variables include those connected to the efficacy of the segmentation, which any segmentation research should take into consideration. The review and analysis of 42 empirical studies shows that the application of soft computing to the issue of segmentation is still in its infancy, and the capacity of these studies to create information may not be adequate. This conclusion was reached as a result of the findings [12].

Ko et al. (2010) provide a synopsis of the results obtained via a comprehensive analysis of previously published research papers that investigate the implementation of soft computing strategies into supply chain management (SCM). Since several aspects of SCM, such as CRM and reverse logistics, have received little attention in previously published works, it is recommended that more investigation be conducted into these and other areas [13].

M. Blaga (2011) describes the use of soft computing methods in the engineering of knitted fabric. Some fundamental information on the knitting process as a complex system based on interactions between yarn qualities, process parameters, and knitted fabric attributes is presented. This information may be found in more detail in subsequent sections. The modeling of knitted textiles, the production of knitted fabrics, the quality monitoring of knitted fabrics, and the marketing of knitted fabrics have all benefited from the utilization of soft computing methods such as artificial neural networks, fuzzy logic, and genetic algorithms [14].

(Bharat et al., 2022) Soft computing methods are gaining popularity as a solution of choice due to the unpredictability and susceptibility of the different process types. The genetic algorithm, ant colony optimization, swarm intelligence, and PSO are some of the most important soft computing technologies that have been applied to this problem. The major objective of this study is to provide a synopsis of some of the streamlining procedures for recognizing and making use of their application in order to dominate in-depth work [15].

3.3   Soft Computing

Soft Computing is the antithesis of Hard Computing, often known as Conventional Computing. It is a collective term for a set of computational methods that are based on artificial intelligence (AI) as well as natural selection. Soft computing offers answers to difficult real-life situations for which there are no hard computer solutions that are both cost-effective and efficient. The concept of soft computing refers to the practice of doing computations in an approximative manner in order to provide answers to difficult computational problems that are not entirely accurate but may nevertheless be used. The technique allows answers for issues that may not be solvable at all or may simply take too much time to solve with the technology that is available today. The term "soft computing" may also be used interchangeably with "computational intelligence." The concept of soft computing is an approach to problem-solving that makes use of methods other than computers. Soft computing, which takes the human mind as its model, is tolerant of partial truths, ambiguity, imprecision, and approximation. This stands in contrast to conventional computer models. Researchers are able to address some issues that cannot be processed by standard computers because of soft computing's more forgiving nature. The following is a condensed explanation of the soft computing methods that are used in applications using metamaterials.

(i) Particle Swarm Optimization (PSO): PSO is a kind of stochastic optimization that mimics the behavior and intelligence of swarms. In PSO, the idea of social interaction is applied to the process of finding a solution to a problem. It does this by using a number of particles, also known as agents, that move about in the search space in a swarm fashion in order to locate the optimal answer. Each individual particle in the swarm searches for its positional coordinates in the solution space. These coordinates are connected to the best solution that the individual particle has been able to accomplish up to this point. It is often referred to as a "personal best" or *pbest*. The PSO also keeps track of another greatest value, which is known as the *gbest*, or the "global best." This is the best value that could possibly be produced by any other particle in the vicinity of that particle up to this point [16].

(ii) Bacterial Foraging Optimization (BFO): The bacterial foraging optimization algorithm, often known as BFO, is a biologically inspired swarm intelligence optimization algorithm. It mimics the foraging behavior of bacteria in order to acquire the most amount of energy possible while the bacteria are hunting for food. Since the beginning, it has attracted a significant amount of interest from researchers. Over the course of the last several decades, there has been a discernible increase in the total number of papers written on BFO and the many forms it takes, and this trend is expected to continue. Bacterial foraging optimization, sometimes known as BFO, is a revolutionary bio-inspired heuristic optimization technique that has recently garnered a lot of interest and been extensively applied to a variety of different practical optimization issues. The typical BFO method, on the other hand, has a number of possible flaws, the most notable of which are a lack of swarm communication and a lack of strength in the convergence accuracy.

(iii) Genetic Algorithm (GA): GA is a soft computing search strategy that replicates the principles of natural selection and genetic inheritance. The method begins with a population of potential solutions to a problem, which is represented as a collection of strings, each string representing a candidate answer.

Then, for each string or candidate solution, two genetic operators are applied: crossover and mutation. Crossover involves selecting two parent strings at random and combining their genetic information to create a new child string. A random bit, or gene, in a string gets modified or flipped during mutation.

The effectiveness of the new offspring strings in solving the issue is then assessed. The fitness of a candidate solution is determined by how near it is to the intended outcome. The best candidate solutions are chosen for reproduction, and the genetic operators are used to generate a new generation of candidate solutions.

This process of assessment, selection, and replication is repeated for many generations until a good solution is discovered or the algorithm hits a halt.

Genetic algorithms are employed in a variety of applications, including optimization, machine learning, robotics, and bioinformatics [26]. It is especially beneficial when working with complicated, non-linear issues where typical optimization strategies may fail.

(iv) Neural Network: A neural network is a key component of soft computing that models human brain activity. It is made up of linked nodes, or artificial neurons, that process, analyze, and identify data patterns. By altering the strengths of the connections between neurons depending on sample data, neural networks may be taught to detect complicated patterns, categorize data, make predictions, and perform other tasks.

Input, hidden, and output layers are only a few of the neuronal components that make up a typical artificial neural network. The input layer receives input data, which the hidden layers process via a sequence of mathematical operations. The neural network's ultimate outcome is produced by the output layer.

The design, training technique, and activation function of a neural network influence its performance. The number of layers and neurons in the network are defined by the design, while the training algorithm modifies the strengths of the connections between the neurons depending on sample data. The activation function defines how the output of a neuron is decided based on its input.

Image and audio recognition, natural language processing, robotics, and finance are just a few of the applications of neural networks. It is an excellent tool for dealing with complex challenges because of its ability to learn from data.

3.4 Applications of Soft Computing

Soft computing is an artificial intelligence branch that is used to handle complicated issues that are difficult to solve using standard computer approaches.

It is based on the concept of approximate reasoning and allows for the handling of imprecise, uncertain, or incomplete information (Figure 3.2).

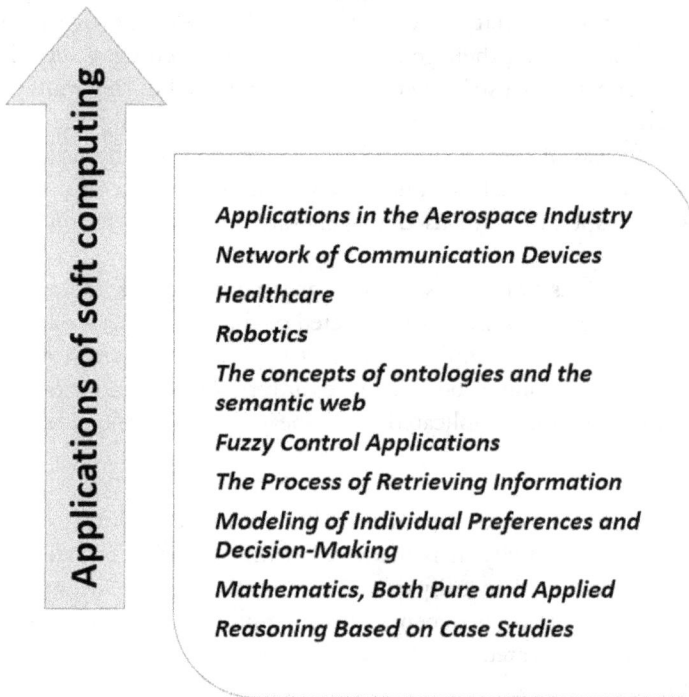

Applications of soft computing

Applications in the Aerospace Industry

Network of Communication Devices

Healthcare

Robotics

The concepts of ontologies and the semantic web

Fuzzy Control Applications

The Process of Retrieving Information

Modeling of Individual Preferences and Decision-Making

Mathematics, Both Pure and Applied

Reasoning Based on Case Studies

Figure 3.2 Application of soft computing.

The applications of soft computing are diverse and can be found in many areas, including the following below.

3.4.1 Applications in the Aerospace Industry

Werbos began working on his theory of linear optimum neural control in the early 1990s (adaptive critics). The aerospace industry and aviation control systems have both made use of it. The high degrees of nonlinearity, unpredictability, and complexity of these issues, as well as the participation of human beings, necessitate the usage of soft computing, which includes neural, fuzzy, and evolutionary computing. Soft computing is employed for aeronautical systems. Berenji suggested use of soft computing in NASA's space programs such as the space shuttle orbital operations. These operations include rendezvous docking and attitude control.

3.4.2 Network of Communication Devices

Since communication networks include people, it is possible to successfully apply the principles of soft computing to these kinds of systems. The use of soft computing techniques makes it possible to find answers to issues that, using traditional computer approaches, have not been able to be resolved satisfactorily. The synchronization and modulation of spread sequences in digital networks of communication may be accomplished quite well with the help of chaos computing. Neuro-fuzzy techniques are applied for data reduction and equalizers. The topologies of networks are discovered via the use of evolutionary computing. In addition to this, it is anticipated that soft computing would play a significant part in the development of systems for wireless communication. Soft computing is a method that may be used to great advantage in the field of communication systems, and it can be used to find answers to problems that hard computing has not been able to address. Neuro-fuzzy techniques are used for both data compression and equalization purposes, and are the result of the combination of artificial neural networks with fuzzy logic.

3.4.3 Healthcare

The use of computer technology is very important in the healthcare industry. The use of Soft Computing approaches provides better and more advanced tools that support the physician in many circumstances, allowing for the speedy detection of illnesses and diagnosis in real time. This is made possible by the advancements in computer technology. Various medical applications, like Registration of Medical Image Using Optimization Techniques, Machine Learning techniques to solve prognostic problems in the medical domain, neural network algorithms in diagnosing cancer, and Fuzzy Logic in various diseases, all use techniques from the field of Soft Computing [28].

3.4.4   Industries Related to Paper-Making

Some knowledgeable individuals used a neural network to create a model of the paper-making process. The innovative model generated findings that were compatible with those reported in planar stochastic fibrous structures along arbitrary scanning lines. Profiles, histograms of local area density, variances, and histograms of local free-fiber lengths were among the findings. These findings are very similar to the experimental data collected from commercial paper samples using optical transmission pictures or radiographic images and then analyzed using image processing software [27].

3.4.5   Robotics

Soft computing approaches have the potential to improve a variety of subfields within this area. Robot driving control is a popular application for neuro-fuzzy systems. This system receives input from the vision subsystem and the goal identifying device, which then sends action commands to the motors. Then, neural networks are frequently in charge of providing fuzzy inference techniques. Furthermore, the systems are taught how to behave by modifying their knowledge bases using a neural network learning approach [29].

3.4.6   The Concepts of Ontologies and the Semantic Web

While conducting Internet research, keep two things in mind: first, there is a distinction to be made between data generated primarily for human consumption and data generated primarily by machines; second, there is a degree of uncertainty that must be tracked. The standard representations of belief-based, ontology-based, possibility and probabilistic information, as well as other types of uncertainty, are propelling soft computing techniques for unpredictability representation and computation to the forefront of semantic web research. Probabilistic modeling, possibility analysis, and belief-based analysis are examples of these approaches. As a consequence of a series of landmark workshops and seminars, both the soft computing and fuzzy logic communities, as well as the Semantic Web community, have been increasingly interested in these difficulties during the past few years. With the use of fuzzy logic, the gap between intuitive knowledge and machine-readable knowledge systems has been bridged. A significant amount of research is also being conducted on methods for extracting partial, incomplete, or uncertain knowledge, as well as on the management of uncertainty in the process of representing information extracted using ontologies, for example, to achieve semantic interoperability between many different systems. The Semantic Web requires the management of large amounts of fuzzy data as well as the retrieval of fuzzy information.

3.4.7 Fuzzy Control Applications

The creation of a fuzzy approach for operating a steam engine by Assilian and Mamdani is regarded as the earliest use of fuzzy logic in the context of control systems. At this moment, both fuzzy control research and its applications were moving at a rapid rate. The use of hard-computing approaches is ineffective in the development of cost-effective robot control systems. The use of soft computing approaches, on the other hand, is what permits the complexity issue in control systems to be addressed. Soft computing approaches are valuable because they allow control systems to accept inaccurate input while maintaining high levels of efficiency and performance.

3.4.8 The Process of Retrieving Information

The purpose of information retrieval is to define systems capable of providing effective and efficient content-based retrieval to a large amount of stored information. At the present, methodologies from the area of soft computing are being used to simulate partiality and subjectivity in order to create adaptive environments for information retrieval that learn the user's perception of what constitutes relevance. Soft computing components responsible for knowledge representation, such as rough sets, fuzzy logic, and probabilistic reasoning, carry out the modeling. In this regard, the use of soft computing technologies may be beneficial in the pursuit of more flexibility in IR systems.

3.4.9 Modeling of Individual Preferences and Decision-Making

Standard methods to decision-making issues include the implicit assumption that all of the information is stated in a single preference representation format by default; however, in actual reality, this is very unlikely to be the case. As a consequence of this, developing innovative fuzzy methods for incorporating various representation formats into the decision-making process is of utmost significance. When dealing with actual decision-making issues, the presence of missing information creates extra challenges that need to be handled.

3.4.10 Mathematics, Both Pure and Applied

Various soft-computing methods have their roots in abstract mathematical ideas. Topology (including tolerance spaces, commonality spaces, and approximation spaces), differential equation theory (with the addition of fuzziness), and the development and algebraic study of new logical systems have all been rethought in light of the soft computing and fundamental mathematical formalisms of fuzzy systems.

3.4.11 Reasoning Based on Case Studies

This model of thinking involves not only the processes of understanding, learning, and problem-solving, but also combines those processes with memory operations. It entails making use of previously implemented solutions in order to fulfill newly formulated requirements, referring to previously decided cases in order to justify newly implemented solutions or explain newly formulated situations, and basing one's reasoning on precedents in order to interpret newly formulated scenarios. In order to execute different tasks of reasoning based on cases with practical applications, new studies are showing the function of soft computing tools, both separately and in combination. These activities may be performed either by themselves or in conjunction with one another.

3.5 Challenges and Solution Soft Computing

Soft Computing, like any other field of technology, faces its own set of challenges. Some of the common challenges are below.

1. **Lack of standardization:** There is no standard definition, framework, or methodology to guide the development of soft computing tools, which makes it harder to create a cohesive set of guidelines for researchers.
2. **Computational complexity:** The various soft computing techniques, such as genetic algorithms and fuzzy logic, require a vast amount of computation time and resources, which can be a significant challenge for researchers.
3. **Dependence on data quality:** Soft computing methods are heavily data-driven, and the quality and quantity of data sources heavily impact their effectiveness.
4. **Lack of transparency:** Soft computing techniques may be "black boxes," making it difficult to comprehend how they work or how to diagnose and enhance them.

3.5.1 Solutions to the Challenges

Some potential solutions to these problems include the following:

1. **Standardization and regulation:** The creation of a standard definition, framework, and technique may be beneficial in providing a much-needed structure for researchers to adhere to.
2. **Enhancing computational power:** Researchers may design and run more complicated soft computing experiments and obtain more insights with the introduction of cloud computing [21], high-performance computing (HPC), and the ever-increasing processing capacity supplied by hardware [25].

3. **Improving data quality:** Improved data collection methods, cleaning procedures, and enhanced processing may increase data quality and accuracy, hence increasing the usefulness of soft computing approaches.
4. **Promoting transparency:** To improve the transparency of soft computing systems, researchers might create visualization approaches, statistical methodologies, and interpretability frameworks.
5. **Integrating different soft computing techniques:** Combining methods such as neural networks, fuzzy logic, and evolutionary algorithms may result in a more resilient and powerful soft computing tool.
6. **Collaborative research:** Collaborative research may bring people from many industries and views together to strive toward a more thorough knowledge of soft computing. This may assist in ensuring that researchers take a coordinated approach, contribute to standardization, and build on each other's abilities.
7. **Education and training:** Education and training may assist researchers in gaining knowledge and abilities in soft computing approaches as well as developing a deeper grasp of their applications. Academic and industrial certifications, short courses, seminars, and e-learning platforms are all options.

3.6   Conclusion

There has been a significant rise in the use of soft computing across the board, including in physics, material sciences, computer chemistry, statistics, and so on. This chapter provided an overview of a variety of soft computing approaches as well as a variety of application areas in which these techniques have been employed. There are a few distinguishing features of soft computing, including its resilience, cost efficiency, and simplicity. Tracking imprecision and uncertainty is a task that lends itself very well to fuzzy logic. ANN, on the other hand, has excellent predictive powers thanks to its generalization and learning capabilities. On the other hand, it has been shown that evolutionary computing approaches may be extremely effective in solving optimization issues. The development of soft computing is advancing at a rapid pace, which will result in an expansion of application areas in the years to come. The number of goods using the kind of computing known as soft computing is growing. The vast majority of these kinds of products make use of one of many different forms of soft computing techniques inside the subsystems, all of which are hidden from the end user. The crux is that, in the not-too-distant future, diverse applications will increasingly make use of soft computing approaches because of their capacity to solve imprecise issues. Within the scope of this chapter, we have provided information on the application area of soft computing. Experts are given the opportunity to choose their work for a certain domain using this document. Those individuals who are interested in making a contribution to this job area will find this material beneficial.

References

[1] Liang, B., van der Wal, C. N., Xie, K., Chen, Y., Brazier, F. M., Dulebenets, M. A., & Liu, Z. (2023, February). Mapping the knowledge domain of soft computing applications for emergency evacuation studies: A scientometric analysis and critical review. *Safety Science*, 158, 105955. https://doi.org/10.1016/j.ssci.2022

[2] Esonye, C., Onukwuli, O., Anadebe, V., Ezeugo, J., & Ogbodo, N. (2021, March). Application of soft-computing techniques for statistical modeling and optimization of Dyacrodes edulis seed oil extraction using polar and non-polar solvents. *Heliyon*, 7(3), e06342. https://doi.org/10.1016/j.heliyon.2021.e06342

[3] Kumar, P., Singh, S., & Deo Choudhary, S. (2021). Reliability prediction analysis of aspect-oriented application using soft computing techniques. *Materials Today: Proceedings*, 45, 2660–2665. https://doi.org/10.1016/j.matpr.2020.11.518

[4] Harirchian, E., Aghakouchaki Hosseini, S. E., Jadhav, K., Kumari, V., Rasulzade, S., Işık, E., Wasif, M., & Lahmer, T. (2021, November). A review on application of soft computing techniques for the rapid visual safety evaluation and damage classification of existing buildings. *Journal of Building Engineering*, 43, 102536. https://doi.org/10.1016/j.jobe.2021.102536

[5] Zafar, A., & Iqbal, A. (2022, June). Application of soft computing techniques in machine reading of Quranic Kufic manuscripts. *Journal of King Saud University – Computer and Information Sciences*, 34(6), 3062–3069. https://doi.org/10.1016/j.jksuci.2020.04.017

[6] Ray, R., Kumar, D., Samui, P., Roy, L. B., Goh, A., & Zhang, W. (2021, January). Application of soft computing techniques for shallow foundation reliability in geotechnical engineering. *Geoscience Frontiers*, 12(1), 375–383. https://doi.org/10.1016/j.gsf.2020.05.003

[7] Yadav, R. S. (2021). Application of soft computing techniques to calculation of medicine dose during the treatment of patient. *Handbook of Computational Intelligence in Biomedical Engineering and Healthcare*, 151–178. https://doi.org/10.1016/b978-0-12-822260-7.00003-0

[8] Dwarakish, G., & Nithyapriya, B. (2016, December). Application of soft computing techniques in coastal study – A review. *Journal of Ocean Engineering and Science*, 1(4), 247–255. https://doi.org/10.1016/j.joes.2016.06.004

[9] Dileep, G., & Singh, S. (2017, January). Application of soft computing techniques for maximum power point tracking of SPV system. *Solar Energy*, 141, 182–202. https://doi.org/10.1016/j.solener.2016.11.034

[10] Yue, Z., & Jia, Y. (2013, May). An application of soft computing technique in group decision making under interval-valued intuitionistic fuzzy environment. *Applied Soft Computing*, 13(5), 2490–2503. https://doi.org/10.1016/j.asoc.2012.11.045

[11] Loebis, D., Sutton, R., Chudley, J., Naeem, W., Dalgleish, F., & Tetlow, S. (2004, July). The application of soft computing techniques to an integrated navigation system of an AUV. *IFAC Proceedings Volumes*, 37(8), 66–71. https://doi.org/10.1016/s1474-6670(17)31952-3

[12] Hiziroglu, A. (2013, November). Soft computing applications in customer segmentation: State-of-art review and critique. *Expert Systems With Applications*, 40(16), 6491–6507. https://doi.org/10.1016/j.eswa.2013.05.052

[13] Ko, M., Tiwari, A., & Mehnen, J. (2010, June). A review of soft computing applications in supply chain management. *Applied Soft Computing*, 10(3), 661–674. https://doi.org/10.1016/j.asoc.2009.09.004

[14] Blaga, M. (2011). Soft computing applications in knitting technology. *Soft Computing in Textile Engineering*, 217–245. https://doi.org/10.1533/9780857090812.3.217

[15] Bharat, N., Kumar, A., & Bose, P. (2022). A study on soft computing optimizing techniques. *Materials Today: Proceedings*, 50, 1193–1198. https://doi.org/10.1016/j.matpr.2021.08.068

[16] Kumar, N., Shukla, H., & Tripathi, R. (2017). Image restoration in noisy free images using fuzzy based median filtering and adaptive particle swarm optimization – richardson-lucy algorithm. *International Journal of Intelligent Engineering and Systems*, 10(4), 50–59. https://doi.org/10.22266/ijies2017.0831.06

[17] Sohal, A. S., Sandhu, R., Sood, S. K., & Chang, V. (2018). A cybersecurity framework to identify malicious edge devices in fog computing and cloud-of-things environments. *Computers and Security*, 74. https://doi.org/10.1016/j.cose.2017.08.016

[18] Alli, A. A., & Alam, M. M. (2020). The fog cloud of things: A survey on concepts, architecture, standards, tools, and applications. *In the Internet of Things (Netherlands)*, 9. https://doi.org/10.1016/j.iot.2020.100177

[19] Parikli, S., Dave, D., Patel, R., & Doshi, N. (2019). Security and privacy issues in the cloud, fog, and edge computing. *Procedia Computer Science*, 160. https://doi.org/10.1016/j.procs.2019.11.018

[20] Kumar, N., Shukla, H., & Tripathi, R. (2017). Image restoration in noisy free images using fuzzy based median filtering and adaptive particle swarm optimization – richardson-lucy algorithm. *International Journal of Intelligent Engineering and Systems*, 10(4), 50–59. https://doi.org/10.22266/ijies2017.0831.06

[21] Suneja, B., Negi, A., Kumar, N., & Bhardwaj, R. (2022). Cloud-based tomato plant growth and health monitoring system using IOT. *2022 3rd International Conference on Intelligent Engineering and Management (ICIEM)*. https://doi.org/10.1109/iciem54221.2022.9853170

[22] Elazhary, H. (2019). IoT(Internet of Things), mobile cloud, cloudlet, mobile IoT, IoT cloud, fog, mobile edge, and edge emerging computing paradigms: Disambiguation and research directions. *In Journal of Network and Computer Applications*, 128. https://doi.org/10.1016/j.jnca.2018.10.021

[23] Martín, C., Garrido, D., Llopis, L., Rubio, B., & Díaz, M. (2022). Facilitating the monitoring and management of structural health in civil infrastructures with an Edge/Fog/Cloud architecture. *Computer Standards and Interfaces*, 81. https://doi.org/10.1016/j.csi.2021.103600

[24] Kumar, K., Saini, G., Shah, R., Kumar, N., & Gupta, M. (2023). IOT-based dam and barrage monitoring system. *Enabling Methodologies for Renewable and Sustainable Energy*, 151–161. https://doi.org/10.1201/9781003272717-9

[25] Kumar, N. (2022). Future challenges in fog and edge computing applications. *Bio-Inspired Optimization in Fog and Edge Computing Environments*, 39–54. https://doi.org/10.1201/9781003322931-3

[26] Kumar, K., Kumar, N., Kumar, A., Mohammed, M. A., Al-Waisy, A. S., Jaber, M. M., Pandey, N. K., Shah, R., Saini, G., Eid, F., & Al-Andoli, M. N. (2022). Identification of cardiac patients based on the medical conditions using machine

learning models. *Computational Intelligence and Neuroscience*, 2022, 1–15. https://doi.org/10.1155/2022/5882144

[27] Dote, Y., & Ovaska, S. J. (2001). Industrial applications of soft computing: A review. *Proceedings of the IEEE*, 89(9), 1243–1265.

[28] Laghari, R. A., Li, J., Laghari, A. A., & Wang, S. Q. (2020). A review on application of soft computing techniques in machining of particle reinforcement metal matrix composites. *Archives of Computational Methods in Engineering*, 27, 1363–1377.

[29] Harirchian, E., Hosseini, S. E. A., Jadhav, K., Kumari, V., Rasulzade, S., Işık, E., & Lahmer, T. (2021). A review on application of soft computing techniques for the rapid visual safety evaluation and damage classification of existing buildings. *Journal of Building Engineering*, 43, 102536.

Chapter 4

Service-Oriented Computing: Challenges, Benefits, and Emerging Trends

Rohit Verma[1] and Dheeraj Rane[2]

[1]National College of Ireland, Dublin, Ireland

[2]IITI Drishti CPS Foundation, Indian Institute of Technology Indore, India

4.1   Introduction

In the rapidly evolving landscape of technology, service-oriented computing (SOC) has emerged as a paradigm that holds transformative potential for developing flexible, scalable, and modular software systems (Papazoglou 2003). By embracing a service-oriented approach, organizations can effectively tackle the intricate challenges presented by complex business processes, dynamic market demands, and ever-evolving technological advancements. SOC offers a multitude of benefits, encompassing improved flexibility, reusability of services, heightened agility, enhanced interoperability, and cost-effectiveness (Verma & Srivastava 2014).

Here, we comprehensively comprehend SOC by extensively exploring its challenges, benefits, and emerging trends. Our aim is to unravel the intricacies of service composition and orchestration, skillfully navigate the complexities surrounding quality of service (QoS; Wu et al. 2022), security, and governance, and shed illumination into the inherent advantages of SOC. By doing so, we equip researchers and

DOI: 10.1201/9781032716718-4

practitioners with invaluable knowledge and perspectives, enabling them to comprehensively understand this multifaceted domain.

First, we present the challenges confronted by organizations during the adoption and implementation of SOC (Niknejad et al. 2020). From unraveling the intricacies of service composition and orchestration to addressing the critical considerations of QoS, security, and governance, we actively explore the obstacles that require meticulous attention and astute resolution. A firm grasp of these challenges is imperative to maximize the potential benefits that SOC has to offer.

Next, we endeavor to highlight the myriad of benefits that SOC bestows upon organizations. By wholeheartedly embracing SOC, organizations can achieve remarkable improvements in flexibility, scalability, reusability, and responsiveness within their software systems. Additionally, SOC contributes to the reduction of costs and expedited time-to-market, endowing organizations with a distinct competitive advantage within the fast-paced and ever-evolving business landscape of today.

Moreover, this chapter endeavors to present the emerging trends that shape the future trajectory of SOC. We explore the ascendancy of microservices (Lu et al. 2023) architecture, the transformative potential harbored by serverless computing, and the seamless integration of AI and machine learning into service-oriented systems. These emerging trends invite researchers and practitioners alike to explore uncharted territories, discover novel approaches, and harness cutting-edge technologies to propel the development of more efficient and intelligent service-oriented systems.

In conclusion, this chapter stands as an all-encompassing guide, ushering readers into the intricate realm of service-oriented computing. By meticulously addressing challenges, uncovering benefits, and illuminating emerging trends, we aspire to empower readers with the necessary knowledge and insights to adeptly navigate the dynamic SOC landscape and unleash its transformative potential within their respective domains. Armed with a comprehensive understanding of SOC, organizations can effectively drive innovation, seamlessly adapt to evolving market demands, and construct resilient software systems that meet the ever-changing needs of the digital era.

4.1.1 Background and Motivation

In today's interconnected and ever-evolving business landscape, the demand for flexible and scalable software systems has reached new heights. Traditional monolithic architectures often struggle to keep pace with the dynamic requirements of modern organizations. Consequently, service-oriented computing has emerged as a compelling paradigm, offering a promising approach to designing and developing distributed software systems. The primary objective of this chapter is to present a comprehensive overview of the challenges, benefits, and emerging trends within the SOC domain (Papazoglou et al. 2007).

The impetus behind this research stems from the recognition that organizations across diverse industries are embracing SOC as a means to surmount the limitations imposed by traditional architectures (Hachem et al. 2014, Kyo"sti & Lindstro"m 2022). By decomposing complex systems into modular and loosely coupled services, SOC empowers businesses to achieve heightened levels of agility, scalability, and reusability. However, despite the growing adoption of SOC, significant research gaps and unresolved questions persist, necessitating further exploration and analysis.

4.1.2 Research Problem and Research Questions

This chapter takes a deep dive into the challenges and opportunities presented by service-oriented computing. Through an extensive literature review and analysis of real-world case studies, our goal is to uncover the hurdles faced during SOC adoption, explore the benefits it offers, and examine the emerging trends in the field. By gaining a comprehensive understanding of SOC's complexities, readers can effectively leverage its potential to drive innovation in their respective domains.

To guide our investigation, we have formulated the following research questions:

■ What are the primary challenges encountered during the adoption and implementation of service-oriented computing? By examining literature and real-world case studies, we aim to identify the key obstacles organizations face on their SOC journey.
■ What are the key benefits that organizations can attain by adopting service-oriented computing? By a thorough review of the literature and analysis of successful SOC implementations, we seek to uncover the transformative impact and wide-ranging advantages that SOC brings to organizations.
■ What are the emerging trends and technologies that influence the evolution of service-oriented computing? By staying abreast of the latest advancements in SOC, we aim to shed light on the cutting-edge trends and technologies that are shaping the future of the field, providing new avenues for researchers and practitioners to explore.

In addressing these research questions, this chapter aims to equip readers with valuable insights into the challenges, benefits, and emerging trends of service-oriented computing, enabling them to navigate the dynamic SOC landscape with confidence and drive innovation in their respective fields.

These research questions serve as the foundation of our investigation, driving us to comprehensively explore the challenges, benefits, and emerging trends within the realm of service-oriented computing. By addressing these questions, we aim to provide valuable insights and contribute to the existing body of knowledge surrounding SOC.

4.1.3 Objectives and Scope of the Chapter

The chapter at hand embarks on a comprehensive exploration of service-oriented computing, meticulously delving into its various facets, including its definition, principles, key components, benefits, challenges, emerging trends, and real-world case studies. The chapter adheres to a structured format, ensuring a systematic and cohesive flow of information. Let us now delve into the distinct sections that comprise this chapter:

1. The chapter commences with a thorough exposition of SOC, providing a comprehensive overview of its foundational elements. This section elucidates the core principles and key components that underpin this paradigm, establishing a solid foundation for the subsequent discussions.
2. A detailed examination of the benefits bestowed by SOC takes center stage in this section. The focus lies on unraveling the advantages that organizations can reap through the adoption of SOC, accentuating its potential to enhance flexibility, promote reusability, and drive cost savings. These benefits are explored in the context of optimizing operational efficiency and enabling organizations to adapt readily to the ever-evolving demands of the market.
3. This section shifts its attention towards the challenges that inevitably accompany the implementation of SOC. In-depth analysis is devoted to various critical aspects, such as service composition, quality of service (QoS), security, and governance. By dissecting these challenges, organizations are empowered to develop robust strategies that mitigate risks and maximize the benefits derived from SOC.
4. Emerging trends and technologies that shape the future trajectory of SOC form the focal point of this section. Meticulous examination is dedicated to the profound impact of microservices, serverless computing, and the integration of artificial intelligence (AI). These emerging trends engender novel possibilities, allowing organizations to fortify their service-oriented systems and gain a competitive edge within the dynamic realm of digital landscapes.
5. The presentation of real-world case studies augments the practicality of this chapter. By showcasing specific examples of SOC implementation across diverse industries, readers gain invaluable insights into the tangible application and implications of SOC. These case studies illuminate the practicality of SOC, rendering it more relatable and tangible to readers across various domains.
6. The chapter culminates with a succinct summary that encapsulates the key points discussed throughout its course. Implications for practice and future research are carefully delineated, offering pragmatic guidance to both practitioners and researchers alike. This conclusive section ensures that readers

depart with a lucid comprehension of SOC's potential and are equipped with insights that will inform their future endeavors within this field.

In summation, this chapter endeavors to holistically comprehend SOC, encapsulating its challenges, benefits, emerging trends, and practical applications through real-world case studies. By distilling implications for practice and future research, it serves as a valuable compendium for researchers, practitioners, and decision-makers seeking to harness the transformative potential of SOC within their organizations.

4.2 Service-Oriented Computing: Definition and Overview

This section provides a comprehensive definition and overview of service-oriented computing (El-Sheikh et al. 2016; Huhns & Singh 2005). We delve into the key concepts and components that form the foundation of SOC, including service-oriented architecture (SOA), service-oriented modeling, service-oriented design principles, and the key components that make up service-oriented computing.

4.2.1 Definition of Service-Oriented Computing

Service-oriented computing is an architectural paradigm that emphasizes creating, deploying, and consuming modular, loosely coupled services to build distributed software systems. These services encapsulate discrete business functionalities and communicate with each other through standardized protocols. SOC aims to enable organizations to achieve greater agility, flexibility, and reusability in their software architectures.

4.2.2 Service-Oriented Architecture

Service-oriented architecture (SOA) has acted as a pivotal architectural style within the service-oriented computing paradigm (Papazoglou 2003; Papazoglou et al. 2007). It encompasses a set of design principles and guidelines that facilitate the creation and orchestration of the services. At its core, SOA emphasizes service composition, wherein multiple services collaborate harmoniously to accomplish complex business processes Zeng et al. (2004). By embracing SOA, organizations can effectively break down monolithic applications into reusable services, enabling them to assemble these services flexibly to fulfill precise business requirements. This approach empowers organizations to enhance their agility and responsiveness, while fostering the development of modular and scalable software systems.

4.2.3 *Service-Oriented Modeling*

Service-oriented modeling serves as a fundamental component of service-oriented computing (SOC), encompassing the analysis, design, and representation of services within a service-oriented architecture (SOA). By employing modeling techniques specific to SOC, organizations can ensure the proper alignment of services with business processes, promote interoperability, and create modular and scalable systems.

A key objective of service-oriented modeling is the establishment of service boundaries. This involves defining the scope and responsibilities of individual services, encapsulating distinct business functionalities within discrete units. Well-defined service boundaries enhance manageability, reusability, and scalability, while also facilitating effective communication and contract establishment between services.

Another critical aspect of service-oriented modeling is the specification of service interfaces. Well-defined interfaces enable service interoperability and loose coupling, allowing services to evolve independently. This involves determining input and output parameters, message formats, and supported protocols. Effective interface modeling ensures seamless integration and interaction among services.

Service compositions and orchestrations are core elements of SOC, and modeling techniques aid in representing these relationships and dependencies. Modeling service compositions entails defining the sequence, conditions, and rules that govern the orchestration of services to achieve specific business objectives. Visualization and modeling of service compositions enable a comprehensive understanding of information flow, service choreography, and overall system behavior.

Various modeling techniques and standards, such as UML (Unified Modeling Language), BPMN (Business Process Model and Notation), and SoaML (Service oriented architecture Modeling Language), are utilized in service-oriented modeling to represent models and artifacts. These standardized notations provide semantic consistency and visual representations for modeling services, interfaces, compositions, and orchestrations.

Service-oriented modeling generates valuable artifacts for documentation, communication, and system understanding. Models facilitate stakeholder visualization and comprehension of the structure and behavior of SOC systems, fostering collaboration. Furthermore, models support decision-making processes, performance analysis, and system governance.

In nutshell, service-oriented modeling plays a critical role in designing and representing services, interfaces, compositions, and orchestrations within an SOA. It ensures alignment with business processes, promotes interoperability, and facilitates the creation of modular and scalable systems. Effective modeling contributes to enhanced system understanding, collaboration, and informed decision-making throughout the software development lifecycle.

4.2.4 Service-Oriented Design Principles

Service-oriented design principles serve as guiding principles for creating services that adhere to the principles of loose coupling, high cohesion, and autonomy Hsieh et al. (2012). These principles promote the development of independent, reusable, and maintainable services within a service-oriented architecture (SOA), enabling organizations to achieve desired levels of flexibility, scalability, and modifiability (Papazoglou et al. 2008).

In SOC, loose coupling is a key design principle, emphasizing minimal dependency and independence between services. It entails defining clear service boundaries, specifying well-defined interfaces, and utilizing standard communication protocols. Loose coupling enables service reuse and composition, enhancing flexibility and adaptability.

High cohesion ensures that services have a clear and well-defined purpose, encapsulating specific business functionalities or capabilities. This promotes reusability, maintainability, and ease of understanding and management.

Autonomy emphasizes the self-contained nature of services, enabling them to operate independently and make decisions without heavy reliance on other services or external entities. Autonomy enhances system resilience, scalability, and distributed decision-making.

Service composability enables the easy composition of services to create complex business processes. Services can collaborate through choreography or orchestration, allowing flexible and dynamic system assembly based on changing requirements.

Adhering to standards and open protocols ensures interoperability and ease of integration. Using standardized protocols facilitates seamless interaction between services from different vendors and heterogeneous systems.

By following these service-oriented design principles, organizations can create loosely coupled, highly cohesive, autonomous, and composable services. Architects and developers can make informed decisions about service boundaries, interfaces, and system structure, resulting in scalable, adaptable, and robust service-oriented architectures that effectively meet business needs.

4.2.5 Key Components of Service-Oriented Computing

The key components of service-oriented computing serve as the foundational elements for implementing and managing service-oriented architectures. These components, namely service registries, service consumers, service providers, and service orchestration engines, work together to enable the creation, discovery, and consumption of services within an SOA. Understanding these components is essential for effectively designing and managing service-oriented systems Nayak et al. (2023).

Service registries act as central repositories, facilitating the publication and discovery of services. They provide a catalog of available services, allowing consumers and providers to locate and interact with each other. Service consumers, which can be applications, devices, or other services, invoke and utilize services to fulfill specific tasks. They interact with services through interfaces, driving the execution of business processes within the SOA. On the other hand, service providers implement the functionalities encapsulated within services and make them available to consumers. They ensure adherence to interfaces and service-level agreements, playing a vital role in maintaining service quality. Finally, service orchestration engines coordinate the execution of service compositions and workflows, managing the sequencing and data flow between services.

These components collectively support the dynamic and distributed nature of service-oriented computing. They enable seamless interaction and collaboration between services, empowering organizations to build scalable, modular, and interoperable systems.

Understanding these key components is crucial within the context of the chapter titled "Service-Oriented Computing: Challenges, Benefits, and Emerging Trends." It allows organizations to address challenges related to service discovery, composition, and orchestration, while leveraging the flexibility, reusability, and interoperability benefits offered by SOC. By keeping informed about emerging trends and advancements in these components, organizations can stay at the forefront of service-oriented computing and adapt to its evolving landscape.

This section builds upon the foundations established in Section I, which provided the background, motivation, research problem, and scope of the chapter. By delving into the key components of SOC, this section aligns with the overarching theme of the chapter, contributing to a comprehensive understanding of the challenges, benefits, and emerging trends in service-oriented computing.

4.3 Benefits of Service-Oriented Computing

SOC provides organizations with a multitude of advantages to improve their software systems and drive business success in the digital era. In this section, we will delve into the fundamental benefits tied to SOC, encompassing heightened flexibility, scalability, reusability, agility, interoperability, and cost-effectiveness (Papazoglou et al. 2008). SOC empowers organizations to quickly adapt to evolving requirements, autonomously scale services, leverage component reusability, promptly meet market demands, enable seamless service communication, and optimize resource allocation. By capitalizing on these advantages, organizations can construct robust software systems that effectively address evolving needs, granting them a competitive edge in the digital age.

4.3.1 Improved Flexibility and Scalability

SOC bestows organizations with a noteworthy edge through its ability to augment flexibility. By breaking down complex systems into modular and loosely coupled services, SOC empowers businesses to swiftly adapt and respond to evolving requirements. The capability to independently add, modify, or replace services allows for precise updates, minimizing disruptions to the entire system. This flexibility also extends to scalability, enabling organizations to scale services horizontally or vertically, optimizing resource utilization and enhancing performance. Embracing SOC's flexibility empowers organizations to achieve agility and responsiveness in their software systems, effectively meeting the dynamic demands of the modern business landscape.

4.3.2   Reusability of Services

SOC embraces the concept of service reuse, empowering organizations to leverage pre-existing services across various applications and scenarios. By designing services with well-defined interfaces and standardized communication protocols, these services become reusable components that seamlessly integrate into different contexts (Verma & Srivastava 2015). Service reuse eliminates the need for redundant development, saving valuable time and effort while ensuring consistency across applications. This approach facilitates modular and incremental development, enabling organizations to enhance their systems gradually by assembling pre-existing services. By embracing service reuse, organizations can maximize productivity, improve development efficiency, and achieve greater consistency and modularity in their software systems (Ahmed et al. 2014).

4.3.3   Increased Agility and Responsiveness

SOC empowers organizations with increased agility and responsiveness to market dynamics. The modular nature of services facilitates rapid composition and re-composition, enabling the creation of new business processes and workflows. This agility allows organizations to quickly adapt to evolving business needs, seize emerging opportunities, and promptly respond to market demands (Papazoglou 2003). By embracing SOC, organizations effortlessly introduce new services and functionalities, fostering an innovative culture and enabling differentiation in a competitive landscape. The ability to swiftly adapt and evolve is a significant advantage offered by SOC, enabling organizations to stay ahead in a rapidly changing business environment.

4.3.4   Better Interoperability

Interoperability is a crucial advantage that SOC brings to the table. By adhering to standardized interfaces and protocols, services can effortlessly communicate and interact with each other, regardless of the underlying technology stack. This seamless interoperability promotes collaboration and integration across diverse systems and applications, allowing organizations to leverage their existing investments while embracing new technologies (Wei & Blake 2010). It also facilitates the integration of internal and external systems, enabling smooth data exchange and empowering organizations to build robust ecosystems of interconnected services. The ability to interoperate with various systems and technologies empowers organizations to construct flexible and scalable architectures that foster collaboration and maximize the value of their service-oriented systems.

4.3.5 Lower Costs and Faster Time-to-Market

SOC presents organizations with an opportunity to achieve cost savings and expedite time-to-market. By leveraging service reuse, organizations can focus their development efforts on building new functionalities, resulting in reduced time and costs. Moreover, by leveraging third-party services and cloud-based offerings, organizations can minimize the need for extensive in-house development. The modular nature of SOC allows for parallel development, enabling teams to work simultaneously on different services and expedite project delivery.

The standardized interfaces and protocols in SOC foster interoperability, simplifying the integration process and reducing complexity. This streamlined integration facilitates faster time-to-market, enabling organizations to rapidly deploy new services and features. The ability to respond swiftly to market demands enhances competitiveness and improves customer satisfaction. By embracing SOC, organizations can optimize their development processes, reduce costs, and gain a competitive edge in the marketplace.

In summary, SOC offers improved flexibility, scalability, reusability, agility, and interoperability. Service reuse, streamlined development, and simplified integration efforts contribute to lower costs and faster time-to-market. Embracing SOC empowers organizations to drive innovation, enhance software systems, and gain a competitive edge in today's business landscape.

4.4 Challenges of Service-Oriented Computing

Service-oriented computing (SOC) brings significant benefits, but it also poses challenges that organizations must tackle to harness its full potential (Raggett 2015). This section provides insights into the key challenges of SOC, including the complexity of service composition and orchestration, considerations of quality of service (QoS), security and privacy issues, management and governance issues, and integration with legacy systems. Successfully solving these problems is paramount to implementing and operating service-oriented architectures (SOAs) (Niknejad et al. 2020). Identifying these challenges is key to achieving an efficient implementation and operation. By understanding and overcoming these obstacles, organizations can maximize the benefits of SOC and ensure the success of service-oriented systems.

4.4.1 Complex Service Composition and Orchestration

One of the main challenges in SOC is the complexity of the composition and orchestration of services. Service composition (Lemos et al. 2016) involves the combination of individual services to achieve complex business processes. It includes constructing services. Organizations frequently face the task of choosing and coordinating services from large pools of available options. Identification of appropriate services, determining their compatibility, and defining orchestration logic can be complex and time consuming. This can be time and effort consuming. In addition, managing dependencies, handling exceptions, and ensuring consistency of compositions is a problem in itself. Effective tools, methodologies and standards are required to simplify the compositional and orchestration process to simplify (Peltz & Peltz 2003).

4.4.2 Quality of Service (QoS) Issues

Another challenge with SOC is ensuring the quality of services you want (Zeng et al. 2004). As the services are often distributed and designed to meet complex business requirements, it becomes critical to maintain and monitor QoS parameters. Factors such as response time, availability, reliability, security and scalability must be considered and effectively managed. However, in dynamic and heterogeneous environments, it can be difficult to achieve and still guarantee the desired level of QoS across various services and interactions. Organizations need to develop robust mechanisms to monitor, measure, and enforce QoS to ensure that service level agreements (SLAs) are met.

4.4.3 Security and Privacy Concerns

With the increasing adoption of SOC, security and privacy concerns become critical challenges. The distributed nature of services and the exposure of interfaces and data raise potential risks. Organizations must implement appropriate security measures to protect services and their interactions from unauthorized access, data breaches, and malicious attacks. Ensuring secure communication, enforcing authentication and authorization mechanisms, and implementing data encryption are essential. Privacy concerns also arise due to the sharing and exchange of data between services. Organizations must address privacy regulations, data anonymization, and consent management to protect sensitive information Li et al. (2021).

4.4.4 Management and Governance Challenges

Effective management and governance are vital for successful SOC implementation. Managing a large number of services, their versions, dependencies, and lifecycle can become complex. Organizations must establish robust service management processes, including service discovery, registration, versioning, and retirement. Service-level agreements (SLAs) must be defined, monitored, and enforced to meet business and customer expectations. Governance frameworks and policies need to be established to ensure compliance, service quality, and accountability. Furthermore, managing service providers, handling service changes, and ensuring appropriate documentation and communication add to the management challenges.

4.4.5 Legacy System Integration

Integrating legacy systems into an SOC environment poses a significant challenge for many organizations. Legacy systems are often built on older technologies, use different data formats, and lack service-oriented capabilities. Integration efforts must be undertaken to enable these systems to participate in the service-oriented architecture seamlessly. Organizations may need to invest in modernization approaches, such as service enablement or legacy system encapsulation, to bridge the gap between legacy systems and the SOC ecosystem. The coexistence of legacy systems and services requires careful planning, integration frameworks, and middleware solutions to ensure smooth interoperability and data exchange.

Overcoming these challenges requires a systematic approach, careful planning, and adoption of best practices in SOC. Organizations must invest in research and development efforts to advance the field, improve tooling and frameworks, and develop methodologies to address these challenges effectively.

As researchers, it is imperative to explore innovative solutions and propose novel approaches to tackle these challenges. Collaborative research efforts, industry partnerships, and knowledge sharing play a vital role in advancing the understanding and resolution of these challenges. By addressing these obstacles head-on, organizations can fully realize the benefits of SOC and create robust, scalable, and secure service-oriented architectures that drive digital transformation and enable business success.

4.5 Emerging Trends in Service-Oriented Computing

As service-oriented computing continues to evolve, new trends and technologies are shaping the future of service-oriented architecture (SOA). In this section, we will explore several emerging trends in SOC that have gained traction in the field. These trends include microservices architecture, serverless computing, cloud-native computing, containerization and orchestration, and the integration of artificial intelligence (AI) and machine learning. Understanding these trends is vital for researchers and practitioners in SOC, as they provide insights into the direction of SOC and open up opportunities for innovation and progress.

4.5.1 Microservices Architecture

Microservices architecture is an architectural style that emphasizes building applications as a collection of small, independent, and loosely coupled services (Lu 2023). Each service focuses on a specific business capability and can be developed, deployed, and scaled independently. This approach offers benefits such as modularity, scalability, and ease of maintenance. It allows organizations to evolve and update individual services without disrupting the entire system. Researchers in SOC are actively exploring effective ways to design, deploy, and manage microservices architectures, while addressing challenges related to service discovery, inter-service communication, and data consistency.

4.5.2 Serverless Computing

Serverless computing, also known as Function as a Service (FaaS), is a programming paradigm that enables developers to focus on writing code for specific tasks without the need to manage underlying infrastructure. In a serverless environment, services are triggered by events and automatically scale up or down based on demand. This approach offers advantages such as reduced operational burden, enhanced scalability, and cost-effectiveness. Researchers are actively exploring techniques to optimize serverless architectures, address security concerns, and overcome challenges such as cold start latency, efficient resource allocation, and effective service composition.

4.5.3 Cloud-Native Computing

Cloud-native computing is an innovative approach that leverages cloud computing platforms and technologies to develop, deploy, and manage applications (Hsieh et al. 2012). It revolves around the principles of containerization, microservices, and dynamic orchestration, enabling the creation of highly scalable and resilient systems. By adopting cloud-native architectures, organizations can fully utilize the capabilities of cloud infrastructure and services, unlocking benefits such as increased agility, scalability, and resilience. Researchers are actively investigating methodologies and best practices for building cloud-native applications, with a focus on addressing challenges associated with container management, service discovery, and dynamic resource allocation.

4.5.4 Containerization and Orchestration

Containerization has gained significant popularity in SOC as it provides a lightweight and portable approach to packaging and deploying applications. Containers offer isolation, flexibility, and reproducibility, allowing services to be deployed consistently across different environments. Container orchestration frameworks like

Kubernetes enable the management and scaling of containers in a distributed system. Researchers are exploring containerization techniques, investigating orchestration strategies, and addressing challenges related to container security, networking, and data management.

4.5.5 AI and Machine Learning in Service-Oriented Computing

The integration of AI and machine learning techniques in SOC introduces exciting possibilities for intelligent and autonomous systems. AI and machine learning can be leveraged in various areas of SOC, including service composition, resource optimization, QoS prediction, and anomaly detection. Researchers are exploring how AI techniques like natural language processing, knowledge representation, and reinforcement learning can enhance service-oriented systems. The combination of AI and SOC enables intelligent service discovery, self-adaptive service compositions, and intelligent service monitoring and management.

These emerging trends in SOC provide researchers with a fertile landscape for exploration and innovation. However, further research is needed to address the challenges and opportunities associated with these trends, such as scalability, performance, security, and interoperability. Interdisciplinary collaborations between computer science, software engineering, and domain-specific areas will play a crucial role in advancing these emerging trends and realizing their potential in real-world applications.

In summary, the emerging trends in SOC—including microservices architecture, serverless computing, cloud-native computing, containerization and orchestration, and the integration of AI and machine learning—are shaping the future of service-oriented architectures. Researchers have the opportunity to contribute to these trends by developing novel approaches, methodologies, and tools while addressing the challenges they present. By embracing these emerging trends, organizations can unlock new levels of agility, scalability, and intelligence in their service-oriented systems, driving innovation and delivering value to users and stakeholders.

4.6 Case Studies: Real-World Examples of Service-Oriented Computing

In addition to understanding the theoretical foundations and emerging trends of service-oriented computing, exploring real-world examples that demonstrate the practical applications and benefits of SOC is crucial. In this section, we present three case studies showcasing successful implementations of SOC in the healthcare, finance, and transportation sectors.

4.6.1 Case Study 1: Service-Oriented Computing in Healthcare

SOC has played a transformative role in enhancing patient care, streamlining processes, and improving collaboration among healthcare providers. One example is the implementation of a service-oriented architecture in a hospital setting. By decomposing complex healthcare systems into modular services, interoperability among disparate systems is achieved, enabling seamless data exchange and communication. SOC facilitates the integration of electronic health records (EHRs), medical devices, and clinical decision support systems, supporting evidence-based healthcare practices and providing a holistic view of patient information.

4.6.2 Case Study 2: Service-Oriented Computing in Finance

In the finance industry, SOC has revolutionized the operations of financial institutions, enabling faster, more efficient, and secure transactions. An example is the adoption of a service-oriented architecture in payment processing systems. By encapsulating payment services as independent and reusable components, financial institutions achieve scalability, modularity, and interoperability. SOC facilitates the integration of different payment gateways, banking systems, and fraud-detection mechanisms, providing a seamless experience for customers and ensuring secure and reliable financial transactions.

4.6.3 Case Study 3: Service-Oriented Computing in Transportation

SOC has played a pivotal role in optimizing logistics, enhancing passenger experience, and improving operational efficiency in the transportation industry. In a transportation management system, service-oriented computing enables the integration of various services such as route planning, vehicle tracking, and real-time information dissemination. By leveraging a service-oriented architecture, transportation companies achieve seamless communication and collaboration among different stakeholders, leading to improved fleet management, enhanced customer satisfaction, and efficient resource utilization.

These case studies illustrate the diverse applications of SOC across different industries and emphasize the benefits organizations can achieve by adopting a service-oriented approach. These benefits include improved interoperability, streamlined processes, enhanced customer experience, and increased operational efficiency. By leveraging service-oriented computing, organizations can effectively address industry-specific challenges and drive innovation in their respective domains.

It is important to note that these case studies represent only a subset of the potential applications of SOC. The principles and benefits of SOC can be applied to various other industries, including manufacturing, retail, telecommunications, and more. As SOC continues to evolve, it is expected that more organizations will adopt service-oriented architectures to gain a competitive edge and meet the ever-changing demands of their industries.

In conclusion, the case studies presented in this section provide practical illustrations of successful implementations of service-oriented computing in healthcare, finance, and transportation. These examples demonstrate the transformative impact of SOC in streamlining processes, enhancing collaboration, and achieving business goals. Analyzing these real-world examples enables organizations to gain valuable insights and inspiration for applying SOC principles to their own industry-specific challenges.

4.7 Conclusion

Titled "Service-Oriented Computing Challenges, Benefits, and Emerging Trends," this chapter provides a comprehensive exploration of service-oriented computing. We have examined the fundamental aspects of SOC, beginning with the background and motivation for this research. We identified the research problem and formulated research questions to guide our investigation. Our study covered the essential components of SOC, including its definition, service-oriented architecture (SOA), service-oriented modeling, and service-oriented design principles. We delved into the wide-ranging benefits of SOC, such as enhanced flexibility, scalability, service reusability, agility, interoperability, and cost-effectiveness. Additionally, we addressed the challenges associated with SOC, including complex service composition and orchestration, quality of service (QoS) considerations, security and privacy concerns, management and governance challenges, and legacy system integration. Furthermore, we explored the emerging trends in SOC, including microservices architecture, serverless computing, cloud-native computing, containerization and orchestration, and the integration of AI and machine learning.

The insights gathered from this chapter have significant implications for practitioners. Organizations embarking on SOC initiatives should carefully consider the outlined benefits and challenges to make informed decisions and develop effective strategies. It is crucial to focus on designing loosely coupled and autonomous services, leveraging service composition and orchestration techniques, and ensuring desired levels of service quality. Furthermore, attention should be given to security and privacy measures, effective management and governance processes, and approaches for integrating legacy systems. Embracing emerging trends—such as microservices architecture, serverless computing, cloud-native computing, containerization and orchestration, and AI and machine learning integration—can drive innovation and enhance service-oriented systems.

Regarding future research, there are several promising avenues to explore. Researchers can concentrate on refining service-oriented modeling techniques, developing methodologies for effective service composition and orchestration, and advancing the understanding of QoS management in SOC. Additionally, exploring novel approaches to address security and privacy concerns, tackle management and governance challenges, and enhance legacy system integration can contribute to the advancement of SOC. Further investigations into emerging trends, such as optimizing microservices architecture, improving serverless computing platforms, refining cloud-native computing practices, enhancing containerization and orchestration frameworks, and exploring the full potential of AI and machine learning in SOC, hold significant research potential.

As technology continues to evolve and the demand for scalable and adaptive systems grows, service-oriented computing will continue to play a pivotal role in enabling organizations to meet their ever-changing business needs. By understanding the challenges, capitalizing on the benefits, and embracing the emerging trends, organizations can harness the power of SOC to drive innovation, enhance competitiveness, and deliver value to their stakeholders.

References

Ahmed, T., Verma, R., Bakshi, M. & Srivastava, A. (2014), Membrane computing inspired approach for executing scientific workflow in the cloud, *in* M. Gheorghe, G. Rozenberg, A. Salomaa, P. Sos´ık & C. Zandron, eds, '*Membrane Computing*', Springer International Publishing, Cham, pp. 51–65.

El-Sheikh, E., Zimmermann, A., Jain, L. C. & Jain, L. C. (2016), 'Emerging trends in the evolution of service-oriented and enterprise architectures', *Emerging Trends in the Evolution of Service-Oriented and Enterprise Architectures*. Intelligent Systems Reference Library, vol. 111, pp.1–35.

Hachem, S., Pathak, A. & Issarny, V. (2014), 'Service-oriented middleware for large-scale mobile participatory sensing', *Pervasive and Mobile Computing*. Vol. 10, pp. 66–82.

Hsieh, S.-H., Hsieh, S.-L., Hsieh, S.-L., Cheng, P.-H. & Lai, F. (2012), 'Ehealth and healthcare enterprise information system leveraging serviceoriented architecture', *Telemedicine Journal and E-health*. Vol. 18, no. 3, pp. 205–212.

Huhns, M. N. & Singh, M. P. (2005), 'Service-oriented computing : Key concepts and principles', *IEEE Internet Computing*. Vol. 9, no. 1 (2005), pp/ 75–81.

Kyo¨sti, P. & Lindstr¨om, J. (2022), 'Soa-based platform use in development and operation of automation solutions: Challenges, opportunities, and supporting pillars towards emerging trends', *Applied Sciences*. Vol. 12, no. 3, pp. 10–74.

Lemos, A. L., Daniel, F. & Benatallah, B. (2016), 'Web service composition: A survey of techniques and tools', *ACM Computing Surveys*.

Li, X., Li, X., Li, X., Zheng, Z., Zheng, Z., Zheng, Z., Dai, H.-N. & Dai, H.-N. (2021), 'When services computing meets blockchain: Challenges and opportunities', *Journal of Parallel and Distributed Computing*. Vol. 150, pp. 1–14.

Lu, Z., Delaney, D. & Lillis, D. (2023), 'A survey on microservices trust models for open systems', *IEEE Access*. Vol. 11, pp. 28840–28855.

Nayak, N., Ambalavanan, U., Thampan, J. M., Grewe, D., Wagner, M., Schildt, S. & Ott, J. (2023), 'Reimagining automotive service-oriented communication: A case study on programmable data planes', *IEEE Vehicular Technology Magazine*. Vol. 82, pp. 1–19.

Niknejad, N., Niknejad, N., Ismail, W., Ghani, I., Nazari, B., Bahari, M., Bahari, M., Hussin, A. R. C. & Hussin, A. R. C. (2020), 'Understanding service-oriented architecture (soa): A systematic literature review and directions for further investigation', *Information Systems*. Vol. 91, pp. 1–27.

Papazoglou, M. P. (2003), 'Service-oriented computing: Concepts, characteristics and directions', *Proceedings of the Fourth International Conference on Web Information Systems Engineering, 2003. WISE 2003*.

Papazoglou, M. P., Traverso, P., Dustdar, S. & Leymann, F. (2007), 'Service-oriented computing: State of the art and research challenges', *IEEE Computer*. Vol. 40, no. 11, pp. 38–45.

Papazoglou, M. P., Traverso, P., Dustdar, S. & Leymann, F. (2008), 'Service-oriented computing: A research roadmap', null.

Peltz, C. & Peltz, C. (2003), 'Web services orchestration and choreography', *IEEE Computer*. Vol. 36, no. 10, pp. 46–52.

Raggett, D. (2015), 'The web of things: Challenges and opportunities', *IEEE Computer*. Vol. 48, no. 5, pp. 26–32.

Verma, R. & Srivastava, A. (2014), 'A novel web service directory framework for mobile environments', *in 2014 IEEE International Conference on Web Services*, pp. 614–621.

Verma, R. & Srivastava, A. (2015), 'Towards service description for mobile environments', *in 2015 IEEE International Conference on Services Computing*, pp. 138–145.

Wei, Y. & Blake, M. B. (2010), 'Service-oriented computing and cloud computing: Challenges and opportunities', *IEEE Internet Computing*. Vol. **14**, no. 6, pp. 72–75.

Wu, D., Zhang, P., He, Y. & Luo, X. (2022), 'A double-space and doublenorm ensembled latent factor model for highly accurate web service qos prediction', *IEEE Transactions on Services Computing*. Vol. 16, no. 2, pp. 802–814.

Zeng, L., Benatallah, B., Ngu, A. H. H., Dumas, M., Kalagnanam, J. R. & Chang, H. (2004), 'Qos-aware middleware for web services composition', *IEEE Transactions on Software Engineering*. Vol. 30, no. 5, pp. 311–327.

Chapter 5

Role of Soft Computing Methodologies in Service-Oriented Computing

Pradeep Singh Rawat[1] and Prateek Kumar Soni[2]

[1]*School of Computing, DIT University, Dehradun, India*

[2]*ABV-IIITM, Gwalior, Madhya Pradesh, India*

5.1 Introduction

Service-Oriented Computing (SOC) is a paradigm that revolutionizes the way software functionalities are organized and provided in distributed systems. It offers a flexible and scalable approach to building and integrating applications by treating them as a collection of self-contained services. In SOC, services represent autonomous units of functionality that can be accessed and combined to fulfill specific business requirements. At the core of service-oriented computing is the concept of service granularity. Services are designed to encapsulate specific business logic or functionality, operating independently of each other. This granularity allows services to be easily reused and combined to create new applications or compose complex functionalities. By leveraging service composition, organizations can rapidly build and adapt applications by optimizing existing services rather than developing new ones from scratch. Service-oriented computing also promotes service reusability, where services are designed to be modular and independent, allowing them to be utilized in various contexts and applications. This reusability leads to improved

DOI: 10.1201/9781032716718-5

development efficiency, reduced redundancy, and increased overall system flexibility. Additionally, service governance plays a vital role in managing the lifecycle, deployment, and management of services, ensuring compliance with organizational policies and standards. One of the significant benefits of SOC is its scalability. By breaking down applications into individual services, organizations can scale and distribute resources independently, enabling horizontal scalability and flexible resource allocation. This capability allows systems to adapt to changing demands and effectively utilize available resources, leading to improved performance and cost-efficiency. Service-oriented computing has found widespread adoption across industries and domains, offering a holistic approach to building and integrating complex systems. It enables organizations to leverage existing services, promote interoperability, and quickly respond to changing business requirements. By embracing SOC principles, enterprises can enhance their agility, achieve greater flexibility, and unlock the potential for efficient service-oriented architectures [1].

On the other hand, Soft Computing (SC) is a computational paradigm that addresses the challenges of solving complex problems that involve uncertainty, imprecision, and approximate reasoning. Unlike traditional binary logic, which relies on precise and deterministic representations, soft computing techniques embrace the notion of handling ambiguity and incomplete information. At the heart of soft computing is the integration of various methodologies, including fuzzy logic, neural networks, evolutionary computation, and probabilistic reasoning. Fuzzy logic provides a framework for representing and manipulating imprecise or uncertain information, allowing for flexible reasoning and decision-making. Neural networks, inspired by the structure and functionality of the human brain, excel at pattern recognition, data classification, and prediction tasks, leveraging their ability to learn and generalize from examples. Evolutionary computation algorithms, such as genetic algorithms, mimic the process of natural selection to solve optimization and search problems by iteratively evolving candidate solutions. Probabilistic reasoning, encompassing Bayesian networks and statistical models, facilitates reasoning under uncertainty by assigning probabilities to different events and utilizing them for decision-making. Soft computing techniques are particularly valuable in domains where the problems are complex, involve incomplete or noisy data, or require human-like decision-making. They offer a flexible and adaptive approach to problem-solving, enabling systems to handle real-world complexities more effectively. Soft computing methods excel in scenarios where precise mathematical models are impractical or insufficient to capture the inherent uncertainty and imprecision of the problem domain. The application of soft computing spans a wide range of domains, including data analysis, image and speech recognition, natural language processing, optimization, control systems, and many more. By harnessing the power of soft computing, organizations can tackle complex problems that traditional computational approaches struggle to address, leading to improved decision-making, enhanced system performance, and increased efficiency [2].

In service-oriented computing (SOC), soft computing (SC) techniques enhance service composition by incorporating fuzzy logic, neural networks, evolutionary computation, and probabilistic reasoning. Fuzzy logic handles imprecise information and enables flexible composition based on multiple criteria. Neural networks optimize service selection and composition by learning patterns and predicting suitable compositions. Evolutionary computation efficiently explores the composition space for optimal solutions. Probabilistic reasoning supports decision-making by considering uncertainties and probabilities. SC improves the intelligence and adaptability of service composition, leading to more effective and flexible composite services in SOC systems.

5.2 Fundamentals of Soft Computing Methodologies

Fundamentals of soft computing encompass a collection of computational techniques that aim to model and emulate human-like intelligence, reasoning, and decision-making processes. This interdisciplinary field combines various methodologies, including fuzzy logic, neural networks, evolutionary computation, and swarm intelligence. Soft computing techniques offer powerful tools for handling uncertainty, vagueness, and complex problem domains, making them particularly well-suited for applications in areas such as pattern recognition, optimization, control systems, and decision support. By integrating these methodologies, soft computing enables the development of intelligent systems capable of adapting, learning, and providing robust solutions in dynamic and uncertain environments. In this chapter, we will discuss the essential concepts and principles underlying Fuzzy Logic, Neural Networks, Evolutionary Computation, and their hybridization, exploring their applications and significance in various domains, including service-oriented computing.

5.2.1 Fuzzy Logic

Fuzzy logic is a branch of soft computing that provides a mathematical framework for dealing with uncertainty and imprecision in decision-making processes. Unlike classical logic, which relies on binary values of true or false, fuzzy logic allows for the representation and manipulation of partial truths or degrees of membership. It provides a means to handle and reason with vague or ambiguous information, making it well-suited for domains where precise measurements or boundaries are difficult to define. It provides a means to represent and reason with vague or ambiguous information using fuzzy sets, membership functions, fuzzy rules, and fuzzy inference mechanisms [3].

A fuzzy set is characterized by a membership function, which assigns a level of membership to each element within a given universe of discourse. In other words, the membership function determines the degree to which an element belongs to the fuzzy set. A membership function characterizes the shape and behavior of a fuzzy set, denoted as $\mu A(x)$, maps an element x to a value between 0 and 1, indicating the degree to which x belongs to the fuzzy set A. Triangular, trapezoidal, Gaussian, and sigmoidal functions are typical varieties of membership functions. Fuzzy rules capture expert knowledge or heuristics in the form of "if–then" statements. Each fuzzy rule consists of an antecedent (input) and a consequent (output), both expressed as fuzzy sets. The antecedent represents the conditions or criteria for activating the rule, and the consequent represents the output of the rule. The process of fuzzy inference involves combining the fuzzy sets from the activated rules to generate a fuzzy output. This is done through fuzzy logic operators, such as AND, OR, and NOT, which operate on the membership values of the fuzzy sets [4].

Fuzzy logic has proven to be highly valuable in various applications within the domain of SOC. In service discovery, fuzzy logic techniques are employed to improve matching and similarity measures, enabling more flexible and approximate service matching. This accommodates variations in user requirements and service offerings, leading to more accurate and context-aware service discovery. Fuzzy logic also plays a crucial role in service composition by enabling intelligent and adaptive selection of services based on both functional and non-functional aspects, such as Quality of Service (QoS) attributes. Fuzzy rules guide the composition process, allowing for dynamic and uncertain environments. Additionally, fuzzy logic models can predict and optimize QoS attributes, enabling better decision-making in service selection and composition. Overall, fuzzy logic provides powerful and adaptive solutions for addressing the complexities and uncertainties present in SOC, enhancing service discovery, composition, QoS management, resource allocation, Service Level Agreement (SLA) management, and security.

5.2.2 Neural Networks

Soft computing (SC) combines various computational techniques to handle uncertainty, imprecision, and complexity. Neural networks, as a key component of SC, provide a flexible and robust approach to problem-solving. Neural networks in SC are designed to mimic the behavior of biological neural networks. They consist of interconnected nodes, or artificial neurons, that process and transmit information. These networks can learn from data, adapt to changing conditions, and make predictions or decisions based on the patterns and relationships they discover. SC methodologies, including neural networks, offer several advantages in problem-solving. They can handle imprecise or uncertain data by incorporating fuzzy logic, allowing for more flexible reasoning and decision-making. Additionally, neural networks can be combined with other soft computing techniques, such as genetic algorithms or swarm intelligence, to further enhance their performance and optimization capabilities [5].

Neural networks have emerged as a powerful tool in the realm of service-oriented computing (SOC), providing valuable solutions to a range of challenges. One notable application of neural networks in SOC is service recommendation, where neural networks analyze user preferences and historical usage data to offer personalized service recommendations. By learning patterns and relationships from this data, neural networks enable users to discover relevant services that align with their needs and preferences. Another key application of neural networks in SOC is SLA management. Neural networks can analyze historical data on service performance, user feedback, and resource utilization to predict and optimize quality of service (QoS) attributes. This proactive approach allows for effective monitoring of SLA compliance, prediction of potential SLA violations, and decision-making to prevent or mitigate such violations. Neural networks also excel in service performance prediction, leveraging historical data on service usage, resource utilization, and environmental factors to estimate QoS attributes such as response time, throughput, and availability. These predictions facilitate informed decision-making in service selection and composition to ensure optimal performance

.By leveraging the learning capabilities and pattern recognition of neural networks, SOC can benefit from intelligent decision-making, improved user experience, and efficient resource utilization [6].

5.2.3 Evolutionary Computation

In evolutionary computation, solutions to a problem are represented as individuals in a population. Each individual has a set of characteristics, or "genes," that define its properties or attributes. The population undergoes a process of evolution through successive generations, driven by the principles of selection, reproduction, and variation. Evolutionary computation is a subfield of soft computing that draws inspiration from principles of natural evolution and genetic algorithms to solve complex optimization and search problems. It provides a robust and adaptive approach to finding optimal solutions in diverse domains, including service-oriented computing. It encompasses a set of computational techniques that emulate the process of evolution, including genetic programming, genetic algorithms, evolutionary strategies, and evolutionary programming [7].

Genetic Algorithms are a powerful subfield of evolutionary computation within soft computing. They are inspired by the principles of natural evolution and genetic inheritance and provide a robust optimization technique for solving complex problems. At the core of genetic algorithms is the concept of a population, which represents a collection of potential solutions to a given problem. Each solution is encoded as a chromosome, typically represented as a string of binary or real-valued values. These chromosomes undergo a process of evolution through successive generations, driven by genetic operators such as selection, crossover, and mutation.

Genetic algorithms have found applications in various domains, including optimization problems, machine learning, scheduling, and resource allocation. They offer the advantage of being able to handle complex and multi-dimensional search spaces, where traditional optimization techniques may struggle. Additionally, genetic algorithms are flexible and can be adapted to different problem domains by customizing the selection, crossover, and mutation operators [8].

Evolutionary computation is a powerful approach that is well-suited for solving complex optimization problems, particularly those characterized by vast search spaces, multidimensional parameter spaces, and non-linear relationships. Traditional optimization techniques may struggle to find solutions in such scenarios due to the computational complexity and the lack of explicit problem information. However, evolutionary computation provides a robust and efficient solution. One key advantage of evolutionary computation is its ability to handle problems with multiple objectives, constraints, and uncertainties. Many real-world optimization problems involve conflicting objectives, where improving one aspect may lead to the degradation of another. Evolutionary algorithms, such as genetic algorithms, employ a population-based approach where multiple solutions coexist and compete with each other. Through mechanisms such as fitness assignment, selection, and reproduction, evolutionary computation can effectively navigate the trade-offs between competing objectives, resulting in a set of Pareto-optimal solutions that represent the best compromises.

Additionally, evolutionary computation excels at handling constraints, both hard and soft. Constraints can be incorporated directly into the fitness evaluation process, guiding the search towards feasible solutions. Furthermore, evolutionary algorithms can handle uncertain problem environments by exploring the search space and adapting their solutions over time. This adaptability is particularly valuable in dynamic optimization scenarios, where the problem or its constraints may change over time. The underlying principle of evolutionary computation is inspired by the mechanisms of natural evolution, such as selection, reproduction, and variation. The population of candidate solutions evolves over generations through the application of genetic operators like crossover and mutation. By combining the fittest individuals and introducing random variations, evolutionary algorithms explore the search space in a systematic manner, gradually converging towards optimal or near-optimal solutions. One of the key strengths of evolutionary computation is its ability to effectively search and explore large and complex solution spaces. The use of stochastic operators, such as mutation and crossover, allows for exploration of different regions of the search space, avoiding premature convergence to suboptimal solutions. This makes evolutionary computation well-suited for optimization problems where the landscape is rugged or contains multiple local optima [9].

Evolutionary computation techniques have several applications in service-oriented computing (SOC). They can be used for automating service composition, optimizing service placement and resource allocation, improving service scheduling and load balancing, enhancing service-level agreement (SLA) management, and addressing service selection and recommendation problems. By leveraging the principles of evolution and natural selection, evolutionary computation provides effective solutions to complex optimization and search problems in SOC, enabling efficient and intelligent service provisioning and management [10].

5.3 Soft Computing in Service Discovery and Composition

Fuzzy logic-based service discovery is a prominent application of fuzzy logic in service-oriented computing (SOC). Service discovery involves the identification and selection of relevant services that match the user's requirements and preferences. In fuzzy logic-based service discovery, the user's preferences and requirements are expressed using linguistic terms, such as "high," "low," "good," or "bad." These linguistic terms are associated with fuzzy sets, which capture the degree of membership of a service to a particular term. Fuzzy rules define the relationships between input variables (user requirements) and output variables (service attributes), guiding the selection and ranking of services based on their compatibility with the user's preferences. During the service discovery process, fuzzy logic-based techniques evaluate the degree of match between the user's requirements and the service attributes using fuzzy inference mechanisms. This involves applying fuzzy operators, such as fuzzy AND, fuzzy OR, and fuzzy implication, to calculate the degree of membership and perform fuzzy reasoning. The result is a ranked list of services that best match the user's preferences, considering the imprecision and uncertainty inherent in the discovery process [11].

Fuzzy logic-based service discovery offers several benefits in SOC. It accommodates subjective user preferences, allowing users to express their requirements in a more natural and intuitive manner. It also enables the handling of imprecise or incomplete information, allowing for robust service matching and recommendation. Additionally, fuzzy logic-based techniques can adapt to dynamic changes in user preferences or service availability, enhancing the agility and responsiveness of service discovery in evolving environments.

5.4 Soft Computing for Service Quality Assurance

Soft computing techniques have proven to be effective in addressing the challenges of service quality assurance. Service quality assurance involves monitoring and managing various aspects of service delivery to ensure that customer expectations are met or exceeded. Fuzzy logic, a key component of soft computing, enables the modeling and reasoning of imprecise and uncertain quality indicators. It allows for the representation of linguistic variables, which capture the subjective nature of service quality. By using fuzzy logic, service quality metrics can be defined and evaluated based on linguistic terms, allowing for a more human-like and flexible approach to quality assessment. Fuzzy logic-based systems can handle complex, ambiguous, and non-linear relationships between input variables, enabling accurate evaluation and decision-making in service quality assurance. Neural networks, another essential component of soft computing, excel in pattern recognition, learning, and prediction tasks. They can be utilized to analyze historical service quality data and identify patterns and trends that may affect future quality levels. By training neural networks with relevant data, they can predict potential quality issues and deviations before they occur. Neural network-driven quality assurance systems can help service providers proactively identify and resolve problems, leading to improved service performance and customer satisfaction.

Evolutionary computation algorithms offer optimization capabilities for service quality assurance. By leveraging principles inspired by natural evolution, these algorithms can search for optimal solutions in large and complex search spaces. In the context of service quality assurance, evolutionary computation techniques can optimize service parameters, resource allocation, and network configurations to maximize quality and minimize performance bottlenecks. These algorithms can adapt and learn from past experiences, continuously improving service quality over time. The integration of soft computing methodologies in service quality assurance enables service providers to monitor, analyze, and optimize service quality parameters in real-time. By leveraging fuzzy logic, neural networks, and evolutionary computation, organizations can proactively identify and address quality issues, minimize downtime, and enhance overall customer experience. Soft computing techniques provide a powerful framework for intelligent decision-making, enabling service providers to make data-driven and informed choices to improve service quality [12].

5.5 Soft Computing for Service Optimization

Soft computing techniques play a vital role in service-level optimization, where the objective is to enhance the performance and efficiency of services in various domains. Resource allocation and scheduling are critical aspects of service-oriented systems, where efficient utilization of resources and effective task scheduling can significantly impact system performance and customer satisfaction. Fuzzy logic-based resource allocation and scheduling is an approach that leverages the power of fuzzy logic to optimize the allocation of resources and scheduling of tasks in various domains.

The use of fuzzy logic in resource allocation and scheduling allows for the consideration of various constraints and objectives simultaneously. By defining fuzzy rules that capture the relationships between input variables and desired output actions, service providers can determine the optimal allocation of resources and scheduling of tasks based on multiple criteria. Fuzzy logic-based systems can handle complex and dynamic environments, adapt to changing conditions, and make real-time adjustments to resource allocations and task schedules.

Fuzzy logic-based resource allocation and scheduling have been successfully applied in various domains, including cloud computing, telecommunications, and transportation. In cloud computing, fuzzy logic-based approaches can optimize the allocation of virtual machines, storage resources, and network bandwidth to meet user demands while minimizing resource wastage. In telecommunications, fuzzy logic-based scheduling can prioritize network traffic, allocate bandwidth, and manage network resources efficiently. In transportation, fuzzy logic-based scheduling can optimize the routing and scheduling of vehicles, considering factors such as traffic conditions, delivery deadlines, and driver preferences.

By employing fuzzy logic-based resource allocation and scheduling techniques, organizations can achieve improved resource utilization, task completion times, and overall system performance. Fuzzy logic-based approaches offer a flexible and adaptive framework for resource allocation and scheduling, taking into account both quantitative and qualitative factors. By intelligently managing resources and scheduling tasks, service providers can enhance operational efficiency, meet service level agreements, and deliver high-quality services to customers [13].

Also, in neural network-driven service optimization, neural network models are trained on historical data to learn patterns and relationships between input variables and optimization objectives. These models can then be used to make predictions, recommendations, and informed decisions for optimizing service-oriented systems. By leveraging the learning capabilities of neural networks, service providers can uncover insights, identify optimization opportunities, and drive improvements in system performance. One key area where neural network-driven service optimization is applied is in resource allocation. Neural networks can analyze historical usage patterns, user demands, and other relevant factors to predict resource requirements and allocate resources optimally. By accurately predicting resource needs and dynamically adjusting allocations, service providers can enhance resource utilization, reduce wastage, and improve system efficiency. Furthermore, neural networks can be utilized for service optimization in areas such as task scheduling, load balancing, and quality of service (QoS) management. Neural network models can analyze real-time data, monitor system performance, and make proactive decisions to optimize task scheduling, balance workloads, and maintain desired QoS levels. This enables service providers to adaptively respond to changing conditions, mitigate bottlenecks, and optimize service delivery in real-time [14].

5.5.1 System Architecture

Here's a high-level system architecture diagram illustrating the role of soft computing methodologies in service-oriented computing as shown in Figure 5.1.

Service-Oriented Computing: This is the overarching concept that focuses on building and delivering services in a distributed environment.

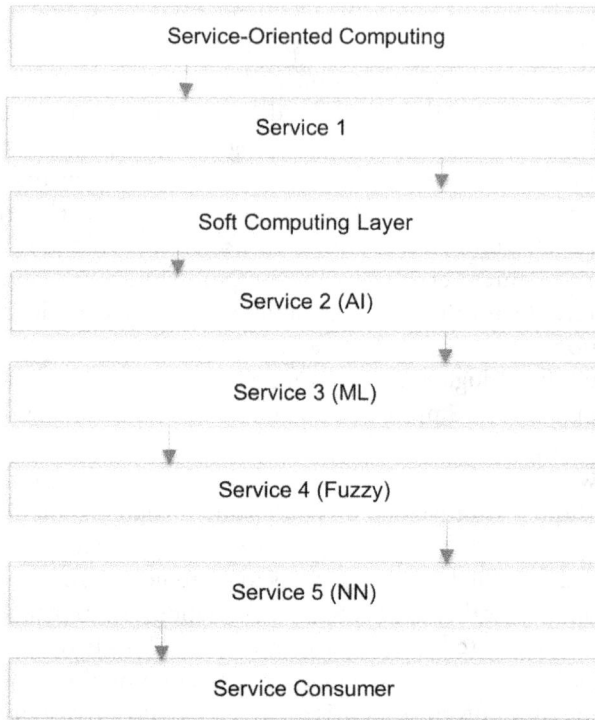

Figure 5.1 System architecture of soft computing methodologies in service-oriented computing.

Service 1 to Service n: These represent individual services offered in a service-oriented architecture. Each service provides a specific functionality or capability to service consumers.

Soft Computing Layer: This layer incorporates various soft computing methodologies to enhance the capabilities of the services. It acts as an intermediary layer between the service providers and consumers.

Service 2 to Service 5: These services demonstrate the integration of specific soft computing methodologies into the service-oriented architecture. For example, Service 2 might utilize artificial intelligence techniques, Service 3 might employ machine learning algorithms, Service 4 could utilize fuzzy logic, and Service 5 might incorporate neural networks.

Service Consumers: These are the end-users or clients who interact with the services provided by the service-oriented architecture. They can access and utilize the services exposed by the architecture, taking advantage of the soft computing methodologies embedded within the services.

Overall, the diagram highlights how soft computing methodologies are integrated into the service-oriented computing paradigm, enabling the development of intelligent and adaptive services to meet the diverse needs of service consumers.

5.6   Soft Computing in Service Security and Privacy

In soft computing, fuzzy logic-based intrusion detection systems utilize fuzzy sets, linguistic variables, and fuzzy rules to handle uncertainty and imprecision in security events. Fuzzy sets represent linguistic terms, such as "normal," "suspicious," or "malicious," to describe the degree of membership of an event or behavior to a particular category. Fuzzy rules define the relationships between these linguistic variables and guide the detection process.

The detection phase involves collecting and preprocessing relevant data, such as network traffic, system logs, and other security-related information. Fuzzy logic-based techniques, such as fuzzy inference systems, are then employed to evaluate the collected data. Fuzzy rules are used to determine the degree of suspicion or risk associated with observed events. Fuzzy inference mechanisms calculate the degree of membership of events to different linguistic terms, allowing for more accurate and robust detection of intrusions [15].

Fuzzy logic-based intrusion detection systems in soft computing offer several advantages. They can handle uncertainty and imprecision in security events, enabling the detection of complex and evolving threats. These systems can also incorporate human expertise and domain knowledge by defining linguistic variables and rules based on expert input. Furthermore, fuzzy logic-based techniques can adapt and learn from new patterns or emerging threats, enhancing their ability to detect previously unseen attacks. On the other hand, neural network approaches have proven to be highly effective for anomaly detection in soft computing. Anomaly detection involves identifying patterns or instances that deviate significantly from normal behavior or expected patterns. Neural networks offer powerful capabilities to detect anomalies by learning from large amounts of data and identifying complex patterns.

One popular neural network approach for anomaly detection is the auto encoder. Auto encoders are unsupervised neural networks that aim to reconstruct the input data at the output layer. During the training process, the auto encoder learns to encode the input data into a lower-dimensional representation and then decode it back to reconstruct the original input. Anomalies in the data can be identified by measuring the discrepancy between the input and the reconstructed output. If the reconstruction error exceeds a predefined threshold, it indicates the presence of an anomaly [16]. Also, by emulating the principles of natural selection and evolution, genetic algorithms offer effective methods for addressing security challenges and enhancing security measures. Furthermore, genetic algorithms contribute to malware detection and classification. By representing malware features as chromosomes and assessing their fitness based on classification accuracy, genetic algorithms evolve effective models for malware detection. This approach enables the development of accurate and efficient malware detection systems, enhancing the ability to combat evolving and sophisticated malware threats.

For intrusion detection systems (IDS), genetic algorithms optimize system configurations and parameters. They encode IDS settings as chromosomes and assess their effectiveness using fitness functions. By iteratively refining these settings through genetic operators, such as mutation and crossover, genetic algorithms improve the performance and adaptability of IDS, leading to more effective detection and prevention of intrusions. In firewall rule optimization, genetic algorithms optimize rule sets by evaluating their fitness in terms of effectiveness, coverage, and efficiency. By evolving and refining rule sets, genetic algorithms minimize redundancy, enhance rule priority, and optimize overall firewall performance [17]. In conclusion, soft computing techniques play a vital role in enhancing service security and privacy. By leveraging fuzzy logic, neural networks, evolutionary computation, and other soft computing methodologies, innovative solutions can be developed to address the challenges associated with service-oriented computing. These techniques enable the detection and prevention of intrusions, facilitate secure service composition, provide robust anomaly detection, and optimize security solutions. Moreover, soft computing approaches can handle the uncertainty and complexity of security-related data, adapt to evolving threats, and incorporate human expertise into the decision-making process. By integrating soft computing into service-oriented computing, organizations can strengthen their security measures, protect sensitive data, and ensure the privacy of their services and users.

5.7 Case Studies and Applications of Soft Computing in Service-Oriented Computing

Soft computing techniques have found practical application in various domains, showcasing their versatility and effectiveness. Real-life case studies provide concrete examples of how these techniques have been successfully implemented in diverse fields.

5.7.1 Adaptive Service Composition in Healthcare Systems

In a healthcare setting, the utilization of soft computing techniques has revolutionized the way adaptive service composition is achieved based on patient needs and preferences. The complexity and variability of patient conditions, medical history, and treatment requirements call for intelligent approaches to customize and optimize healthcare services. Fuzzy logic algorithms have emerged as a valuable tool in this context. By leveraging fuzzy logic algorithms, the system can effectively evaluate the compatibility and suitability of various healthcare services in real-time. The algorithm considers multiple factors, including patient medical history, current diagnosis, treatment guidelines, and individual preferences, to make informed decisions about service composition. Fuzzy logic allows for the representation and manipulation of imprecise or uncertain information, enabling the system to handle the inherent ambiguity and vagueness in healthcare data. The adaptive service composition enabled by fuzzy logic algorithms leads to several benefits in healthcare delivery. First, it allows for tailored treatment plans that align with the individual needs and preferences of patients, promoting patient-centered care. Second, it optimizes the allocation of healthcare resources by considering factors such as resource availability, cost-effectiveness, and treatment outcomes. This ensures efficient resource utilization and enhances the overall effectiveness of healthcare services. Moreover, the system can continuously adapt and update the service composition based on changes in the patient's condition, treatment response, or new medical information. It allows for real-time adjustments to the treatment plan, ensuring that patients receive the most appropriate and up-to-date care. The flexibility and adaptability of fuzzy logic-based service composition empower healthcare providers to deliver personalized and responsive healthcare services [18].

5.7.2 Intelligent Service Recommendation in Online Retail

An online retail platform successfully implemented an intelligent service recommendation system by leveraging the power of neural networks. With a vast array of products available, it became essential to provide personalized recommendations to customers based on their browsing behavior, purchase history, and product features. Neural networks, known for their ability to identify intricate patterns and relationships within data, were employed to analyze and understand customer preferences. The system trained neural network models on a large dataset that included customer behavior, historical purchases, and product attributes. By processing this information, the models were able to learn and identify patterns in customer preferences, enabling the generation of accurate and targeted service recommendations.

The neural network models leveraged various techniques, such as collaborative filtering and content-based filtering, to generate recommendations. Collaborative filtering compared a customer's behavior with that of similar customers, identifying products or services that other customers with similar tastes and preferences had engaged with. Content-based filtering, on the other hand, focused on analyzing the characteristics and attributes of products to suggest similar items. Through continuous learning and refinement, the neural network models became more adept at capturing the nuances of customer preferences. They took into account factors such as the types of products customers frequently purchased, the frequency of their visits, and their interactions with specific product categories. By considering these variables, the system could make increasingly accurate predictions about which products or services would resonate with individual customers.

The implementation of the intelligent service recommendation system had significant benefits for both the online retail platform and its customers. Customers experienced a highly personalized shopping experience, with relevant recommendations tailored to their preferences and interests. This improved customer satisfaction, as customers felt that the platform understood their needs and made relevant suggestions, saving them time and effort in finding desirable products [19].

5.7.3   Fault Detection and Diagnosis in Industrial Automation

In the context of industrial automation, the implementation of soft computing techniques has revolutionized the detection and diagnosis of faults in complex systems. The intricate nature of these systems, coupled with the potential for numerous interconnected components, necessitates intelligent approaches to ensure their smooth operation and minimize downtime. Soft computing techniques, particularly genetic algorithms, have been instrumental in addressing this challenge. By leveraging genetic algorithms, the system is capable of evolving fault detection and diagnosis rules based on a variety of inputs, including sensor data, historical fault records, and system behavior. The algorithms learn patterns and correlations from this data, enabling them to proactively identify and diagnose faults before they escalate into more significant issues [20].

The genetic algorithms employ a population-based approach to optimize the fault detection and diagnosis rules. Initially, a population of potential rules is created, representing different combinations and configurations. Each rule undergoes evaluation against historical fault records and sensor data to assess its performance in accurately detecting and diagnosing faults. The genetic algorithms then apply selection, crossover, and mutation operations to produce new generations of rules that exhibit improved performance. Through this iterative process, the genetic algorithms gradually refine the fault detection and diagnosis rules, focusing on identifying patterns and correlations within the data that indicate specific fault conditions. The rules become increasingly specialized and accurate in detecting and diagnosing faults, allowing for timely troubleshooting and maintenance interventions.

Additionally, soft computing techniques aid in maintenance efficiency. The ability to accurately diagnose faults based on learned patterns and correlations streamlines the troubleshooting process, allowing maintenance personnel to quickly identify the root causes and apply the necessary repairs or adjustments. This reduces the time required for troubleshooting and maintenance activities, optimizing the utilization of resources and minimizing operational disruptions [21]. These real-life case studies demonstrate the practical application of soft computing techniques across various domains. From healthcare and retail to industrial automation, cloud computing, and network security, soft computing has proven to be a powerful tool for enhancing efficiency, improving decision-making, and achieving better outcomes. As these technologies continue to evolve, we can expect even more innovative applications and solutions in the future. In conclusion, soft computing methodologies play a crucial role in advancing service-oriented computing by addressing complex problems and enabling intelligent decision-making. Fuzzy logic, neural networks, and evolutionary computation are fundamental techniques that have found numerous applications in service-oriented computing domains.

Soft computing techniques have been successfully applied in service discovery, service composition, intrusion detection, anomaly detection, security solutions, and resource allocation, among others. They provide robust solutions that adapt to changing conditions, handle uncertainty, and optimize service quality, efficiency, and security. The future of soft computing in service-oriented computing is promising, with emerging trends and research directions that focus on integration with emerging technologies, development of explainable models, handling big data and real-time processing, adaptive and self-learning systems, and ethical considerations. These trends aim to address emerging challenges and leverage new opportunities, ensuring the trustworthy, efficient, and responsible use of soft computing techniques.

By embracing these advancements, service-oriented computing can continue to evolve and provide innovative solutions across various industries, including healthcare, retail, industrial automation, cloud computing, and network security. Soft computing methodologies empower organizations to optimize service delivery, enhance customer satisfaction, improve system reliability, and achieve better outcomes in an increasingly interconnected and data-driven world. Overall, the role of soft computing methodologies in service-oriented computing is indispensable. They offer powerful tools to tackle complex problems, make intelligent decisions, and deliver high-quality services. As technology continues to advance, soft computing techniques will play a vital role in shaping the future of service-oriented computing and driving innovation in diverse domains.

5.8   Conclusions

The soft computing technique plays a prominent role in optimization of the resources in service oriented computing environment. The chapter covers the basic terminology of the soft computing techniques and its application in a service oriented computing paradigm. The case studies provide the closer understanding about the role of the two paradigm in integration manner. It also covers the background knowledge about the soft computing and service oriented computing paradigm. It covers the applications of the technologies in industrial automation, retail system, health care system and cloud resource optimization with optimal layered architecture.

5.9 Future Trends and Research Directions in Soft Computing for Service-Oriented Computing

The future of soft computing in service-oriented computing is shaped by several emerging trends and research directions that aim to address evolving challenges and capitalize on new opportunities. One prominent trend is the integration of soft computing with emerging technologies like blockchain and the Internet of Things (IoT). This integration enhances security and privacy in service-oriented computing by leveraging the inherent decentralized and immutable nature of blockchain, while also enabling intelligent service provisioning in IoT environments. This integration opens up possibilities for secure and efficient service delivery in various domains, such as supply chain management, healthcare, and smart cities [22].

Another important research direction is the development of explainable and interpretable soft computing models. As these models become more complex and powerful, understanding their decision-making process becomes crucial. Explainable models provide transparency, enabling users to comprehend the reasoning behind soft computing decisions and building trust in their outcomes. Interpretable models also help in compliance with regulatory requirements, such as the General Data Protection Regulation (GDPR), where the right to explanation is mandated [23].

Handling big data and real-time processing is another significant focus in soft computing for service-oriented computing. With the exponential growth of data, scalable algorithms are required to efficiently process and analyze large volumes of data. This involves the development of distributed computing frameworks, parallel processing techniques, and efficient data mining algorithms that can operate in real-time and provide timely insights for decision-making and service optimization. Furthermore, the ethical and responsible use of soft computing is gaining increasing attention. Research efforts are focused on establishing frameworks for fairness, transparency, and accountability in soft computing algorithms and systems. Ethical considerations such as bias detection and mitigation, fairness in decision-making, and privacy-preserving techniques are being integrated into the design and deployment of soft computing models to ensure responsible and trustworthy systems.

By pursuing these future trends and research directions, soft computing can further advance service-oriented computing and enable the development of efficient, intelligent, and ethical systems. The integration with emerging technologies, the focus on explain ability and interpretability, the handling of big data and real-time processing, the development of adaptive systems, and the emphasis on ethical considerations collectively contribute to the evolution and enhancement of soft computing for service-oriented computing.

References

[1] Shen, J., Kim, S.D. and Venkatasubramanian, N. (2012). Service oriented computing and applications. *Computer Systems Science And Engineering*, 27(2), pp. 87–87.

[2] Kumari, U. (2017). "Soft computing applications: A perspective view." 2017 2nd *International Conference on Communication and Electronics Systems (ICCES)*, IEEE.

[3] Arun M, Shanavaz S. (2022, Aug 11). Forecasting of weld parameters by soft computing techniques. *In 2022 Third International Conference on Intelligent Computing Instrumentation and Control Technologies (ICICICT)* (pp. 381–385), IEEE.

[4] Tarannum S, Jabin S. (2018, Oct 12). A comparative study on fuzzy logic and intuitionistic fuzzy logic. *In 2018 International Conference on Advances in Computing, Communication Control and Networking (ICACCCN)* (pp. 1086–1090), IEEE.

[5] Ibrahim D. (2016, Jan 1). An overview of soft computing. *Procedia Computer Science*, 102, pp. 34–38.

[6] Wang H, Yang Z, Yu Q, Hong T, Lin X. (2018, Nov 1). Online reliability time series prediction via convolutional neural network and long short term memory for service-oriented systems. *Knowledge-Based Systems*, 159, pp. 132–147.

[7] Zhang, B., Wu, Y., Lu, J. and Du, K.L. (2011). Evolutionary computation and its applications in neural and fuzzy systems. *Applied Computational Intelligence and Soft Computing*, vol. 2011, pp. 1–21.

[8] Ko, M., Tiwari, A. and Mehnen, J. (2010). A review of soft computing applications in supply chain management. *Applied Soft Computing*, 10(3), pp. 661–674.

[9] Slowik, A. and Kwasnicka, H. (2020). Evolutionary algorithms and their applications to engineering problems. *Neural Computing and Applications*, 32, pp. 12363–12379.

[10] Squillero G, Burelli P, editors. (2016). *Applications of Evolutionary Computation*, Springer.

[11] Buvanesvari, R., Prasath, V. and SanofarNisha, H. (2013). A review of fuzzy based QoS web service discovery. *International Journal of Advanced Networking and Applications*, 4(5), pp. 1752.

[12] Kumar, M., Sharma, A. and Kumar, R. (2011). Optimization of test cases using soft computing techniques: A critical review. *WSEAS Transactions on Information Science and Applications*, 8(11), pp. 440–452.

[13] Chandran K, Shanmugasudaram V, Subramani K. (2016, Jan 1). Designing a fuzzy-logic based trust and reputation model for secure resource allocation in cloud computing. *International Arab Journal of Information Technology (IAJIT)*, vol. 13(1), pp 30–37

[14] Mirahadi, F. and Zayed, T. (2016). Simulation-based construction productivity forecast using neural-network-driven fuzzy reasoning. *Automation in Construction*, 65, pp. 102–115.

[15] Dotcenko S, Vladyko A, Letenko I. (2014, Feb 16). A fuzzy logic-based information security management for software-defined networks. *In 16th International Conference on Advanced Communication Technology* (pp. 167–171), IEEE.

[16] Naseer S, Saleem Y, Khalid S, Bashir M.K, Han J, Iqbal M.M, Han K. (2018, Aug 17). Enhanced network anomaly detection based on deep neural networks. *IEEE Access*, 6, pp. 48231–48246.

[17] Sujatha K.S, Dharmar V, Bhuvaneswaran R.S. (2012, Apr 19). Design of genetic algorithm based IDS for MANET. *In 2012 International Conference on Recent Trends in Information Technology* (pp. 28–33), IEEE.

[18] Das S, Sanyal M.K. (2020). Application of AI and soft computing in healthcare: A review and speculation, *International Journal of Scientific & Technology Research*, vol. 8(11), pp. 1786–1806.

[19] Malik, M.S.I. (2020). Predicting users' review helpfulness: The role of significant review and reviewer characteristics. *Soft Computing*, 24(18), pp. 13913–13928.

[20] Parvaresh, A., Hasanzade, A., Mohammadi, S.M.A. and Gharaveisi, A. (2012). Fault detection and diagnosis in HVAC systems based on a soft computing approach. *International Journal of Soft Computing and Engineering*, 2(3), pp. 2231–2307.

[21] Dai X, Gao Z. (2013, Jan 30). From model, signal to knowledge: A data-driven perspective of fault detection and diagnosis. *IEEE Transactions on Industrial Informatics*, 9(4), pp. 2226–2238.

[22] Ibrahim, D. (2016). An overview of soft computing. *Procedia Computer Science*, 102, pp. 34–38.

[23] Sharma, S., Shakya, H.K. and Mishra, A. (2022). Medical data security using blockchain with soft computing techniques: A review. *The Internet of Medical Things (IoMT) Healthcare Transformation*, vol. 1 pp. 269–288.

Chapter 6

Fundamental Principles for Service-Oriented Computing Paradigm

Narendra Kumar

School of Computing, DIT University Dehradun, Dehradun, Uttarakhand, India

6.1   Introduction

A service-oriented architecture (SOA) is an approach for designing software in which individual application components expose their services to one another over a communications channel, typically the Internet [26]. The ideas that underpin a service-oriented approach are universal and do not rely on any particular product, provider, or technology. Simply put, service-oriented architecture simplifies the process by which software components located on different networks may collaborate effectively. Service-oriented architecture is a technical term for an architectural paradigm in which networked programs interact with and rely on remote services. In this framework, applications are built using a combination of different services that are accessed via an online network connection [21]. SOA uses common forms of communication to make service integration into applications quicker and easier. Each SOA service is a discrete, self-sufficient enterprise-level operation. With the services supplied in this fashion, it is much easier for developers to put together their apps. Please be aware that SOA and microservice architecture are not the same thing. Users can build apps with SOA by mixing a wide range of features from many current services. The breadth of the service-oriented architecture framework encompasses a collection of architectural concepts that structure system

DOI: 10.1201/9781032716718-6

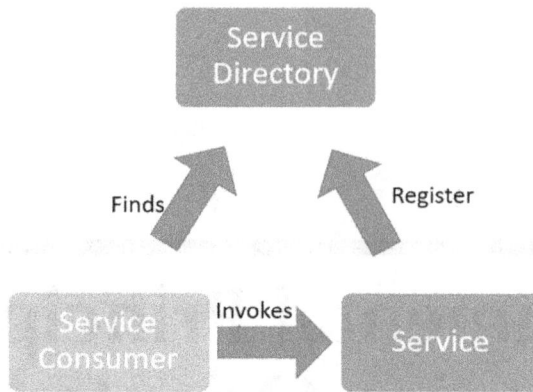

Figure 6.1 Service-oriented architecture.

development and provide mechanisms for combining components into a cohesive and autonomous system. Computing that is based on SOA organizes its functions into a collection of interoperable services. These services may then be included in a variety of software systems that are associated with distinct business areas. Users are able to create apps consisting of a multitude of features by combining a selection of those offered by preexisting services, thanks to SOA (see Figure 6.1) SOA refers to a collection of design principles that organize system development and provide mechanisms for integrating components into a cohesive and decentralized system. These principles are referred to as "design principles." Computing that is based on SOA organizes its capabilities into a collection of interoperable services. These services may then be included in a variety of software systems that correspond to distinct business areas.

Service-oriented architecture leads all of us to understand it as a kind of architecture that centers on services. The term "service" refers to an independent software component that is built with well-specified interface standards.

The service is not made available to other developers until the directory or registry in which it is stored has been built and verified. Until then, the service is supplied in Figure 6.2. A repository containing information on the published service is also made available by the registry. This repository includes instructions on how to construct an interface, the needed levels of service, and methods for retaining authorization, among other things.

In the context of service-oriented architecture, there are two primary roles:

Service provider: The supplier of a service can be either the business or individual responsible for keeping it running and making it available to clients. Service providers can increase awareness of their offerings by including them in registries alongside service contracts that specify the service's kind,

Service response

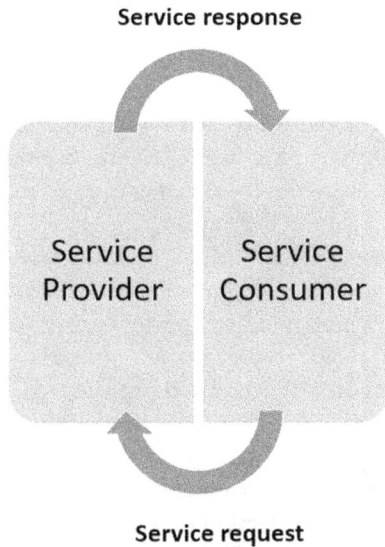

Figure 6.2   **Primary roles of service-oriented architecture.**

its intended use, any necessary preconditions for getting the service, and its price.

Service consumer: The service consumer is the individual who is able to locate the service information in the registry and produce the essential client parts in order to bind to and make use of the service.

6.2   Related Work

The authors Goodall et al. (2011) offer an interface architecture for presenting water resource modeling as web services and explain how it may be used to simulate a rainfall or runoff event inside a watershed system. This research was carried out as part of the Water Resources Modeling Initiative (WRMI). Having followed a discussion of both the benefits and drawbacks of employing service-oriented computing in the modeling of water resource systems, we come to a conclusion by outlining the kinds of work that will be required in the near future to advance the implementation of service-oriented computing in the modeling of water resource systems [1].

Moghaddam et al. (2015) provides a brief overview and analysis of the growing partnership between cooperative e-manufacturing and SOA, which is leading to the formation of a new manufacturing paradigm based on a distributed network of "cloud sendees" that make possible the concept of "Manufacturing as a Service" (MaaS) [2].

Beer Mohamed et al. (2021) offer an adaptive security architecture paradigm for SOA-compliant public-key infrastructure-based identity federation across and inside organizations. To achieve these goals, the suggested architecture is deployed and evaluated in a production-ready, federated-identity-enabled corporate computing setting using security-centric financial data. Existing and new solutions are compared side by side to verify the enhancement in the security of the identity federation environment [3].

In an article by Hustad & Olsen (2021), we learn more about digital infrastructure, SOA, and microservices. It highlights the pros and cons of using cloud services as a component of a service-oriented environment to establish an environmentally friendly infrastructure [4], [29].

Researchers Cabrera et al. (2017) carried out a comprehensive mapping project by developing a review procedure that combines automated and human searches from a variety of sources. In order to obtain the articles for evaluation, researchers used a method that was both systematic and exhaustive to extricate the keywords from the research questions and selection criteria [5].

Service-oriented computing (SOC) is gaining importance as a reference paradigm for a new category of distributed computing technologies, such as web services and the grid. In [6] the author explains the three most crucial aspects of service-oriented computing, namely communication latency, informal coupling, and open-endedness, and link these characteristics to conventional process algebra operators. In addition, researchers note that the combination of these three factors creates new problems that necessitate the research and development of new process algebra operators [6].

Systematizing and optimizing management processes in complex transport systems is essential to the growth of the transport sector in the Arctic, which is why the idea of a complex transport system is based on a service-oriented architecture [7].

An article by Rojas et al. (2021) describes SOA design, administration, and implementation for medium, small, and micro organizations using infrastructure and cost optimization. The architecture is defined by the conceptual model and physical model needed to carry it out. The conceptual model abstracts the business model into three core services: business service, Chat Service, and company service. The service contract layer was removed, web services had no influence, and data storage was decentralized. Optimizing infrastructure and software development firm expenses improved business agility [8].

Niknejad et al. (2020) investigated the issues that already exist with SOA, and then reported findings to the academic community. As a result, a systematic literature review was carried out to investigate previously published research on SOA and the variables that contributed to the success or failure of SOA implementations between the years 2009 and 2019. In order to thoroughly cover all of the research that is associated with SOA in the area of IS (Infrastructure Services), a two-stage review process was performed. This protocol comprised both automated and human searching, and it resulted in 103 main papers. The papers have been organized according to four distinct study topics, which are SOA concepts, SOA impact, SOA adoption, and SOA practice [9].

(LUO et al., 2011) by referring to a philosophy that is centered on service. The IAAS platform is going through reconstruction. A strategy management system is offered in order to maximize service monitoring and service scheduling. This system is built on loosely connected physical resources, which are supplied via virtualization technology [32]. The prototype implementation demonstrates that the proposed change would successfully enhance the performance of the service operating on IAAS [10].

(Chen et al., 2020) The goal of the provided identification approach is to map the main activity aspects with the intelligent abilities in order to elicit the service needs that are involved in the user activity cycle. In addition, a brand new approach called the rough-fuzzy best-worst method is presented to prioritize the criteria that have been determined while concurrently managing intrapersonal and interpersonal uncertainty [11].

(Deventer et al., 2017) The goal of the provided identification approach is to map the main activity aspects with the smart capabilities in order to elicit the service needs that are involved in the user activity cycle. In addition, a brand new approach called the rough-fuzzy best-worst method is presented to prioritize the criteria that have been determined while concurrently managing intrapersonal and interpersonal uncertainty [12].

The objective of research by Pulparambil and Baghdadi (2019) was to provide a complete comparison of current SOAMMs (Service Oriented Architecture Maturity Model) in order to identify issues that need improvement as well as potential for study. For the purpose of investigating the SOA adoption maturity studies, a comprehensive literature study was carried out. Just a few SOAMMs provide prioritizing improvement measures and directions for choosing them, despite the fact that all SOAMMs include a measurement framework in their proposals. The present state of the study demonstrates that there is a knowledge gap regarding the prescriptive as well as descriptive purposes of SOAMM utilization, and it points to the need for further studies in this area [13].

In a 2021 study, Bora and Bezboruah used a cluster-based web server to provide a unique evaluation approach that will evaluate a prototype web service-based system for a COVID-19 disease processing system. This methodology has been introduced in this study. Researchers refer to it as the PwCOV. The service will create clinical instructions and analyze related information for widely dispersed illness data sets. For each individual request from an end user, it applies the business processes and general concepts of service-oriented computing [14].

In research by Wang et al. (2017), a service-oriented system-on-chip architecture called SoSoC is proposed. With this architecture, a single chip may provide computing functions from both integrated processors and app-defined hardware accelerators. Programmers are able to make effective use of a wide variety of computing resources because of the well-defined programming interfaces made available by SoSoC, which models and realizes the design concepts of SOA [15].

An article by Hasic et al. (2022) takes a systematic approach to the challenge of distinguishing between decision modeling and process modeling. It does this by delivering a Decision as a Service (DaaS) layered Service-Oriented Architecture (SOA) in which decisions are seen as automated, and external services that processes all on demand services to receive the conclusion [33]. A formalization of DMN constructions and the appropriate layer components sheds light on the DaaS process so that it may be understood. In addition, DaaS is analyzed in relation to the core features of the SOA paradigm, demonstrating its contribution in terms of abstraction, loose coupling, reusability, and several other applicable SOA concepts. In addition, the advantages that the DaaS architecture offers in terms of process-decision modeling and mining are explored. At the end, the SOA maturity of DaaS is evaluated, and the DaaS architecture is presented using the approval process for a bank loan and a real-life event log of the application [16].

Service-oriented computing (SOC) provides agility in systems development and business process management. End-users and technology providers love these technology-independent services and this modular approach to business operations. Service-oriented architectures (SOAs) have great promise, but there is little study on how they are used in reality [17].

Cloud computing and service-oriented computing have a connection that is mutually beneficial; one offers computing services, while the other provides computing services in the form of services. The authors feel that the combination of SOC and cloud computing settings brings a new set of research obstacles; nevertheless, they also believe that the combination presents potentially game-changing prospects [18].

6.3   Principles of Service-Oriented Architecture (Also Known as SOA)

Soft computing is the antithesis of hard computing, often known as conventional computing. Soft computing is a collective term for a set of computational methods that are based on artificial intelligence (AI) as well as natural selection [24]. It offers answers to difficult real-life situations for which there is no hard computer solution that is both cost-effective and efficient. The concept of soft computing [35] refers to the practice of doing computations in an approximative manner in order to provide answers to difficult computational problems that are not entirely accurate but may nevertheless be used [25]. The technique allows answers for issues that may not be solvable at all or may simply take too much time to solve with the technology that is available today. The term "soft computing" may also be used interchangeably with "computational intelligence." The concept of soft computing is an approach to problem-solving that makes use of methods other than computers. Soft computing, which takes the human mind as its model, is tolerant of partial truths, ambiguity, imprecision, and approximation. This stands in contrast to conventional computer models. Researchers are able to address some issues that cannot be processed by standard computers using soft computing's techniques inspired from nature. The following is a condensed explanation of the soft computing methods that are used in applications using metamaterials.

(i)   *Modularity*
In the design of systems, the idea of modularity is an essential component. A module may be thought of as a subsystem that has good cohesion. After that, the explanation discusses both the positive and negative aspects of using modular systems. In light of the fact that a service-oriented system is really an enterprise, we not only combed through the research published in the area of computer science, but also the research published in the field of the organizational sciences. The services included in the design are created as individual modules of functionality, each of which provides its respective consumers with well-defined interfaces. The services provide a logical picture of separate business-level functions (for example, customer verification), and their scope may be described (see Figure 6.3) as either very granular or relatively coarse-grained.

(ii) *Loosely Coupled*
This is made easier by the encapsulation of the underlying functionality, which makes it possible to conceptually isolate the implementation from the object doing the calling. As long as services reflect distinct significant business tasks, they are allowed to encapsulate functionality at a variety of different levels, ranging from the components that are contained inside an application to the components or subsystems that are interacting across companies. Because of this, the synthesis of these services into more complicated services and applications is made easier.

(iii) *Service Abstraction*
The contract includes only important information that is made available to customers. Finding the optimal mix of knowledge disclosure and finding the best solution. You should conceal any information about a software that is not strictly necessary for other people to successfully utilize the program. The notion of service abstraction is considered to be one of the most significant aspects of service design. With the use of service abstraction, providers are able to shield customers from the technical and implementation details of service logic. With the use of this idea, services are transformed into back boxes. The only necessary functional and technical information is included in the service contract. Why is it necessary to use Service Abstraction?

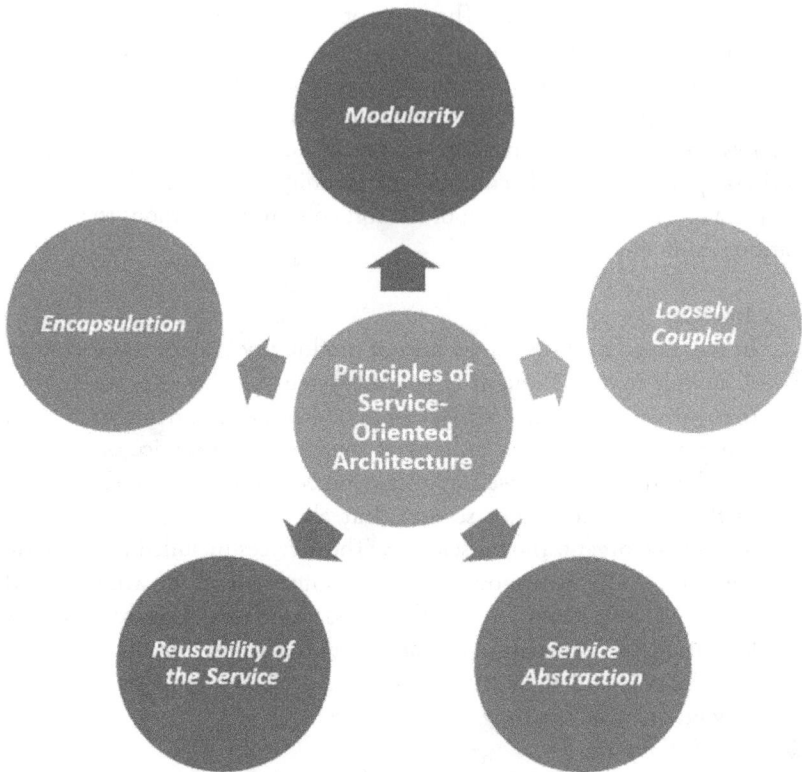

Figure 6.3   Principles of service-oriented architecture.

The supplier should be encouraged to disclose less information with the outside world. Provide customers the flexibility to deploy the service in the most effective way possible, without making any assumptions or incorrect judgements .Urge the service provider to improve the service by using various information technologies (IT) and information systems (I).

(iv)   *Reusability of the Service*

With the goal of achieving the highest possible rate of reuse, logic has been partitioned into services. The concept of reusability is an important one for any organization that focuses on software development. This is due to the fact that no one wants to waste time and energy reproducing the same piece of code for each of the various apps that have the same need. Hence, once the code for a web service has been built, it needs to be capable of working with a variety of different kinds of applications. Reusing existing capabilities to their fullest extent rather than developing new ones from scratch is a key tenet of SOA design. The idea behind it is to design something only once and then use it to several uses. When it comes to creating services, it is necessary to think critically and strategically in order to locate re-usable patterns and then construct services that can be reused as and when the need arises. Reusable services, made possible by SOA design, are a huge boon to businesses' efforts to save costs and uphold industry standards.

(v) Encapsulation

Encapsulation is the act of enclosing something, as in a capsule. During the process of encapsulation, both the business logic and the implementation are concealed from the outside world. A number of encapsulation types may be used with a Component-Based service. They include white box, which exposes all aspects of the component's implementation; gray box, which exposes certain aspects of the component's implementation; and black box. In the scenarios of white box and gray box, the customers of the component have the freedom to make changes to the component in order to fulfill certain requirements for their solutions.

6.4 Components of Service-Oriented Architecture

Service-Oriented Architecture (SOA) is a software design pattern where components, called services, communicate and interact with each other in order to achieve a common goal (see Figure 6.4). The main components of SOA include:

1. **Service:** This is the most important aspect of SOA. A service is a self-contained unit of functionality accessible through a well-defined interface. It may be programmed to do a specific job or to deliver data to other services.
2. **Service provider:** This is the entity that provides services to customers. Service providers might come from inside or outside the corporation.
3. **Service consumer:** This is the entity that makes use of the service provider's offerings. Service users might be both inside and external to the company.
4. **Service registry:** This is a centralized repository that maintains information about the organization's services. It assists customers in locating the services they need.
5. **Service broker:** This component serves as a go-between for the service provider and the service customer. It is capable of performing duties such as authentication, authorization, and mediation.
6. **Service interface:** This is the public interface of a service that is available to customers. It specifies the methods and parameters for gaining access to the service.
7. **Service Bus:** A service bus is a middleware component that allows services to communicate with one another. It offers a unified messaging architecture that supports a wide range of communication protocols and message formats.

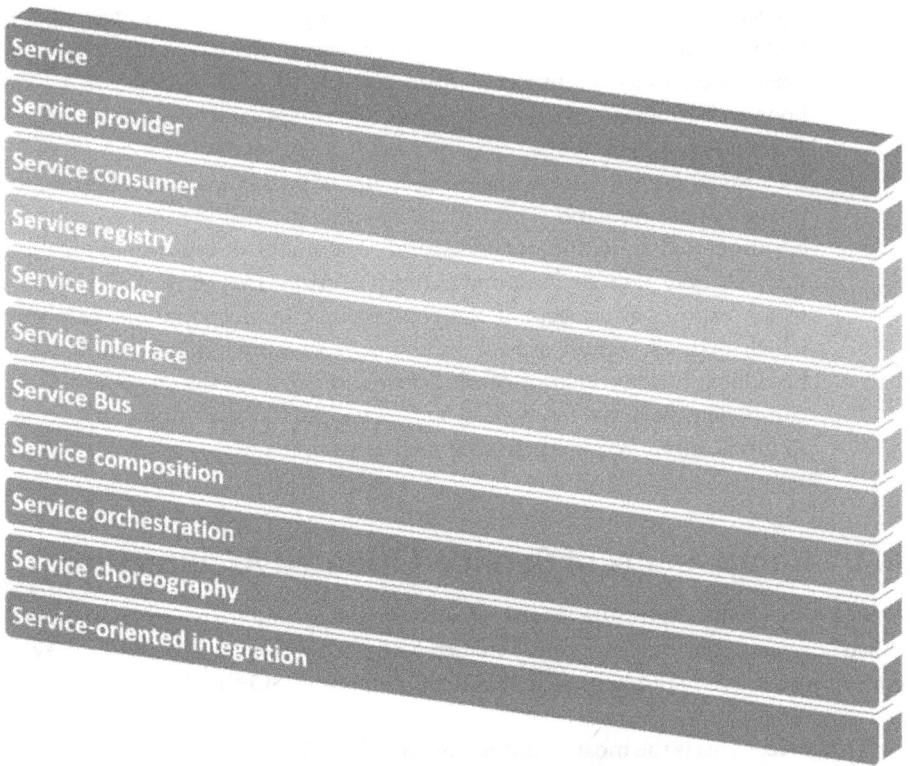

Figure 6.4 Components of service-oriented architecture.

8. **Service composition:** This refers to the process of combining many services into a single complete offering in order to deliver a more comprehensive service. Workflow, orchestration, and choreography are some of the processes that may be used to compose services.

9. **Service orchestration:** This is the process of establishing and organizing different services to accomplish a given purpose.

10. **Service choreography:** This is the process of specifying the interactions of many services in a distributed system that lacks centralized control.

11. **Service-oriented integration:** The process of integrating numerous applications utilizing SOA principles, in which each application produces and consumes services.

SOA is appropriate for big and complex corporate systems because it offers a flexible and modular design that allows for the simple addition and removal of services. It encourages service reuse, shortens development time, and increases system compatibility.

6.5 Applications of Service-Oriented Computing

Service-oriented computing (SOC) has several uses, including:

1. **E-commerce:** In Figure 6.5, SOC may be utilized in e-commerce systems to offer web-based services such as payment processing, inventory management, and delivery tracking.

2. **Healthcare:** SOC allows healthcare practitioners to securely communicate medical information and photos, as well as get access to services such as test results and pharmaceutical databases.

3. **Education:** Course management systems, online tutoring, and distant learning are all examples of how SOC may be utilized to deliver educational services.

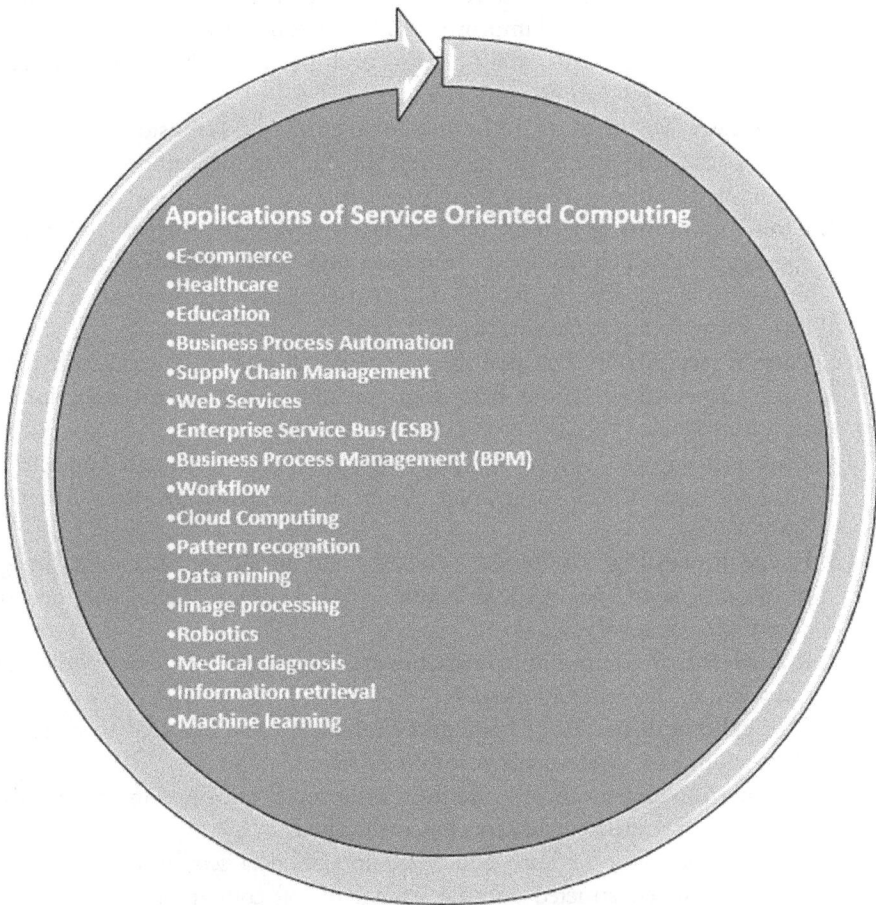

Applications of Service Oriented Computing

- E-commerce
- Healthcare
- Education
- Business Process Automation
- Supply Chain Management
- Web Services
- Enterprise Service Bus (ESB)
- Business Process Management (BPM)
- Workflow
- Cloud Computing
- Pattern recognition
- Data mining
- Image processing
- Robotics
- Medical diagnosis
- Information retrieval
- Machine learning

Figure 6.5   Applications of service-oriented computing.

4. **Business Process Automation:** SOC may help a company automate difficult business processes and integrate numerous systems.
5. **Supply Chain Management:** SOC may assist firms in coordinating the actions of many supply chain players to guarantee effective production and delivery.
6. **Web Services:** This is the most basic and popular use of Service Oriented Computing. A web service is a software system that allows various applications to communicate with one another through the Internet. They mostly interact via HTTP and XML.
7. **Enterprise Service Bus (ESB):** This is a platform for messaging-based integration. It enables you to rapidly and simply link apps and systems without the need to create code. It implements service-oriented architecture (SOA) concepts such as loose coupling and service reuse.
8. **Business Process Management (BPM):** BPM is a technology that allows businesses to manage and improve their business operations. It employs SOA to offer a flexible means of automating and integrating business operations across several applications.
9. **Workflow:** Workflow is a technique for managing tasks inside a process. It enforces the sequence of the tasks and the circumstances under which they should be completed using a set of preset rules.
10. **Cloud Computing:** Cloud computing is a service-oriented computing approach in which computer resources are made available on-demand through the Internet. Scalability and cost-efficiency are advantages of this sort of computing for businesses [20], [23].
11. **Pattern recognition:** For identifying patterns in massive datasets, soft computing approaches such as fuzzy logic, neural networks, and evolutionary algorithms are used [22].
12. **Data mining:** By looking for patterns and correlations, soft computing methods are utilized to extract important information from massive datasets.
13. **Image processing:** For object detection and image enhancement, image processing techniques such as neural networks, fuzzy logic, and genetic algorithms are used [19].
14. **Robotics:** Soft computing approaches are being used to create robots that can adapt to their surroundings.
15. **Medical diagnosis:** Fuzzy logic and neural networks are used to diagnose ailments and provide therapy recommendations.
16. **Information retrieval:** To identify important information in massive datasets, soft computing approaches are applied.
17. **Machine learning:** To learn and adapt to new data sets, machine learning algorithms are constructed utilizing a range of soft computing methodologies such as fuzzy logic, neural networks, and evolutionary algorithms [27], [28], [30], [31], [34].

6.6 Conclusion

Due to its capacity to securely and efficiently connect dispersed computing systems, the service-oriented computing paradigm has grown in popularity. Thus, understanding this computing paradigm's core concepts is crucial. Service-oriented computing is based on modularity, loose coupling, abstraction, encapsulation, and reusability. Modularity divides a system into smaller, more manageable parts. This simplifies system maintenance, updating, and scaling. In service-oriented computing, a system is divided into services that may be independently built, deployed, and maintained. Loose coupling means separating system components. This simplifies component replacement without compromising other parts. In service-oriented computing, services are autonomous and may be modified or replaced without impacting the others. Abstraction involves concealing system specifics and only revealing relevant information to other components. This simplifies system maintenance. Service-oriented computing applies this approach by abstracting services and only exposing essential information to other services. Data and procedures are bundled together under encapsulation. This simplifies maintenance and updating. Encapsulating services in service-oriented computing makes data and procedures easier to maintain and update. Reusability means employing system components in different systems. This simplifies component maintenance, updating, and scaling. In service-oriented computing, services are reusable across systems to make maintenance and updating easier. These concepts may help enterprises build safe, efficient distributed computing systems.

References

[1] Goodall, J. L., Robinson, B. F., & Castronova, A. M. (2011, May). Modeling water resource systems using a service-oriented computing paradigm. *Environmental Modelling & Software*, 26(5), 573–582. https://doi.org/10.1016/j.envs oft.2010.11.013

[2] Moghaddam, M., Silva, J. R., & Nof, S. Y. (2015). Manufacturing-as-a-Service—From e-work and service-oriented architecture to the cloud manufacturing paradigm. *IFAC-PapersOnLine*, 48(3), 828–833. https://doi.org/10.1016/j.ifacol.2015.06.186

[3] Beer Mohamed, M. I., Hassan, M. F., Safdar, S., & Saleem, M. Q. (2021, June). Adaptive security architectural model for protecting identity federation in service oriented computing. *Journal of King Saud University – Computer and Information Sciences*, 33(5), 580–592. https://doi.org/10.1016/j.jksuci.2019.03.004

[4] Hustad, E., & Olsen, D. H. (2021). Creating a sustainable digital infrastructure: The role of service-oriented architecture. *Procedia Computer Science*, 181, 597–604. https://doi.org/10.1016/j.procs.2021.01.210

[5] Cabrera, O., Franch, X., & Marco, J. (2017, July). Ontology-based context modeling in service-oriented computing: A systematic mapping. *Data & Knowledge Engineering*, 110, 24–53. https://doi.org/10.1016/j.datak.2017.03.008

[6] Bravetti, M., & Zavattaro, G. (2006, September). Service oriented computing: A new challenge for process algebras. *Electronic Notes in Theoretical Computer Science*, 162, 121–125. https://doi.org/10.1016/j.entcs.2005.12.116

[7] Terentyev, A., Andreev, A., Yegorov, V., & Omarov, A. (2021). Digital services as tools for implementing service-oriented architecture in transport systems. *Transportation Research Procedia*, 57, 672–678. https://doi.org/10.1016/j.trpro.2021.09.099

[8] Rojas, H., Arias, K. A., & Renteria, R. (2021). Service-oriented architecture design for small and medium enterprises with infrastructure and cost optimization. *Procedia Computer Science*, 179, 488–497. https://doi.org/10.1016/j.procs.2021.01.032

[9] Niknejad, N., Ismail, W., Ghani, I., Nazari, B., Bahari, M., & Hussin, A. R. B. C. (2020, July). Understanding service-oriented architecture (SOA): A systematic literature review and directions for further investigation. *Information Systems*, 91, 101491. https://doi.org/10.1016/j.is.2020.101491

[10] Luo, X. X., Song, M. N., & Song, J. D. (2011, September). Research on service-oriented policy-driven IAAS management. *The Journal of China Universities of Posts and Telecommunications*, 18, 64–70. https://doi.org/10.1016/s1005-8885(10)60208-7

[11] Chen, Z., Ming, X., Zhou, T., Chang, Y., & Sun, Z. (2020, April). A hybrid framework integrating rough-fuzzy best-worst method to identify and evaluate user activity-oriented service requirement for smart product service system. *Journal of Cleaner Production*, 253, 119954. https://doi.org/10.1016/j.jclepro.2020.119954

[12] Deventer, J. V., Derhamy, H., Atta, K., & Delsing, J. (2017, June). Service oriented architecture enabling the 4 th Generation of district heating. *Energy Procedia*, 116, 500–509. https://doi.org/10.1016/j.egypro.2017.05.096

[13] Pulparambil, S., & Baghdadi, Y. (2019, January). Service oriented architecture maturity models: A systematic literature review. *Computer Standards & Interfaces*, 61, 65–76. https://doi.org/10.1016/j.csi.2018.05.001

[14] Bora, A., & Bezboruah, T. (2021). PwCOV in cluster-based web server. *Data Science for COVID-19*, 195–212. https://doi.org/10.1016/b978-0-12-824536-1.00038-1

[15] Wang, C., Li, X., Chen, Y., Zhang, Y., Diessel, O., & Zhou, X. (2017, October 1). Service-Oriented architecture on FPGA-Based MPSoC. *IEEE Transactions on Parallel and Distributed Systems*, 28(10), 2993–3006. https://doi.org/10.1109/tpds.2017.2701828

[16] Hasic, F., De Smedt, J., Broucke, S. V., & Serral, E. (2022, March 1). Decision as a Service (DaaS): A service-oriented architecture approach for decisions in processes. *IEEE Transactions on Services Computing*, 15(2), 904–917. https://doi.org/10.1109/tsc.2020.2965516

[17] Luthria, H., & Rabhi, F. (2009, April 1). Service oriented computing in practice – An agenda for research into the factors influencing the organizational adoption of service oriented architectures. *Journal of Theoretical and Applied Electronic Commerce Research*, 4(1), 39–56. https://doi.org/10.4067/s0718-18762009000100005

[18] Wei, Y., & Blake, M. B. (2010, November). Service-Oriented computing and cloud computing: Challenges and opportunities. *IEEE Internet Computing*, 14(6), 72–75. https://doi.org/10.1109/mic.2010.147

[19] Kumar, N., Shukla, H., & Tripathi, R. (2017). Image restoration in noisy free images using fuzzy based median filtering and adaptive particle swarm

optimization – richardson-lucy algorithm. *International Journal of Intelligent Engineering and Systems*, 10(4), 50–59. https://doi.org/10.22266/ijies2017.0831.06

[20] Kumar, K., Kumar, A., Kumar, N., Mohammed, M. A., Al-Waisy, A. S., Jaber, M. M., Shah, R., & Al-Andoli, M. N. (2022). Dimensions of internet of things: Technological taxonomy architecture applications and open challenges—A systematic review. *Wireless Communications and Mobile Computing*, 2022, 1–23. https://doi.org/10.1155/2022/9148373

[21] Kumar, N. (2022). Future challenges in fog and edge computing applications. *Bio-Inspired Optimization in Fog and Edge Computing Environments*, 39–54. https://doi.org/10.1201/9781003322931-3

[22] Dawar, I., & Kumar, N. (2023). Text categorization by content using naïve Bayes approach. 2023 11th International conference on internet of everything, *Microwave Engineering, Communication and Networks (IEMECON)*. https://doi.org/10.1109/iemecon56962.2023.10092372

[23] Enayati, R., Ravanmehr, R., & Aghazarian, V. (2023). A service-oriented framework for remote sensing big data processing. *Earth Science Informatics*, 1–26.

[24] Ma, T., Xu, C., Yang, S., Huang, Y., An, Q., Kuang, X., & Grieco, L. A. (2023). A mutation-enabled proactive defense against service-oriented man-in-the-middle attack in Kubernetes. *IEEE Transactions on Computers*, 27(7), 1843–1856.

[25] Nayak, N., Ambalavanan, U., Thampan, J. M., Grewe, D., Wagner, M., Schildt, S., & Ott, J. (2023). Reimagining automotive service-oriented communication: A case study on programmable data planes. *IEEE Vehicular Technology Magazine*, 8(2), 69–79.

[26] Kokila, S., & Sivaradje, G. (2023). Dynamic service oriented resource allocation system for interworking broadband networks. *International Journal of Advanced Intelligence Paradigms*, 24(1–2), 70–91.

[27] Liu, Y., Zhang, K., Hou, B., Li, Q., Feng, J., & de La Fortelle, A. (2023). Real-time traffic impedance and priority based cooperative path planning mechanism for SOC-ITS: efficiency and equilibrium. *Simulation Modelling Practice and Theory*, 122, 102683.

[28] Ibrahim, A. M. A., Abdullah, N. S., & Bahari, M. (2023). Software as a service challenges: A systematic literature review. In *Proceedings of the Future Technologies Conference* (pp. 257–272). Springer, Cham.

[29] Suneja, B., Negi, A., Kumar, N., & Bhardwaj, R. (2022). Cloud-based tomato plant growth and health monitoring system using IOT. *2022 3rd International Conference on Intelligent Engineering and Management (ICIEM)*. https://doi.org/10.1109/iciem54221.2022.9853170

[30] Kumar, N., Shukla, H., & Tripathi, R. (2017). Image restoration in noisy free images using fuzzy based median filtering and adaptive particle swarm optimization – richardson-lucy algorithm. *International Journal of Intelligent Engineering and Systems*, 10(4), 50–59. https://doi.org/10.22266/ijies2017.0831.06

[31] Ahsani, V., Rahimi, A., Letafati, M., & Khalaj, B. H. (2023). Unlocking Metaverse-as-a-service The three pillars to watch: Privacy and security, edge computing, and blockchain. *Cryptography and Security*, arXiv preprint arXiv:2301.01221, pp 1–21.

[32] Mattia, S., Paolo, M., & Stefano, N. (2023). Virtual earth cloud: A multi-cloud framework for enabling geosciences digital ecosystems. *International Journal of Digital Earth*, 16(1), 43–65.

[33] Kumar, K., Saini, G., Shah, R., Kumar, N., & Gupta, M. (2023). IOT-based dam and barrage monitoring system. *Enabling Methodologies for Renewable and Sustainable Energy*, 151–161. https://doi.org/10.1201/9781003272717-9

[34] Kumar, K., Kumar, N., Kumar, A., Mohammed, M. A., Al-Waisy, A. S., Jaber, M. M., Pandey, N. K., Shah, R., Saini, G., Eid, F., & Al-Andoli, M. N. (2022). Identification of cardiac patients based on the medical conditions using machine learning models. *Computational Intelligence and Neuroscience*, 2022, 1–15. https://doi.org/10.1155/2022/5882144

[35] Laghari, R. A., Li, J., Laghari, A. A., & Wang, S. Q. (2020). A review on application of soft computing techniques in machining of particle reinforcement metal matrix composites. *Archives of Computational Methods in Engineering*, 27, 1363–1377.

Chapter 7

Trends and Future Opportunities of Service-Oriented Computing in Social Benefits

Rohit Verma,[1] Surendra Shukla,[2] and Shivani Jaswal[1]

[1]*National College of Ireland, Dublin, Ireland*

[2]*Department of Computer Science and Engineering, Graphic Era, Deemed to be University, Dehradun, Uttarakhand, India*

7.1 Introduction

The paradigm shift of service-oriented computing (SOC) (Huhns & Singh 2005) has transformed the manner in which organisations provide and utilise services with the aim of achieving societal advantages. The service-oriented computing paradigm has significant potential for addressing social challenges and generating positive impacts across various domains due to its emphasis on modular, loosely coupled services and standard communication protocols. The present chapter delves into the analysis of service-oriented computing in social benefits, elucidating the progressions and potential prospects that are anticipated in the future (Papazoglou 2003).

In recent years, there has been a growing recognition of the importance of leveraging technology to address social issues and improve the well-being of individuals and communities (Narayan 2020). Rapid advances in digital technologies, connectivity, and data availability have opened new avenues for service-oriented computing to drive social impact (Ostrom et al. 2010). By breaking down complex systems into

DOI: 10.1201/9781032716718-7

modular services, SOC enables organisations to deliver tailored solutions, promote collaboration, and enhance service delivery across the healthcare, education, disaster response, and public safety domains. Understanding the background and context of service-oriented computing in the social context is crucial to unlocking its full potential.

Service-oriented computing has its roots in the broader field of software architecture and distributed computing. Service-oriented architecture (SOA) was introduced in the late 1990s as a response to the need for flexible and adaptable systems.[1] SOA emphasised the use of loosely coupled services that could be invoked and combined to fulfil specific business requirements. This architectural style has grown in prominence as organisations seek to overcome the limitations of monolithic applications and construct more agile and scalable systems.

Service-oriented computing is an architectural approach that concentrates on building up systems by transforming them into a collection of services. The entity comprises a diverse range of services. These services are designed to encapsulate discrete business functions and can be independently deployed and orchestrated. The utilisation of standardised protocols facilitates seamless integration and communication with disparate systems. The core tenets of service-oriented computing are comprised of loose coupling, service re-use, service discovery, and dynamic composition, as posited by scholarly sources (Verma & Srivastava 2014, 2015). Comprehending the basic tenets and doctrines of service-oriented computing enables an individual to explore its practical implementations and potential societal advantages.

The concept of loose coupling pertains to the level of interdependence among services, allowing them to function autonomously and be integrated in diverse arrangements. The provision of flexibility enables organisations to modify their services in response to evolving demands, autonomously expand their scope, and substitute or upgrade them without causing disruption to the entire system. The practise of reusing services has been found to enhance productivity by promoting the development of reusable components that can be utilised across various domains and applications. Organisations can economise on system development while maintaining quality and consistency by utilising pre-existing services. Service discovery facilitates the identification and accessibility of services, thereby easing their incorporation and composition. It permits service providers to publicise their capabilities, thereby making them discoverable and accessible to other services. The dynamic composition combines services on demand to create new functionality, enabling flexibility and adaptability. This dynamic nature of service composition enables organisations to respond quickly to evolving needs and orchestrate complex processes by assembling preexisting services.

Service-oriented computing is important in the management of social challenges and realizing tangible benefits. It is also important to gain service-orientated computing. By adopting SOC principles, organisations can improve service delivery, improve access to resources and promote collaboration between stakeholders. The flexibility and scalability of SOC allow custom solutions that can be adjusted to change needs, ensuring efficient resource utilisation. Furthermore, SOC's modular nature facilitates service reuse, reduces redundant development effort, and promotes cost effectiveness. Understanding the importance of service-oriented computing in social benefits helps us appreciate its transformative potential and potential positive effects.

The use of service-oriented computing in various areas has shown its effectiveness in achieving social benefits. It has shown that for health care application, SOC has facilitated the integration of disparate systems and improved patient care through seamless medical data exchange and cooperation between health providers (Azoui et al. 2021). For example, using a service-oriented approach, healthcare providers can integrate electronic medical records, medical devices, and clinical decision-support systems.

Service-oriented computing has helped to improve learning experiences and enable personalised education in the educational sector. There was an interesting work by Mircea (Mircea & Andreescu 2012) that presents how, by using modular services, educational institutions can create adaptive learning environments, offer customised content and resources, and facilitate collaboration between students and educators. SOC makes it possible to integrate learning management systems, digital content repositories, and online collaboration tools while emphasizing innovative and interactive learning experiences for students and educators (Akhrif et al. 2019).

Service-oriented computing was crucial for disaster response and humanitarian assistance in coordinating efforts, optimizing resource allocation, and facilitating communication between aid organisations and affected communities (Li et al. 2023). Services-oriented computing is required. SOC enables the integration of many services like emergency systems, geospatial data (Fang et al. 2023), logistics management, and communication platforms such as GPS systems. It enables organizing these services; organisations can accelerate response time, increase situational awareness, and streamline coordination during crises and natural disasters. This will accelerate response, improve situational awareness, and increase coordination. Through increased capacity, organisations can accelerate crisis and disaster response time, increase situational awareness, and mitigate crisis and disaster situations.

Similarly, service-oriented computing has been applied in public safety to create integrated systems that support law enforcement, emergency management, and public safety agencies (Xu et al. 2019). It is used in the field of public safety and security. By incorporating services such as video surveillance, sensor networks, incident-management systems, and communication platforms, an SOC enables effective monitoring, prompt response, and information sharing in emergency situations. These applications illustrate the capacity of service-oriented computing to provide social benefits and address societal issues.

Understanding the significance of service-oriented computing for social advantages enables us to comprehend its potential influence on various fields. By leveraging SOC power, organisations can foster innovation, enhance service delivery, and generate positive social change. By investigating service-oriented computing trends and future opportunities, we can identify new ways to apply this paradigm to address emergent social problems and maximise its capacity for social good.

In the rest of this chapter, we look at the social benefits of service-oriented computing, our applications, and our success in a variety of areas as part of our examination of the social benefits of service-oriented computing. Subsequently, an analysis is conducted on the patterns that impact service-oriented computing within social welfare domains, including but not limited to healthcare, education, emergency response, and public safety, thereby exerting an influence on service computing within the aforementioned domains. Furthermore, an examination of prospective prospects and potential advancements in service-oriented computing will be conducted, which could potentially enhance societal advantages. In conclusion, the present discourse will address the impediments and constraints that need to be overcome to fully actualise the social advantages that service-oriented computing has to offer. The objective of this chapter is to gain an understanding of the present status and prospective opportunities of service-oriented computing in the context of social impact. The objective of this course is to provide an introduction to the core concepts of service-oriented computing and to offer an opportunity for students to effect change in this field.

7.2   Social Benefits of Service-Oriented Computing

Service-oriented computing is a paradigm shift that is changing how organisations provide and use services for the public good. By using modular, loosely coupled services and standardised communication protocols, SOC has a huge potential to solve social problems and make positive changes in many different areas. This section looks at the many ways service-oriented computing helps society.

SOC allows organisations to improve the delivery, collaboration, access and use of services, leading to better social results. By breaking up complicated systems into modular services, SOC lets organisations tailor their responses to specific social problems. This encourages collaboration among stakeholders and makes it easier to get services to people quickly. Understanding the social benefits of service-oriented computing is important if you want to use it to its fullest and help make good changes in society.

Service-oriented computing can be used in many different areas to help solve social problems and make people and communities happier and healthier (Zhang & Li 2022). SOC makes it easy for healthcare workers to share information, work together, and connect different systems so that patient care can be improved. By implementing a service-oriented strategy, for example, healthcare providers can integrate electronic health records, medical devices, and clinical decision support systems, resulting in more precise diagnoses, individualised treatments, and enhanced care coordination.

Service-oriented computing has revolutionised learning experiences in the education sector by establishing adaptive learning environments, personalised education, and interactive platforms. By integrating modular services, educational institutions can provide customised content and resources, facilitate collaborative learning, and provide students with individualised feedback. SOC facilitates the incorporation of learning management systems, digital content repositories, and online collaboration tools, thereby empowering students and educators with innovative and interactive learning experiences.

In the realm of disaster response and humanitarian assistance, service-oriented computing is indispensable for coordinating efforts, optimising resource allocation and facilitating communication between relief agencies and affected communities. SOC enables the incorporation of diverse services, such as emergency response systems, geospatial data, logistics management, and communication platforms, enabling efficient response coordination, rapid information sharing, and effective deployment of resources during crises and disasters.

Public safety and security also benefit from service-oriented computing through the creation of integrated systems that support law enforcement, emergency management, and public safety agencies. By integrating services such as video surveillance, sensor networks, incident-management systems, and communication platforms, SOC enables effective monitoring, rapid response, and information sharing in critical situations, thereby enhancing public safety and security.

7.2.1 Examples: Social Benefits

Numerous successful initiatives demonstrate the potential of service-oriented computing to create social impact. In healthcare, initiatives have utilised SOC to integrate electronic health records, telemedicine systems, and clinical decision support tools, leading to improved patient outcomes, reduced healthcare costs, and enhanced care coordination. By seamlessly exchanging medical data, healthcare providers can make more informed treatment decisions, minimise errors, and improve the overall quality of care.

Using service-oriented computing, educational institutions have created personalised learning platforms, virtual classrooms, and online collaboration tools, thereby transforming the learning experience. Through the incorporation of learning management systems, digital content repositories, and collaborative platforms, educational institutions have increased student engagement, facilitated personalised learning pathways, and promoted collaborative knowledge sharing between students and teachers.

Service-oriented computing has facilitated efficient coordination and resource allocation within the realms of disaster response and humanitarian assistance. By integrating emergency response systems, geospatial data, logistics management, and communication platforms, organisations have improved their ability to respond quickly and effectively during disasters, mitigating the impact on affected communities and ensuring efficient resource distribution.

For effective incident-management, public safety agencies have effectively implemented service-oriented computing-based systems to integrate surveillance networks, emergency response platforms, and communication systems. SOC has enhanced the ability to prevent, detect, and respond to threats to public safety, thereby assuring the safety and security of communities by facilitating communication and collaboration between multiple agencies.

These examples illustrate the efficacy of service-oriented computing in attaining social benefits in diverse domains. Organisations can address social challenges, improve service delivery, and improve the well-being of individuals and communities by leveraging service-oriented computing.

7.2.2   Challenges and Limitations of Service-Oriented Computing in Social Benefits

While service-oriented computing presents enormous potential for social benefits, it is also subject to obstacles and limitations. Ethical and legal challenges associated with data privacy, security, and ownership must be carefully considered to ensure that SOC initiatives comply with regulatory requirements and safeguard individual rights. When attempting to combine legacy systems with service-oriented architectures, integration and interoperability issues can arise, necessitating careful planning and coordination. In order to assure the long-term viability and sustainability of SOC systems, scalability, performance, and governance must also be addressed. By comprehending and addressing these obstacles, organisations can maximise the social benefits of service-oriented computing.

This section has provided an overview of the social benefits of service-oriented computing. It highlighted its successful applications in healthcare, education, emergency response, and public safety. Using service-oriented computing, organisations can address social challenges, enhance collaboration, optimise resource utilisation, and improve service delivery. The section that follows will examine the trends influencing service-oriented computing in social benefits, as well as the advancements and future opportunities that can increase its impact.

7.2.3   Impact of Service-Oriented Computing in Social Benefits

In recent years, service-oriented computing (SOC) has emerged as a paradigm shift that offers numerous advantages and has a positive impact on a variety of social benefit domains. This section provides an overview of the benefits of SOC and its capacity to promote positive social change. In addition, it provides case studies and examples illustrating the successful implementation of SOC initiatives, highlighting its tangible benefits. In addition, adoption and implementation strategies for SOC are discussed in order to help organisations maximise its potential.

SOC offers numerous advantages that contribute to the enhancement of social benefits across various sectors. One of the primary benefits is service delivery flexibility and agility. By encapsulating services as independent modules, SOC enables the simple composition and recomposition of services, allowing businesses to rapidly adapt to changing requirements and provide customised solutions. This adaptability enhances productivity and responsiveness, resulting in improved service quality and consumer satisfaction.

In addition, SOC facilitates the interoperability and integration of various systems and services. It facilitates communication and data exchange between various applications and platforms, thereby promoting collaboration and information sharing among stakeholders. This interoperability is especially beneficial in domains such as healthcare, education, disaster response, and public safety, where the integration of diverse systems and data sources is essential for effective decision-making and coordination.

Case studies and examples of successful SOC implementations highlight its benefits and positive impact further. SOC has revolutionised patient care in the healthcare industry by facilitating the integration of electronic health records (EHRs) and enabling the transmission of patient data between healthcare providers. This seamless information flow has improved care coordination, decreased medical errors, and increased patient safety.

SOC has transformed learning experiences in the education sector by facilitating the integration of learning management systems (LMS) and various educational services. This integration offers students personalised and adaptive learning environments where they can access pertinent resources, collaborate with peers, and receive individualised assistance. Through the incorporation of online learning platforms and open educational resources, SOC has widened access to education, allowing all learners, regardless of location or socioeconomic status, to receive a quality education.

Adoption and implementation strategies are crucial for effectively maximising the benefits of SOC. Organisations must establish a roadmap for adopting SOC that takes into account organisational readiness, technical infrastructure, and the availability of resources. Establishing governance frameworks and standards that direct the implementation process and ensure consistency and interoperability is essential. Engaging stakeholders and nurturing collaboration are also essential for the successful adoption of SOCs, as the creation of an ecosystem of interconnected services requires the participation of numerous actors.

In addition, organisations should invest in training and capacity building to ensure that their personnel have the skills necessary to effectively implement and manage SOC initiatives. Promoting a culture of innovation and continuous development is essential for adopting SOC as a transformative methodology. By cultivating a supportive environment and incentivizing experimentation, organisations can cultivate a culture that promotes the exploration of new service-oriented solutions and learning from both successes and failures.

In nutshell, SOC has a positive impact on social benefit domains and provides numerous benefits. Its adaptability, interoperability, and capacity to integrate disparate systems and services all contribute to enhanced service delivery and consumer satisfaction. Through case studies and illustrations, we can see how SOC has transformed healthcare, education, and other sectors, resulting in improved outcomes and positive societal change. By employing effective strategies and fostering an innovative culture, organisations are able to harness the potential of SOC and generate significant improvements in social benefits.

7.3 Trends in Service-Oriented Computing for Social Benefits

This section investigates the many trends redefining the landscape of service-oriented computing (SOC) in several sectors, with a focus on healthcare, education, disaster response and humanitarian assistance, and public safety and security. This can provide significant insight into the current and future orientations of SOC, as well as its potential social impact. Naghmeh et al. had presented an exhaustive survey on some trends in SOC (Niknejad et al. 2020), however, we present exclusive trends in the aforementioned domains.

7.3.1 Overview of Trends in Service-Oriented Computing

Service-oriented computing (SOC) has emerged as a paradigm shift that has transformed social service delivery. Several significant SOC trends are reshaping the landscape of service-oriented computing for social good. Healthcare, education, emergency preparedness, and public safety and security are among these trends. Understanding these trends can provide valuable insight into the present and future directions of SOC, as well as its potential effects on society.

7.3.2 Trends in Service-Oriented Computing for Healthcare

In the healthcare industry, service-oriented computing is undergoing remarkable advancements that are resulting in improved patient care and health outcomes. Integration of electronic health records (EHRs) via service-oriented architectures is a prominent trend. This facilitates the transmission of patient information among healthcare providers, resulting in enhanced care coordination and decision-making. Moreover, service-oriented computing enables the integration of clinical decision support systems, telemedicine applications, and mobile health solutions, granting healthcare professionals access to vital information and resources in real time.

Emergence of patient-centric care models is an additional trend in service-oriented computing for healthcare. Integrating various services, such as peripheral devices, remote monitoring systems, and health tracking applications, SOC enables the development of personalised healthcare solutions. Together, these services capture and analyse patient data, enabling individualised interventions and proactive health management. In addition, service-oriented computing enables the integration of healthcare systems with external resources, such as social determinants of health data, in order to provide holistic and comprehensive care.

7.3.3   Trends in Service-Oriented Computing for Education

Service-oriented computing is transforming the delivery and customisation of learning experiences for pupils in the field of education. A notable trend is the adoption of learning management systems (LMS) with service-oriented architectures. This permits educational institutions to integrate various services, such as content repositories, assessment tools, and collaboration platforms, into a unified learning environment. Using service-oriented computing, educators can construct adaptive and interactive learning environments that are tailored to the needs and preferences of each student.

Integration of learning analytics and data-driven decision-making represents an improvement in service-oriented computing for education. SOC facilitates the accumulation and analysis of data from a variety of educational services, such as student performance, participation, and learning activities. This data-driven approach enables educators to gain insight into student progress, pinpoint areas for improvement, and personalise instruction according to each student's unique learning styles and requirements. In addition, service-oriented computing facilitates the integration of external resources, such as open educational resources (OER) and online learning platforms, thereby increasing the accessibility of high-quality education to a diverse learner population.

7.3.4   Trends in Service-Oriented Computing for Disaster Response and Humanitarian Aid

Moreover, service-oriented computing is essential for disaster response and humanitarian aid. Integrating heterogeneous systems and resources through service-oriented architectures is a significant advancement in this discipline. Multiple services, including emergency response systems, geographic information systems (GIS), logistics management, and communication platforms, can be incorporated seamlessly with SOC. During times of crisis, this integration improves situational awareness, enables efficient resource allocation, and enables effective coordination between relief agencies and stakeholders.

Utilising real-time data and analytics for disaster response and humanitarian assistance is an expansion of service-oriented computing. SOC enables the incorporation of sensor networks, social media platforms, and remote sensing technologies, enabling the collection and analysis of real-time data from disaster-affected regions. This data-driven strategy improves decision-making, facilitates predictive modelling, and supports humanitarian interventions based on empirical evidence. Moreover, service-oriented computing enables the development of mobile applications and communication services that facilitate disaster-related information exchange, emergency alerts, and crowdsourced assistance.

7.3.5 Trends in Service-Oriented Computing for Public Safety and Security

In the domain of public safety and security, service-oriented computing contributes to the creation of integrated systems that augment the capabilities of law enforcement, emergency management, and public-safety agencies. Integrating video surveillance systems, sensor networks, and incident-management services using service-oriented architectures is a significant advancement. This integration enables the efficient surveillance of public areas, the early detection of security threats, and the prompt management of emergencies.

Another advancement in service-oriented computing is the application of advanced analytics and artificial intelligence (AI) techniques to public safety and security. SOC enables the incorporation of data analytics services, predictive modelling tools, and anomaly detection algorithms to improve situational awareness and facilitate proactive decision-making. These technologies enable the identification of patterns, the detection of suspicious activity, and the implementation of early warning systems, thereby enhancing efforts to promote public safety and security.

Understanding these trends in service-oriented computing for social benefits provides valuable insight into the current and future opportunities for using SOC to advance society. By incorporating these trends and maximising the potential of service-oriented computing, organisations and stakeholders can foster innovation, enhance service delivery, and achieve significant outcomes in the healthcare, education, disaster response, and public safety and security sectors.

7.4 Future Opportunities of Service-Oriented Computing in Social Benefits

As service-oriented computing continues to evolve, there are a number of promising future opportunities with enormous potential to generate positive social effects.

Understanding these opportunities can provide a road map for harnessing the potential of SOC in order to achieve societal advancements. By investigating these possibilities, we can gain insight into the potential advancements and effects that SOC could have in a variety of domains, such as healthcare, education, disaster response and humanitarian assistance, and public safety and security.

7.4.1 Future Opportunities for Service-Oriented Computing in Healthcare

The future of service-oriented computing in healthcare presents numerous opportunities for enhancing patient care and health outcomes. The advancement of interoperability and data exchange standards is one such opportunity. By enhancing the integration and exchange of electronic health records (EHRs) across multiple healthcare systems, SOC can facilitate the administration of comprehensive and coordinated care. This integration would enable healthcare providers to access patient data from a variety of sources, resulting in more informed decision-making and individualised treatment plans.

Utilising emerging technologies such as artificial intelligence (AI) and machine learning (ML) is another opportunity for the future of service-oriented computing in healthcare. Medical diagnostics, drug discovery, and treatment optimisation may be revolutionised by these technologies. SOC can support data-driven clinical decision support systems, predictive analytics for disease prevention, and personalised treatment recommendations based on patient-specific data by integrating AI and ML algorithms into service-oriented architectures.

In addition, the future of service-oriented computing in the healthcare industry involves the expansion of telemedicine and remote patient monitoring capabilities. SOC can facilitate the smooth incorporation of telemedicine platforms, wearable devices, and remote monitoring systems as the demand for accessible and cost-effective healthcare services increases. This integration would allow healthcare professionals to remotely monitor patients, provide virtual consultations, and implement timely interventions, thereby enhancing access to care and decreasing healthcare disparities.

7.4.2 Future Opportunities for Service-Oriented Computing in Education

The future of service-oriented computing presents promising opportunities for transforming learning experiences in the field of education and improving educational outcomes. The development of adaptive learning environments is one such chance. Educators can create personalised and adaptive learning experiences that are tailored to the requirements, preferences, and learning styles of each student by leveraging service-oriented computing. SOC can facilitate the integration of intelligent tutoring systems, adaptive assessment tools, and personalised content delivery platforms, empowering students to learn at their own tempo and in the manner that best meets their specific learning needs.

Utilising learning analytics and big data represents a future opportunity for service-oriented computing in education. SOC can facilitate data-driven decision-making to improve teaching practises and student performance by collecting and analysing data from various educational services and platforms. Educators can obtain valuable insights into student progress, identify areas for improvement, and provide targeted interventions and support by integrating learning analytics tools. This data-driven methodology can assist educators in optimising instructional strategies, customising learning pathways, and enhancing educational outcomes.

In addition, the future of service-oriented computing in education will involve the expansion of online and distant learning opportunities. SOC can facilitate the integration of online learning platforms, virtual classrooms, and collaborative tools, facilitating seamless access to educational resources and encouraging the development of global learning communities. This expansion would increase access to education, particularly for underserved populations, and encourage continuous learning in the digital age.

7.4.3 Future Opportunities for Service-Oriented Computing in Disaster Response and Humanitarian Aid

Service-oriented computing also holds significant future opportunities in the domains of disaster response and humanitarian aid. One such opportunity lies in the advancement of real-time data integration and analytics. By further enhancing the integration of heterogeneous data sources, including social media, sensor networks, and satellite imagery, SOC can enable more accurate and timely situational awareness during disasters. This integration would facilitate effective resource allocation, rapid decision-making, and improved coordination among relief agencies, ultimately enhancing the efficiency and effectiveness of disaster response efforts.

Utilising emerging technologies such as blockchain and the Internet of Things (IoT) is a future opportunity for service-oriented computing in disaster response and humanitarian assistance. These technologies can facilitate secure and decentralised data sharing, transparent supply chain management, and efficient resource monitoring. By incorporating blockchain and IoT into service-oriented architectures, SOC can improve the transparency, accountability, and traceability of humanitarian operations, ensuring that resources reach those in need more efficiently and effectively.

In addition, the future of service-oriented computing in disaster response and humanitarian assistance will involve the creation of predictive modelling and early warning systems. By utilising historical data, real-time information, and advanced analytics, SOC can enable the prediction and early detection of disasters, thereby allowing proactive measures to be taken to mitigate their impact. This may involve the creation of predictive models for natural disasters, early warning systems for disease outbreaks, and decision-support tools for humanitarian logistics and resource management.

7.4.4 Future Opportunities for Service-Oriented Computing in Public Safety and Security

In the area of public safety and security, the future of service-oriented computing offers exciting opportunities to improve community safety and wellbeing. Integration of smart city technologies and service-oriented architectures is one such opportunity. Using service-oriented computing, cities can incorporate video surveillance systems, sensor networks, and data analytics platforms to develop intelligent and interconnected systems that improve public safety. This integration would facilitate real-time monitoring of public areas, early threat detection, and effective emergency response.

Utilisation of edge computing and edge intelligence represents a future opportunity for service-oriented computing in public safety and security. These technologies can facilitate real-time data processing and analysis at the network's edge, thereby reducing latency and improving the responsiveness of security systems. By integrating edge computing capabilities into service-oriented architectures, SOC can support real-time threat detection, intelligent video analytics, and automated incident response, thereby bolstering public safety and facilitating proactive security.

In addition, the future of service-oriented computing in public safety and security will involve the development of predictive policing and crime prevention techniques. SOC can facilitate the identification of crime patterns, hotspots, and trends by leveraging historical crime data, real-time information, and advanced analytics. This data-driven strategy can support predictive surveillance models, resource allocation optimisation, and proactive crime prevention measures, thereby enhancing community safety and security.

Understanding these prospective opportunities for social benefits in service-oriented computing provides valuable insight into the potential advancements and impacts that SOC can bring to various domains. By embracing these opportunities and maximising the potential of service-oriented computing, organisations, policymakers, and stakeholders can drive innovation, improve service delivery, and create significant societal change in healthcare, education, disaster response and humanitarian aid, and public safety.

7.5 Challenges and Limitations of Service-Oriented Computing in Social Benefits

This section examines the obstacles and constraints that must be overcome in the domain of service-oriented computing (SOC) for social benefits (Alanazi et al. 2019). As SOC continues to advance and shape numerous domains, such as healthcare, education, disaster response and humanitarian assistance, and public safety and security, it is essential to comprehend and overcome these obstacles to maximise its potential for positive societal impacts.

7.5.1 Ethical and Legal Challenges

The ethical and legal considerations surrounding data utilisation and privacy pose a significant obstacle to the widespread adoption of service-oriented computing for social good. SOC requires the acquisition, processing, and dissemination of vast quantities of personal and sensitive information. Therefore, it is essential to establish robust ethical frameworks and adhere to legal regulations in order to safeguard the privacy rights of individuals and ensure the responsible use of data. Additionally, issues pertaining to data ownership, consent, and data sovereignty must be addressed in order to establish trust among SOC ecosystem users and stakeholders.

In addition, the ethical challenges of SOC include algorithmic bias, transparency, and responsibility. As SOC systems increasingly rely on automated decision-making algorithms, ensuring fairness and avoiding discrimination becomes paramount. It is essential to develop algorithms that are unbiased, transparent, and accountable to prevent the perpetuation of social inequalities and uphold ethical standards in the provision of social benefits.

7.5.2 Privacy and Security Challenges

Another critical set of challenges in service-oriented computing for social benefits is related to privacy and security. With the integration and sharing of data across multiple systems and stakeholders, there is an increased risk of data breaches, unauthorised access, and misuse of personal information. Protecting sensitive data from unauthorised disclosure and ensuring the integrity and confidentiality of data are vital considerations in SOC implementation.

Additionally, SOC introduces challenges in preserving privacy while enabling effective data sharing and interoperability. Balancing the need for data accessibility with privacy concerns is a complex task, requiring robust privacy-preserving techniques and mechanisms such as data anonymization, encryption, and access control.

To address these challenges, organisations and policymakers need to implement comprehensive privacy and security frameworks that encompass technical, organisational, and legal measures. Building a data security and privacy culture among users and stakeholders is critical to reducing risks and ensuring data security and integrity.

7.5.3   Social and Cultural Challenges

Social and cultural challenges accompany service-oriented computing for social benefits. For the adoption and implementation of SOC initiatives to be successful, societal and cultural barriers that impede acceptance and utilisation must be removed.

In certain social contexts, resistance to change and reluctance to adopt new technologies and digital transformation are examples of such obstacles. Implementing an SOC may necessitate alterations to workflows, organisational structures, and stakeholder responsibilities, which may be met with resistance and scepticism. To address these obstacles, effective change management strategies, stakeholder engagement, and communication are required to cultivate a positive mindset and establish an environment conducive to SOC adoption.

Moreover, SOC initiatives must account for cultural diversity and inclusiveness. Various cultural norms, values, and practises may impact the acceptability and efficacy of SOC systems. It is essential to design and customise SOC solutions to accommodate cultural differences and ensure that they align with the specific requirements and preferences of diverse user groups. Engaging stakeholders from diverse cultural backgrounds and involving them in the design and decision-making processes can assist in overcoming these obstacles and ensuring the successful integration of SOC in social benefit domains.

7.5.4   Technological Challenges

For effective implementation and long-term sustainability, service-oriented computing for social benefits also confronts technological obstacles that must be overcome. These difficulties include interoperability, scalability, system complexity, and integration of legacy systems.

Interoperability is a significant obstacle in SOC, as it requires the integration of disparate systems, platforms, and services from various vendors and organisations. To ensure seamless communication and data exchange between these systems, it is necessary to develop and employ common standards, protocols, and interfaces. Interoperability enables the efficient integration of SOC components and encourages collaboration and information sharing across domains.

Scalability is an additional technological challenge in SOC, particularly when working with large-scale systems and datasets. As SOC solutions expand to accommodate expanding user bases and increased data volumes, scalability becomes essential for preserving performance and responsiveness. This challenge can be overcome by designing scalable architectures and utilising technologies such as cloud computing and distributed computing.

System complexity arises from the integration of multiple services, applications, and components within SOC ecosystems. Managing this complexity requires effective system design, modularisation, and abstraction techniques. Employing service-oriented architecture (SOA) principles and design patterns can help simplify system complexity and enhance maintainability and reusability.

Furthermore, integrating SOC with existing legacy systems and infrastructure poses challenges in terms of compatibility, data migration, and system modernisation. Legacy system integration often requires careful planning, phased implementation, and collaboration between different stakeholders to ensure smooth transitions and minimise disruptions.

Addressing these technological challenges necessitates a strong technological foundation, continuous innovation, and collaboration between researchers, industry practitioners, and policymakers. It is crucial to invest in research and development efforts that focus on overcoming these challenges to enable the effective implementation and long-term sustainability of service-oriented computing for social benefits.

7.6 Conclusion

In this chapter, we have explored the trends, future opportunities, and challenges of service-oriented computing (SOC) in the context of social benefits. SOC has emerged as a transformative paradigm that has the potential to drive positive social impacts across various domains, including healthcare, education, disaster response and humanitarian aid, and public safety and security. By understanding these trends and prospective opportunities, as well as addressing the obstacles and constraints, we can unlock the full potential of SOC for effecting significant societal change.

Several essential aspects of service-oriented computing for social benefits have been discussed. We began by analysing SOC trends, focusing on advancements in the healthcare, education, emergency response, and public safety and security domains. These trends include the adoption of learning management systems and data-driven decision-making in education, the integration of heterogeneous systems and real-time data analytics in disaster response and humanitarian aid, and the development of integrated systems employing video surveillance, sensor networks, and advanced analytics in public safety and security.

The potential for personalised healthcare solutions, adaptive learning experiences, data-driven decision making, and real-time analytics were then emphasised as we investigated the future opportunities of SOC in these domains. These prospective opportunities pave the way for improved service delivery, collaboration, and outcomes in healthcare, education, emergency response, and public safety and security.

Next, we examined the obstacles and restrictions associated with the adoption of SOC for social benefits. Ethical and legal considerations, privacy and security concerns, social and cultural barriers, and technological complexities are among these obstacles. To assure the responsible and effective use of SOC and to build trust among users and stakeholders, it is essential to address these obstacles. Researchers can use the identified trends and future opportunities to guide their research and develop innovative solutions to the most prevalent issues in healthcare, education, disaster response, and public safety and security. Further research is required to investigate the ethical implications of SOC, to develop robust privacy-protecting techniques, and to design SOC solutions that are culturally sensitive. Understanding the trends and future opportunities in SOC can facilitate decision-making and strategic planning for the adoption and implementation of SOC initiatives among practitioners. To overcome the challenges associated with SOC, organisations must invest in the essential technological infrastructure, develop data governance policies, and foster a culture of data security and privacy. Collaboration between researchers, practitioners, policymakers, and stakeholders is indispensable for the successful implementation and realisation of SOC's prospective benefits in social domains.

Future research should concentrate on addressing the identified obstacles in SOC, such as ethical and legal considerations, privacy and security concerns, social and cultural barriers, and technological complexities. To develop frameworks and guidelines for responsible data usage and governance in SOC and to investigate the social and cultural implications of SOC adoption, additional research is required. In addition, research should address the interoperability issues, scalability concerns, and legacy system integration complexities that arise during SOC implementation.

By addressing these limitations and pursuing future research directions, we can continue to advance the field of service-oriented computing for social benefits and realise its maximum capacity for generating positive societal impacts.

In conclusion, service-oriented computing has the potential to revolutionise the delivery of services across multiple domains and produce significant social benefits. We can harness the power of service-oriented computing to improve service delivery, enhance collaboration, and promote positive societal change in the healthcare, education, disaster response, and public safety and security domains by embracing the identified trends, exploring future opportunities, addressing the challenges, and conducting additional research.

Note

1   www.ibm.com/topics/soa

References

Akhrif, O., Idrissi, Y. E. B. E. & Hmina, N. (2019), Service oriented computing and smart university, *in* M. Ben Ahmed, A. A. Boudhir & A. Younes, eds, '*Innovations in Smart Cities Applications Edition 2*', Springer International Publishing, Cham, pp. 437–449.

Alanazi, S. T., Abdullah, N., Anbar, M. & Al-Wesabi, O. A. (2019), Evaluation approaches of service oriented architecture (soa) – a survey, in '*2019 2nd International Conference on Computer Applications & Information Security (ICCAIS)*', pp. 1–6. IEEE explorer

Azoui, A., Idoughi, D. & Abdelouhab, K. A. (2021), Design of remote pervasive health monitoring system based on cloud computing and soa, *in* '*2020 2nd International Workshop on Human-Centric Smart Environments for Health and Well-being (IHSH)*', 9–10 Feb. 2021, pp. 48–53.

Fang, Z., Yue, P., Zhang, M., Xie, J., Wu, D. & Jiang, L. (2023), 'A service-oriented collaborative approach to disaster decision support by integrating geospatial resources and task chain', *International Journal of Applied Earth Observation and Geoinformation* 117, 103217. URL: www.sciencedirect.com/science/article/pii/S1569843223000390

Huhns, M. N. & Singh, M. P. (2005), 'Service-oriented computing : Key concepts and principles', *IEEE Internet Computing*. Vol. 9, no. 1: 75–81.

Li, W., Wang, S., Chen, X., Tian, Y., Gu, Z., Lopez-Carr, A., Schroeder, A., Currier, K., Schildhauer, M. & Zhu, R. (2023), 'Geographvis: A knowledge graph and geovisualization empowered cyberinfrastructure to support disaster response and humanitarian aid', *ISPRS International Journal of Geo-Information* 12(3). URL: www.mdpi.com/2220-9964/12/3/112

Mircea, M. (2012), 'Soa adoption in higher education: A practical guide to service- oriented virtual learning environment', *Procedia – Social and Behavioral Sciences* 31, 218–223. World Conference on Learning, Teaching & Administration – 2011. URL: www.sciencedirect.com/science/article/pii/S1877042811029740

Mircea, M. & Andreescu, A. I. (2012), 'Service-oriented university: Changes and opportunities towards innovation', *Procedia-Social and Behavioral Sciences* 31, 251–256.

Narayan, R. (2020), 'Leveraging digital intelligence for community wellbeing', *International Journal of Community Well-Being* 3(4), 539–558.

Niknejad, N., Ismail, W., Ghani, I., Nazari, B., Bahari, M. & Hussin, A. R. B. C. (2020), 'Understanding service-oriented architecture (soa): A systematic literature review and directions for further investigation', *Information Systems* 91, 101491. URL: www.sciencedirect.com/science/article/pii/S0306437920300028

Ostrom, A. L., Bitner, M. J., Brown, S. W., Burkhard, K. A., Goul, M., Smith-Daniels, V., Demirkan, H. & Rabinovich, E. (2010), 'Moving forward and making a difference: research priorities for the science of service', *Journal of Service Research* 13(1), 4–36.

Papazoglou, M. P. (2003), 'Service-oriented computing: Concepts, characteristics and directions', *Proceedings of the Fourth International Conference on Web Information Systems Engineering, 2003. WISE 2003*, pp. 3–12. IEEE, 2003.

Verma, R. & Srivastava, A. (2014), A novel web service directory framework for mobile environments, *in* '*2014 IEEE International Conference on Web Services*', IEEE explorer, vol. 1 pp. 614–621.

Verma, R. & Srivastava, A. (2015), Towards service description for mobile environments, *in* '*2015 IEEE International Conference on Services Computing*', 27 June 2015 - 02 July 2015, IEEE explorer, pp. 138–145.

Xu, R., Nikouei, S. Y., Chen, Y., Blasch, E. & Aved, A. (2019), Blendmas: A blockchain-enabled decentralized microservices architecture for smart public safety, *in* '*2019 IEEE International Conference on Blockchain (Blockchain)*' IEEE explorer, 14–17 July 2019, pp. 564–571.

Zhang, H. & Li, M. (2022), 'Integrated design and development of intelligent scenic area rural tourism information service based on hybrid cloud', *Computational and Mathematical Methods in Medicine* 2022, 1–9.

Chapter 8

Cloud Computing-Based Service-Oriented Architecture for Agricultural Applications

Garima Verma[1] and Pradeep Singh Rawat[2]

[1,2]School of Computing, DIT University, Dehradun, India

8.1 Introduction to Cloud Computing and Service-Oriented Architecture

8.1.1 Definition of Cloud Computing

Cloud computing refers to the delivery of computing resources and services (such as servers, storage, applications, and data) over the Internet on a pay-per-use basis. Instead of owning and managing their own infrastructure, businesses and individuals can access and use computing resources and services from third-party providers on a subscription basis. Cloud computing allows for greater flexibility, scalability, and cost-effectiveness than traditional on-premises computing [1]. It also enables users to access their data and applications from anywhere with an Internet connection, using a wide range of devices.

DOI: 10.1201/9781032716718-8

8.1.2 Definition of Service-Oriented Architecture (SOA)

Service-Oriented Architecture (SOA) is a software architecture style that involves the creation of services as independent, reusable components that can be accessed and combined to form more complex software systems. Services are typically designed to perform specific tasks or functions, and are accessed through standardized interfaces using a messaging protocol [2].

SOA is based on the idea of modularization, where the functionality of a system is broken down into smaller, independent parts that can be developed, tested, and deployed separately. This allows for greater flexibility and agility in software development, as changes to one service can be made without affecting other parts of the system [2], [3].

SOA also promotes interoperability between different software systems, as services can be accessed and combined across different platforms and technologies. This allows for greater integration and collaboration between different applications and organizations.

The use of SOA can provide several benefits, including increased scalability, flexibility, and reusability of software components. However, it can also introduce some challenges, such as increased complexity and the need for careful management of service dependencies and versioning [2], [3], [4].

8.1.3 Benefits of Cloud Computing and SOA for Agricultural Business Management

There are several benefits of using cloud computing and Service-Oriented Architecture (SOA) for Agricultural Business Management [2], [3], [5]:

Scalability: Cloud computing and SOA provide a highly scalable infrastructure that can quickly and easily adapt to changing business needs. As agricultural businesses grow and expand, they can quickly scale up their computing resources and services to meet their evolving requirements.

Cost-effectiveness: Cloud computing and SOA can reduce costs by eliminating the need to invest in expensive hardware and software infrastructure. Instead, agricultural businesses can use a pay-per-use model to access and use computing resources and services on an as-needed basis.

Flexibility: Cloud computing and SOA provide the flexibility to access data and applications from anywhere with an Internet connection, using a wide range of devices. This can improve productivity and efficiency by enabling employees to work from anywhere.

Integration: SOA promotes interoperability between different software systems, allowing agricultural businesses to easily integrate their data and applications with those of their partners and suppliers.

Collaboration: Cloud computing and SOA can facilitate collaboration between different teams and organizations, enabling them to share data and applications securely and efficiently.

Data Analytics: Cloud-based data analytics tools can help agricultural businesses make more informed decisions by providing real-time insights into their operations and supply chains. This can help businesses optimize their processes and improve their bottom line.

Agility: Cloud computing and SOA can improve the agility of agricultural businesses by enabling them to quickly respond to changing market conditions and customer demands. They can quickly develop and deploy new applications and services, or modify existing ones, to meet their evolving needs.

Overall, cloud computing and SOA can provide agricultural businesses with a more cost-effective, flexible, and scalable infrastructure that can help them stay competitive in today's fast-paced business environment

8.2 Overview of Agricultural Business Management

8.2.1 Definition and Scope of Agricultural Business Management

Agricultural Business Management is the application of business principles and practices to the management of agricultural enterprises, including farms, ranches, and other agribusinesses. It involves the planning, organizing, directing, and controlling of resources and activities involved in the production, processing, and distribution of agricultural products and services [4], [5].

The scope of Agricultural Business Management includes various functions such as financial management, marketing management, human resource management, production management, and strategic management. These functions are critical for the success of agricultural enterprises, as they help to ensure that resources are effectively and efficiently used to achieve the enterprise's goals [4], [5], [6].

Financial management involves the management of financial resources, including the preparation of budgets, financial statements, and cash flow projections. Marketing management involves the identification of customer needs and preferences, the development of marketing strategies, and the promotion and sale of agricultural products and services. Human resource management involves the recruitment, training, and development of employees, as well as the management of labor relations. Production management involves the planning, organization, and control of production processes, including the management of resources such as land, labor, and capital. Strategic management involves the development of long-term plans and objectives for the enterprise, as well as the identification of opportunities and threats in the business environment [5], [6].

Agricultural Business Management also involves the use of technology and data analytics to improve production processes, optimize resource allocation, and enhance decision-making. It is essential for the sustainability and growth of agricultural enterprises, as it helps them to adapt to changing market conditions and customer demands, while maintaining profitability and social responsibility.

8.2.2 Challenges Faced by India's Agricultural Business Management

Agricultural Business Management in India faces several challenges that affect the productivity, profitability, and sustainability of agricultural enterprises [6], [7]. Here are some of the major challenges:

a. Small and fragmented landholdings: The majority of farmers in India own small and fragmented landholdings, which limits their ability to adopt modern farming practices and technologies and affects their bargaining power in the market.

b. Climate change and natural disasters: Climate change and natural disasters such as floods, droughts, and cyclones have a significant impact on agricultural production in India, leading to crop losses, lower yields, and reduced income for farmers.

c. Lack of irrigation facilities: The majority of agricultural land in India depends on rain-fed agriculture, which makes agriculture vulnerable to variations in rainfall patterns. The lack of irrigation facilities limits the ability of farmers to adopt high-value crops and affects the sustainability of agricultural enterprises.

d. Price volatility: Price volatility in agricultural markets affects the profitability of agricultural enterprises, as farmers are unable to predict the prices of their crops and face significant risks from price fluctuations.

e. Lack of access to credit: Small farmers in India face significant challenges in accessing credit, which limits their ability to invest in modern farming practices and technologies, and affects their ability to expand their businesses.

f. Limited market access: Agricultural enterprises in India face limited market access due to poor infrastructure, inadequate storage and transportation facilities, and a lack of information on market demand and prices.

g. Inadequate extension services: Extension services that provide information and support to farmers are inadequate in India, limiting the adoption of modern farming practices and technologies.

h. Inadequate value chain development: The development of value chains that link farmers to markets and support the processing and distribution of agricultural products is inadequate in India, limiting the ability of agricultural enterprises to capture value from their products.

Addressing the above challenges requires a concerted effort from Indian policymakers, agricultural researchers, and farmers themselves to develop and implement strategies that enhance productivity, profitability, and sustainability in the agricultural sector.

8.2.3 Importance of Cloud Computing and SOA for Indian Agricultural Business Management

India's Cloud Computing and Service-Oriented Architecture (SOA) are increasingly important for India's Agricultural Business Management for several reasons [5], [6], [7], [8]:

Scalability: Cloud Computing and SOA provide scalable and flexible solutions that can be easily customized to meet the specific needs of Indian agricultural enterprises. This is particularly important in the context of agriculture, where production processes can vary significantly depending on factors such as crop types, soil quality, and weather conditions.

Cost-effectiveness: Cloud Computing and SOA can help reduce the cost of managing India's agricultural enterprises by providing cost-effective solutions for data storage, software applications, and hardware infrastructure. This is particularly important for small and medium-sized agricultural enterprises that may have limited resources.

Data analytics: Cloud Computing and SOA enable the collection and analysis of large amounts of data, which can be used to optimize production processes, improve resource allocation, and enhance decision-making. This is particularly important in the context of agriculture, where data on weather patterns, soil quality, and crop yields can provide valuable insights into the performance of agricultural enterprises.

Collaboration: Cloud Computing and SOA provide opportunities for collaboration among different stakeholders in the agricultural sector, including farmers, researchers, extension workers, and policymakers. This can help to promote knowledge sharing, innovation, and the development of best practices in agricultural production and management.

Accessibility: Cloud Computing and SOA can improve the accessibility of agricultural services and information, particularly in rural areas where access to traditional IT infrastructure may be limited. This can help to improve the productivity and profitability of agricultural enterprises, while also enhancing the social and economic development of rural communities.

The importance of Cloud Computing and SOA for India's Agricultural Business Management is likely to grow as the agricultural sector becomes more data-driven, and as the need for scalable and cost-effective solutions becomes more pressing. By leveraging these technologies, agricultural enterprises can enhance their productivity, sustainability, and competitiveness, while also contributing to the overall development of the agricultural sector.

8.3 Cloud Computing Service Models and Platforms for Agricultural Business

8.3.1 Cloud Service Models: IaaS, PaaS, SaaS

Cloud infrastructure refers to the underlying hardware and software components that enable cloud computing services to be delivered to users over the Internet. There are three main types of cloud infrastructure models: Infrastructure-as-a-Service (IaaS), Platform-as-a-Service (PaaS), and Software-as-a-Service (SaaS). Each of these models offers a different level of control, flexibility, and functionality to users, depending on their specific needs and requirements [1], [2].

> *Infrastructure-as-a-Service (IaaS):* IaaS is a cloud computing model in which users rent or lease IT infrastructure resources such as virtual machines, storage, and networking over the Internet. With IaaS, users have complete control over the operating system, applications, and data that are hosted on the infrastructure. This model is typically used by businesses that require a high level of customization and control over their IT infrastructure, such as software development companies, e-commerce platforms, and big data analytics firms.
>
> *Platform-as-a-Service (PaaS):* PaaS is a cloud computing model in which users rent or lease a complete development environment over the Internet. This includes the hardware, software, and tools needed to develop, test, and deploy applications. With PaaS, users have more control over the development environment than with SaaS, but less control than with IaaS. This model is typically used by developers who want to focus on developing and deploying applications, without having to worry about the underlying infrastructure.
>
> *Software-as-a-Service (SaaS):* SaaS is a cloud computing model in which users rent or lease software applications over the Internet. With SaaS, users access the software through a web browser or mobile app, without having to install or maintain the software themselves. This model is typically used by businesses that require a high degree of flexibility and scalability, such as customer relationship management (CRM) software, enterprise resource planning (ERP) software, and productivity tools.

By leveraging IaaS, PaaS, and SaaS, businesses can access the resources they need to run their operations, without having to invest in expensive hardware or software. Additionally, cloud infrastructure allows businesses to scale up or down as needed,

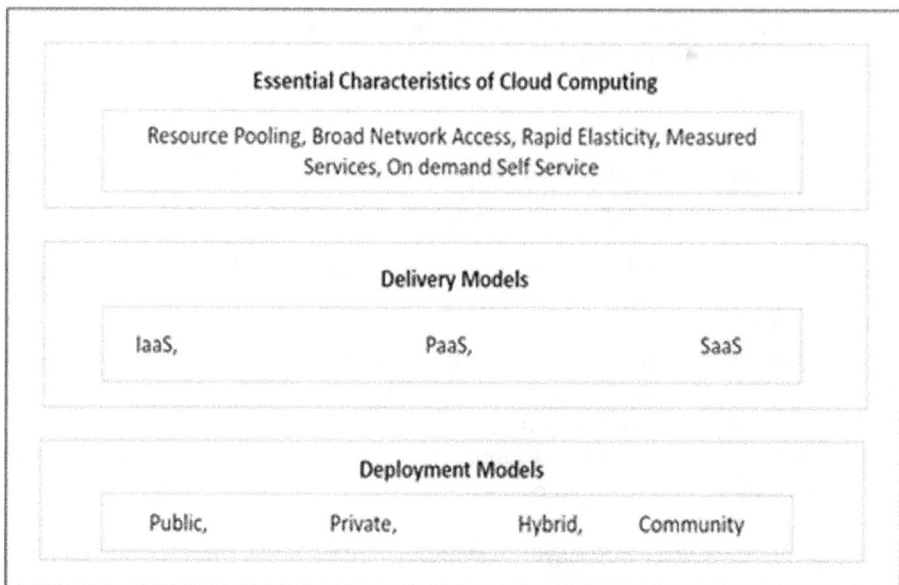

Figure 8.1   NIST model of cloud computing.
Source: [1].

to meet changing demand and business requirements. Figure 8.1 shows the NIST (National Institute of Standards and Technology) model of cloud computing given in 2011.

8.3.2   Popular Cloud Platforms for Agricultural Business Management

Agricultural businesses all over the world employ a number of well-known cloud platforms for agricultural business management. The most well-liked platforms include the following [5], [6], [7]:

Microsoft Azure: Microsoft Azure is a platform for cloud computing that provides a variety of services, such as data analytics, artificial intelligence, and data storage (AI). It offers a flexible and safe way to manage agricultural applications and data, and it integrates well with other Microsoft products and services.

Amazon Web Services (AWS): AWS is a cloud computing platform that provides a variety of services, such as data analytics, machine learning, and data storage. The management of agricultural data and applications is made flexible and scalable, and it is simple to link with other AWS tools and services.

Google Cloud Platform (GCP): GCP is a cloud computing platform that provides a variety of services, such as data analytics, machine learning, and data storage. It offers a flexible and safe way to manage agricultural applications and data, and it is simple to link with other Google tools and services.

IBM Cloud: Data storage, data analytics, and artificial intelligence are just a few of the services provided by IBM Cloud, a cloud computing platform. It offers an easy way to interface with other IBM tools and services while managing agricultural data and applications in a secure and scalable manner.

Oracle Cloud Infrastructure (OCI): OCI is a cloud computing platform that provides a variety of services, such as data analytics, machine learning, and data storage. It is scalable, safe, and easy to combine with other Oracle products and services. It offers a management solution for agricultural data and applications.

DigitalOcean: DigitalOcean is a cloud computing platform that provides a simple and affordable solution for managing data and applications. It is popular among small and medium-sized agricultural enterprises due to its ease of use and low pricing.

Salesforce: Salesforce is a cloud computing platform that provides a wide range of services, including customer relationship management (CRM), marketing automation, and analytics. It is popular in the agricultural industry for managing customer data and improving sales processes [8].

Rackspace: Rackspace is a cloud computing platform that provides managed hosting and cloud services for businesses. It is popular for its customer support and managed services.

The choice of cloud platform for India's Agricultural Business Management will depend on factors such as the specific needs and requirements of the country's agricultural enterprises, the level of scalability and flexibility required, and the level of security and compliance needed.

8.3.3 Pros and Cons of Using Cloud Platforms for Agricultural Business Management

Using cloud platforms for Agricultural Business Management has both advantages and disadvantages. Here are some of the pros and cons of using cloud platforms for agricultural enterprises:

8.3.3.1 Pros

Scalability: Cloud platforms allow agricultural enterprises to scale up or down their IT infrastructure and applications quickly and easily, as needed. This can help agricultural enterprises to better manage their resources and respond to changing business needs.

Flexibility: Cloud platforms offer a wide range of services and solutions that can be tailored to the specific needs of agricultural enterprises. This allows agricultural enterprises to choose the services that are most relevant and beneficial to their operations.

Cost-effective: Cloud platforms can be a cost-effective solution for agricultural enterprises, as they do not require large upfront investments in hardware and software. Instead, agricultural enterprises pay only for the services they use, and can scale up or down their usage as needed.

Collaboration: Cloud platforms allow agricultural enterprises to collaborate with other stakeholders, such as suppliers, customers, and government agencies, in real-time. This can help agricultural enterprises to better manage their supply chain and improve their overall operations.

8.3.3.2 Cons

Security: Cloud platforms can pose security risks for agricultural enterprises, as sensitive data and applications are stored off-site and are accessible over the Internet. This requires agricultural enterprises to take extra precautions to ensure that their data and applications are protected from unauthorized access.

Reliance on third-party providers: Agricultural enterprises that rely on cloud platforms are dependent on third-party providers to ensure that their data and applications are available and accessible at all times. This requires a high level of trust in the provider, as any downtime or disruption could have serious consequences for the agricultural enterprise.

Integration: Cloud platforms may require additional effort to integrate with existing IT systems and applications. This can be a challenge for agricultural enterprises that have legacy systems or applications that are not compatible with cloud platforms.

Regulatory compliance: Agricultural enterprises that use cloud platforms may be subject to regulatory compliance requirements, such as data privacy laws or industry-specific regulations. This requires agricultural enterprises to ensure that their cloud provider is compliant with these regulations, and that their data and applications are stored and managed in compliance with these regulations.

8.4 Service-Oriented Architecture (SOA) for Agricultural Business

8.4.1 Key Components of SOA for Agricultural Business Management

Services: SOA is built around services that are self-contained software components that provide specific functionality. Services can be reused and combined to create more complex applications.

Service Registry: A service registry is a centralized directory that keeps track of available services and their descriptions. This makes it easier for developers to discover and reuse existing services.

Service Bus: A service bus is a middleware component that handles the communication between different services. It provides a layer of abstraction between the services and the underlying infrastructure, making it easier to change or replace services without affecting the rest of the system.

Orchestration: Orchestration is the process of coordinating the execution of multiple services to achieve a specific business goal. This involves defining a sequence of service invocations and managing the flow of data between services.

SOA can provide a range of benefits to agricultural enterprises, including improved integration of systems, flexibility, reusability, and interoperability. The key components of SOA, such as services, service registry, service bus, and orchestration, provide a framework for building and managing complex applications in a more efficient and cost-effective manner. Figure 8.2 shows the three layer SoA architecture.

8.4.2 Best Practices for Implementing SOA in Agricultural Business Management

Here are some best practices for implementing SOA in Agricultural Business Management:

Identify business requirements: Before implementing SOA, it is important to identify the specific business requirements and use cases for the agricultural enterprise. This will help to ensure that the SOA implementation meets the specific needs of the enterprise [10].

Define a service-oriented architecture: It is important to define a clear and well-defined service-oriented architecture that outlines the different services and their relationships. This will help to ensure that the SOA implementation is well-organized and easy to manage [10].

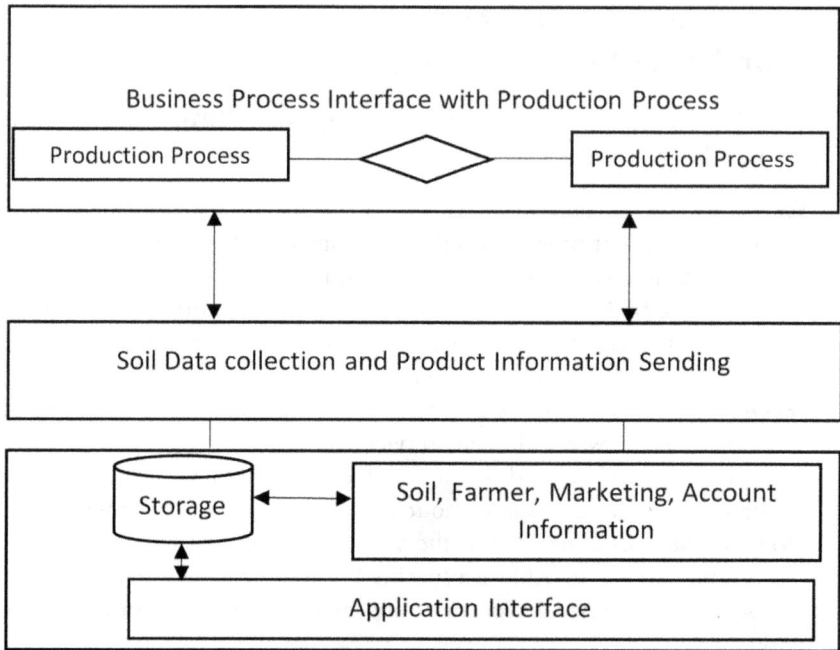

Figure 8.2 Three-layered SOA architecture with some illustrative examples of components from the Arable farming sector.

Source: [9].

> *Use standards-based technologies:* It is important to use standards-based technologies such as SOAP, REST, and WSDL to ensure interoperability between different services and systems. This will help to ensure that the SOA implementation is flexible and can be easily integrated with other systems.
>
> *Focus on service reuse:* One of the key benefits of SOA is the ability to reuse services across different applications and systems. It is important to focus on creating reusable services that can be easily combined to create new applications and systems.
>
> *Implement governance and security:* SOA implementations can become complex, with multiple services and systems interacting with each other. It is important to implement governance and security policies to ensure that the SOA implementation is secure and well-managed.

Use agile development methodologies: Agile development methodologies such as Scrum can be used to develop and manage SOA implementations. This can help to ensure that the SOA implementation is delivered on time and within budget, and can be easily adapted to changing business requirements [11].

Implementing SOA in Agricultural Business Management requires careful planning, well-defined architectures, and the use of standards-based technologies. By focusing on service reuse, governance, and security, agricultural enterprises can ensure that their SOA implementations are flexible, efficient, and secure.

8.5 Indian Case Studies and Success Stories of Cloud Computing in Agricultural Business Management

Here are a few case studies and success stories of cloud computing in agricultural business management in India:

TAFE: TAFE, one of India's largest tractor manufacturers, has adopted cloud computing for its dealer management system. The cloud-based system provides real-time access to data for TAFE's dealers, enabling them to manage sales, inventory, and service more efficiently.

FarmERP: FarmERP is a cloud-based enterprise resource planning (ERP) system designed for the agriculture sector. The system provides a range of features for managing farm operations, including crop planning, inventory management, and financial management. FarmERP has been adopted by several large agricultural enterprises in India, including Mahindra Agribusiness and Jain Irrigation.

AgroStar: AgroStar is a mobile app that provides farmers with real-time information on weather, crop prices, and farming techniques. The app is built on a cloud-based platform, allowing for real-time updates and seamless scalability. AgroStar has been adopted by over 2 million farmers in India and has helped to improve crop yields and reduce waste. Figure 8.3 shows the Agrostar screenshot from google play store.

Figure 8.3   AgroStar application for helping farmers win.

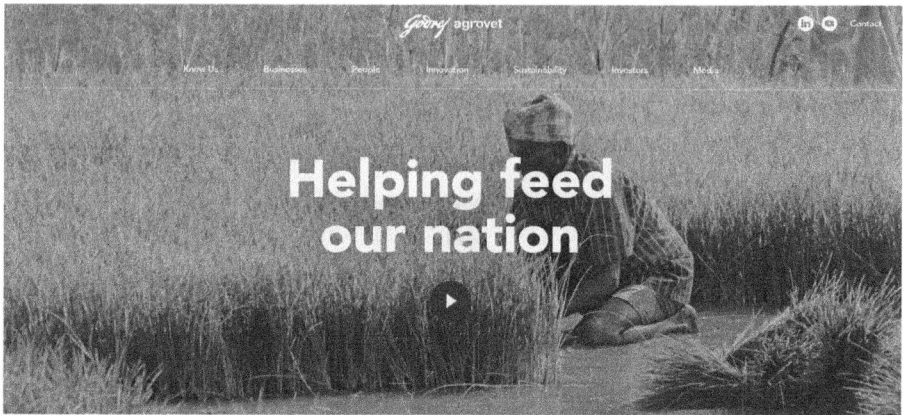

Figure 8.4   Godgej Agrovet snapshot.

Godrej Agrovet: Godrej Agrovet, one of India's largest agribusiness companies, has adopted cloud computing for its supply chain management system. The cloud-based system provides real-time data on inventory, production, and logistics, enabling Godrej Agrovet to optimize its operations and reduce costs. Figure 8.4 shows the portal screenshot of Godrej Agrovet.

KisanHub: KisanHub is a cloud-based platform that provides farmers with real-time data on crop health, weather, and market prices. The platform uses artificial intelligence and machine learning algorithms to provide personalized recommendations to farmers. KisanHub has been adopted by several large agricultural enterprises in India, including Mahyco and PepsiCo.

Cloud computing has been adopted by several agricultural enterprises in India, providing benefits such as real-time access to data, improved supply chain management, and personalized recommendations for farmers. These case studies and success stories demonstrate the potential of cloud computing to transform the agriculture sector in India and improve the livelihoods of farmers. Figure 8.5 shows the portal screenshot of Kisanhub.

IBM Watson Decision Platform for Agriculture: IBM Watson Decision Platform for Agriculture is a cloud-based platform that uses AI and machine learning to provide farmers with data-driven insights to optimize crop yields and reduce costs. The platform enables farmers to monitor and analyze weather data, soil moisture levels, and other factors to make more informed decisions about crop planting, irrigation, and fertilization. Figure 8.6 shows the screenshot of IBM's Watson Decision Platform to Bolster the Indian Agricultural Sector.

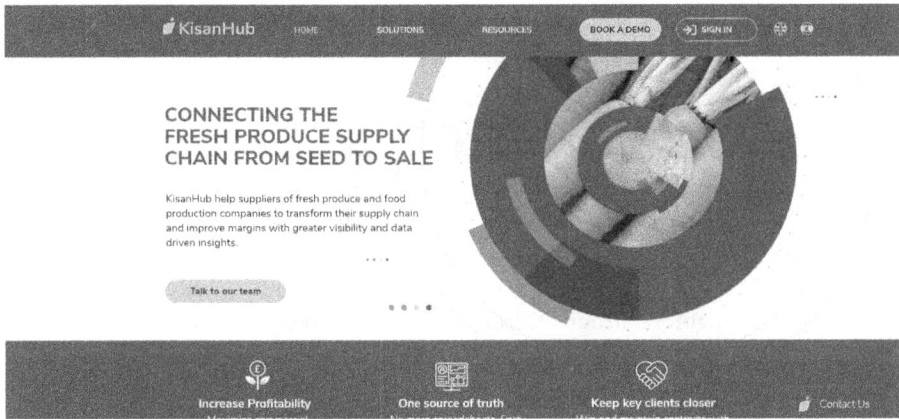

Figure 8.5   KisanHub Portal snapshot.

Figure 8.6   IBM's Watson Decision Platform to bolster the Indian agricultural sector.

The Climate Corporation: The Climate Corporation, a subsidiary of Monsanto, uses cloud computing to provide farmers with real-time weather and climate data, as well as predictive analytics and risk management tools. The company's cloud-based platform, Climate FieldView, enables farmers to make informed decisions about planting, harvesting, and other farm operations based on data-driven insights.

Agrocaelum: Agrocaelum, a Brazilian agribusiness, uses cloud computing to manage and analyze data from its agricultural operations. The company's cloud-based platform, AgroCloud, enables farmers to monitor crop health, track weather conditions, and optimize irrigation and fertilization practices, leading to higher crop yields and increased profitability.

Trimble Agriculture: Trimble Agriculture, a technology company that provides precision agriculture solutions, uses cloud computing to enable farmers to optimize their operations through data analytics and precision farming technologies. The company's cloud-based platform, Connected Farm, enables farmers to analyze data on crop yields, soil conditions, and other factors to make more informed decisions about their farming practices.

8.6 Challenges and Future Directions of Cloud Computing in Agricultural Business Management

8.6.1 Emerging Trends and Technologies for Agricultural Application

The following are some new trends and technologies in cloud computing for managing agricultural businesses. The detailed descriptions are covered in [10], [11], [12]:

Internet of Things (IoT): IoT involves the use of sensors and devices to collect data from various sources, such as soil moisture sensors and weather stations. The data is then analyzed and used to make decisions in real-time. Cloud computing is used to store and process the vast amounts of data generated by IoT devices.

Artificial intelligence (AI): AI is being used in agriculture to help farmers make more informed decisions. Machine learning algorithms can be used to analyze data on weather patterns, soil quality, and crop health to make predictions about crop yields and potential problems.

Blockchain: Blockchain technology is being used to improve supply chain management in agriculture. Blockchain can be used to track the origin and movement of agricultural products, ensuring that they are genuine and have not been tampered with.

Edge computing: Edge computing involves processing data on devices at the edge of a network, rather than sending it to a centralized cloud. This can help to reduce latency and improve the speed of decision-making in real-time applications such as precision agriculture.

Augmented reality (AR): AR can be used to provide farmers with visualizations of their crops, allowing them to quickly identify potential problems and take corrective action. AR can be integrated with cloud-based analytics to provide real-time insights.

The above-mentioned emerging trends and technologies are helping to transform agriculture and improve the efficiency of agricultural business management. Cloud computing is at the forefront of these developments, providing the storage, processing, and analysis capabilities required to make sense of the vast amounts of data generated by modern agriculture.

8.6.2 Future Directions for Cloud Computing in Agricultural Business Management

Here are some potential future directions for cloud computing in agricultural business management:

Integration with autonomous systems: As autonomous systems become more prevalent in agriculture, cloud computing will play an important role in their operation. Autonomous tractors, drones, and other equipment will generate large amounts of data that will need to be processed and analyzed in real-time to optimize their performance.

Use of blockchain for supply chain management: Blockchain technology has the potential to revolutionize supply chain management in agriculture by providing transparency and traceability. In the future, we can expect to see more widespread adoption of blockchain technology in agriculture, particularly in areas such as food safety and certification.

Expansion of precision agriculture: Precision agriculture involves the use of data and technology to optimize crop yields and reduce waste. As cloud computing becomes more affordable and accessible, we can expect to see more widespread adoption of precision agriculture techniques, particularly in developing countries where smallholder farmers can benefit from the use of data and analytics.

Increased use of machine learning: Machine learning algorithms can be used to analyze data on weather patterns, soil quality, and crop health to make predictions about crop yields and potential problems. As machine learning techniques become more sophisticated and accessible, we can expect to see more widespread use of these techniques in agriculture.

Development of new applications: As cloud computing becomes more affordable and accessible, we can expect to see the development of new applications and services that are tailored to the specific needs of agricultural businesses. These could include tools for managing soil health, monitoring water usage, and optimizing fertilizer application.

The future of cloud computing in agricultural business management looks bright, with many exciting developments on the horizon. Cloud computing has the potential to revolutionize agriculture by providing farmers with access to real-time data and analytics, enabling them to optimize their operations and improve crop yields.

8.7 Conclusion

In conclusion, the integration of cloud computing with service-oriented architecture (SOA) has opened up new avenues for agricultural businesses to streamline their operations, improve efficiency, and reduce costs. With the help of cloud-based platforms and services, farmers and agribusinesses can manage their data, applications, and processes in a scalable and cost-effective manner. Cloud computing also enables real-time monitoring and analysis of agricultural data, which helps farmers make informed decisions about crop management, resource allocation, and supply chain optimization.

Moreover, the adoption of SOA architecture in cloud-based agricultural business management provides a modular and flexible framework that allows different components and services to work together seamlessly. This results in improved collaboration and communication between different stakeholders in the agricultural supply chain, including farmers, suppliers, processors, and retailers. Furthermore, the use of web services and APIs in SOA architecture facilitates interoperability and data exchange between different systems and applications, making it easier to integrate with other tools and services.

Overall, the combination of cloud computing and SOA architecture provides a powerful solution for agricultural business management that can help improve productivity, efficiency, and sustainability. As technology continues to evolve, it is expected that cloud-based agricultural management systems will become even more advanced, providing farmers with increasingly sophisticated tools and capabilities to enhance their operations and achieve greater success.

References

[1] Rastogi, G. and Sushil, R., 2015, March. Cloud computing implementation: Key issues and solutions. *In 2015 2nd International Conference on Computing for Sustainable Global Development (INDIACom)* (pp. 320–324). IEEE.

[2] Unnamalai, V.E. and Thresphine, J.R., 2014. Service-oriented architecture for cloud computing. *International Journal of Computer Science and Information Technologies*, 5(1), pp. 251–255.

[3] Zamora-Izquierdo, M.A., Santa, J., Martínez, J.A., Martínez, V. and Skarmeta, A.F., 2019. Smart farming IoT platform based on edge and cloud computing. *Biosystems Engineering*, 177, pp. 4–17.

[4] Rupanagudi, S.R., Ranjani, B.S., Nagaraj, P., Bhat, V.G. and Thippeswamy, G., 2015, January. A novel cloud computing based smart farming system for early detection of borer insects in tomatoes. *In 2015 International Conference on Communication, Information & Computing Technology (ICCICT)* (pp. 1–6). IEEE.

[5] Moysiadis, V., Sarigiannidis, P., Vitsas, V. and Khelifi, A., 2021. Smart farming in Europe. *Computer Science Review*, 39, pp. 100345.

[6] Idoje, G., Dagiuklas, T. and Iqbal, M., 2021. Survey for smart farming technologies: Challenges and issues. *Computers & Electrical Engineering*, 92, pp. 107104.

[7] Triantafyllou, A., Tsouros, D.C., Sarigiannidis, P. and Bibi, S., 2019, May. An architecture model for smart farming. *In 2019 15th International Conference on Distributed Computing in Sensor Systems (DCOSS)* (pp. 385–392). IEEE.

[8] Patil, V.C., Al-Gaadi, K.A., Biradar, D.P. and Rangaswamy, M., 2012. Internet of things (Iot) and cloud computing for agriculture: An overview. *Proceedings of Agro-Informatics and Precision Agriculture (AIPA 2012)* (pp. 292–296). India.

[9] Wolfert, J., Verdouw, C.N., Verloop, C.M. and Beulens, A.J.M., 2010. Organizing information integration in agri-food – A method based on a service-oriented architecture and living lab approach. *Computers and Electronics in Agriculture*, 70(2), pp. 389–405.

[10] Gonçalves, P., Pedreiras, P. and Monteiro, A., 2022. Recent advances in smart farming. *Animals*, 12(6), pp. 705.

[11] Król, D. and Kitowski, J., 2016. Self-scalable services in service oriented software for cost-effective data farming. *Future Generation Computer Systems*, 54, pp. 1–15.

[12] Sharma, V., Tripathi, A.K. and Mittal, H., 2022. Technological revolutions in smart farming: Current trends, challenges & future directions. *Computers and Electronics in Agriculture*, vol. 201, pp. 1–34.

Chapter 9

Service-Oriented Computing Paradigms: Opportunities and Challenges

Rohit Verma,[1] Dheeraj Rane,[2] and Shivani Jaswal[1]

[1]National College of Ireland, Dublin, Ireland

[2]IITI Drishti CPS Foundation, Indian Institute of Technology, Indore, India

9.1   Introduction

Service-Oriented Computing (SOC) (Papazoglou & Georgakopoulos 2003) has established itself as a transformative element within the field of information technology, radically altering the design, conception, and orchestration of software services. The current chapter, "Service-Orientated Computing Paradigm: Opportunities and Challenges," seeks to provide a comprehensive introduction to the world of SOC by examining its vast opportunities and complexities in depth.

SOC introduces a computing framework in which software resources are perceived and treated as services, thereby promoting loose coupling, reusability, interoperability, and abstraction (Papazoglou 2003). This approach stands in stark contrast to traditional monolithic architectures, advocating instead a modular approach. Here, services operate independently but are capable of interacting seamlessly to execute complex business processes. The SOC paradigm offers potential

DOI: 10.1201/9781032716718-9

avenues to improve agility, optimise operational efficiency and promote a flexible IT infrastructure, enabling organisations to maintain their competitive edge amid the accelerating pace of the digital revolution.

However, the path to the successful adoption and implementation of SOC is not devoid of obstacles. Technical and organisational obstacles frequently impede the successful realisation of the full potential of the SOC. The technical aspects include issues such as service discovery and composition (Verma & Srivastava 2014; Driss et al. 2020), Quality of Service (QoS) management (Zeng et al. 2004), security and privacy concerns, governance, scalability, and performance-related concerns (Huhns & Singh 2005). Organisational and management obstacles include human elements, cultural dynamics, and structural factors, such as resistance to change, integration of the legacy system, cultural and political barriers, lack of standardisation, and lack of required skills. For the formulation of effective strategies and best practises for adopting SOC, a thorough understanding of these challenges is essential.

The cornerstones of a successful SOC implementation are strategic planning, meticulous execution, robust governance, and capable change management. Service-Oriented Architecture (SOA) initiatives, including best practises, readiness evaluation, planning, and execution, are discussed in depth in this chapter. It also addresses potential obstacles and provides a roadmap for organisations embarking on their SOC journey.

In addition, this chapter explores the intriguing areas of future SOC trends and directions. Emerging trends that redefine the boundaries of SOC include microservice architecture, serverless computing, event-driven architecture, native cloud computing, and API management and monetization. Additionally, the convergence of SOC with advanced technologies such as Artificial Intelligence (AI) and blockchain (Li et al. 2021) is paving the way for new levels of innovation and value creation. These developments have substantial implications for research, industry, and society, providing impetus for further exploration and driving the SOC paradigm forward.

This chapter's objective is to provide an all-encompassing understanding of SOC, enabling them to exploit its potential while navigating its complexities. It combines theoretical insights with practical considerations to provide a balanced view of the opportunities and obstacles associated with SOC.

The chapter concludes with a comprehensive examination of the Service-Oriented Computing paradigm, highlighting its advantages and disadvantages. It lays a solid foundation for further exploration, experimentation, and evolution, serving as a stepping stone for those who wish to enter the SOC domain. As the journey of Service-Oriented Computing continues, this chapter invites readers to engage with its narrative, gain from its insights, and actively shape its future course.

9.2   Service-Oriented Computing: Overview

The design and delivery of services that are loosely coupled, independent, and interoperable are at the forefront of the innovative architectural approach known as "service-oriented computing" (SOC) (Verma 2020). SOC represents a significant change in the way software systems are designed and implemented, with a focus on the idea of services at its core. In this paradigm, services act as building blocks that can be accessed and combined to complete more complex processes by encapsulating various business functionalities. The core of SOC is the fundamental idea of service orientation, which enables businesses to create modular, adaptable systems that are excellent for collaboration and efficiency (Verma et al. 2014).

The SOC paradigm's core services are not merely random collections of functionalities. They are thoughtfully developed and organised to include particular business functions. For instance, a "payment service" may be present in an e-commerce system and be in charge of managing all transactions. This service is self-sufficient and can run without the assistance of other services. But in order to complete more complicated tasks, it can also collaborate with other services like the "order management service" or the "inventory service." These services can communicate and work together without being inextricably linked to one another; this is due to their loose coupling, which increases their flexibility and adaptability.

Service abstraction, service composition, service reuse, service autonomy, and service discovery are some of the fundamental principles on which SOC is based. Service abstraction suggests that the inner workings of a service are hidden from the user. To access and use the service, users only need to be able to understand the interfaces provided. This principle simplifies interaction and promotes the efficient use of services, since consumers do not need to be concerned with the underlying details.

The ability to create more complex services or processes by combining already existing services is known as the principle of service composition.

This is similar to using Legos to construct a building. Every service functions as a "block" that can be "plugged in" to create more complex systems, resulting in increased operational effectiveness and functionality.

Another important principle, service reusability, emphasises that once a service is developed, it can be used in a variety of situations. This principle increases the efficiency of system development and maintenance, which significantly reduces redundancy. An e-commerce system's payment service, for instance, can be reused in other contexts where a payment mechanism is needed, saving money and hastening time to market.

A key characteristic of SOC, service autonomy guarantees the independence and self-sufficiency of services. The ability to deploy, modify, or even remove services without affecting others is made possible by their autonomy. Consequently, it helps to foster system stability, scalability, and resilience.

In addition, service discovery is a fundamental principle that facilitates the identification and comprehension of services within a system. It includes tools for finding services, comprehending how they work, and efficiently using them. This idea supports the dynamic composition of services and enhances service utilisation.

By adhering to these principles, businesses can develop highly scalable and adaptable modular systems. Improvements in efficiency, lower ownership costs, greater levels of collaboration, and increased business agility are all advantages of such systems. Additionally, these systems are more adaptable to changes in market dynamics, technological advances, and business requirements.

In a nutshell, service-oriented computing is a design strategy that uses the idea of services to build flexible, effective, and scalable systems. Specific business functions are encapsulated into separate, loosely coupled services by SOC, giving organisations the flexibility to quickly adapt to shifting conditions and requirements. Due to this, SOC is no longer just a method for developing software; rather, it is a strategic tool to transform businesses.

9.2.1 Evolution and Development of the Service-Oriented Computing Paradigm

The origins of service-oriented computing (SOC) can be traced back to earlier concepts such as distributed computing and component-based software development. Both of these models served as stepping stones on the path to the modern SOC, providing a theoretical and practical foundation that has been refined over time.

As the initial foundation for SOC, distributed computing enabled the decentralisation of computational resources and functionalities. This computing model is based on the distribution of software system components across multiple networked computers, allowing for more efficient resource utilisation and performance. This idea paved the way for the independent component-based development, another significant SOC predecessor, introduced modular programming. In this development methodology, a system is divided into independent components, each of which encapsulates a particular functionality. These components can be independently developed, tested, and deployed before being assembled into an application. This strategy had a significant impact on SOC, particularly with respect to the principles of reusability, modularity, and composition of services.

As technology progressed, the SOC itself underwent significant transformations, with the emergence of web services functioning as a key impetus for its widespread adoption. Web services are software systems designed to facilitate machine-to-machine communication over a network using standardised protocols. They represented an important evolutionary step in the development of SOC, providing a practical implementation model that adhered to SOC's guiding principles and facilitated its application in real world scenarios (Niknejad et al. 2020).

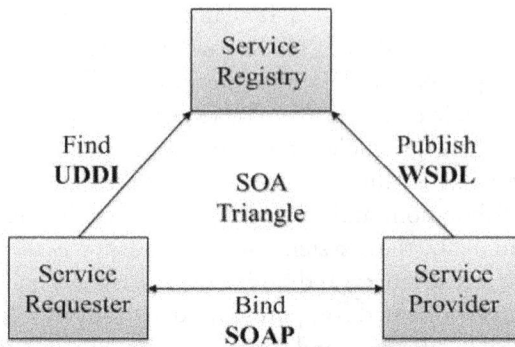

Figure 9.1   Service-oriented architecture and decentralisation of services in the SOC model.

Figure 9.1 presents the realization of service computing using web services, this is one of the most popular use cases of service computing. Web services introduced standard protocols such as the Simple Object Access Protocol (SOAP) and the Web Services Description Language (WSDL). SOAP is a messaging protocol that enables communication between programs running on different operating systems. The WSDL is an XML-based protocol that provides a model for describing web services, essentially acting as a guide for interacting with the web service. These protocols played a crucial role in enabling interoperability and integration between disparate systems, thus improving the applicability of SOC in heterogeneous environments by facilitating communication between different services. However, the development of web services did not mark the end of the SOC's evolution. This architectural paradigm has incorporated even more cutting-edge technologies and methodologies in recent years, including cloud computing (Wei & Blake 2010), microservices, and containerization.

Cloud computing has significantly altered the deployment and accessibility of SOC services (Filippi & Mccarthy 2012). Cloud platforms provide on-demand access to a shared pool of configurable computing resources, enabling dynamic allocation and scaling of services based on demand. This not only improves the scalability and cost-effectiveness of the SOC but also simplifies the deployment and management of services.

Microservices represent a refinement of the SOC paradigm, in which a system is composed of a large number of small independent services, each performing a specific function (Lu et al. 2023). The microservices architecture improves the granularity and modularity of SOC, allowing greater system development flexibility and maintenance agility. Each microservice can be independently developed, deployed, and scaled, enabling the continuous delivery and deployment of large and complex applications (Zimmermann 2017).

Containerization is a lightweight form of virtualization that packages an application and its dependencies as a standard unit for software development. Containers ensure that services run reliably when moved from one computing environment to another, thereby improving the portability and effectiveness of SOC service deployment. Tools such as Docker and Kubernetes have become the backbone of containerization, enabling more robust and scalable SOC systems by ensuring consistent environments for running applications.

The evolution of service-oriented computing is evidence of the continuous development of software architectures, with each new technology or methodology enhancing and refining the SOC's capabilities. SOC continues to evolve from its origins in distributed computing and component-based development, to the proliferation of web services, to the incorporation of cloud computing, microservices, and containerization (El-Sheikh et al. 2016). This development not only improves the scalability, flexibility, and agility of SOC-based systems, but also creates new design, development, and deployment opportunities for software applications. The fundamental principles of SOC, such as service reusability, modularity, interoperability, and autonomy, remain constant despite the complexity of this journey, guiding its evolution, and ensuring its continued relevance in an ever-changing technological landscape.

9.2.2 Key Components and Architecture of Service-Oriented Systems

Service-oriented systems comprise several key components that work together to enable service creation, deployment, and consumption. These components include service providers, service consumers, service registries, and service orchestrators. Service providers implement and expose services, while service consumers utilize these services to fulfil their business requirements. Service registries are repositories of service descriptions and metadata, facilitating service discovery and composition. Service orchestrators coordinate the interaction and invocation of multiple services to achieve desired outcomes. The architecture of service-oriented systems is typically based on a distributed, loosely coupled, and message-oriented model, allowing seamless integration and interoperability between services.

Within the framework of service-oriented systems, several core components work together to make it easier to create, deploy, and use services. These essential parts include service providers, service consumers, service registries, and service orchestrators. Each of these parts has different roles and responsibilities that help make the service-oriented paradigm efficient and robust as a whole.

Service providers are the main parts of the SOC that are in charge of putting services into action and letting people know about them. A service is a separate, self-contained thing that is made to run a specific business process. Service providers design these services, create them using the right software tools and languages, and then make them available to other parts of the system through well-structured network interfaces.

Service consumers, on the other hand, are parts that interact with the above services to meet their own operational needs. These consumers could be other services, applications, or end users who use the interfaces that service providers make available to access services. Most of the time, using a service means making a service request, waiting for the request to be processed, and then receiving and using the service's results.

Service registries are another critical part that holds service descriptions and the metadata that accompany them. Their main job is to make it easier for services to be found and put together. They keep detailed information about each service, such as how the service works, how to get to it, and what protocols or data formats it uses. In large service-oriented systems with hundreds or thousands of services, these registries make it easy for service users to find and understand the services available. This makes services easier to use and reuse.

Service orchestrators play a key role in making sure that multiple services work together and are called when needed to reach more complex goals. In the context of SOC, many business processes need to make use of more than one service at the same time. Orchestrators take care of this by controlling the order of service calls, data transformations, and the handling of errors. When simple services are combined into more complex composite services or business workflows, they do this.

Service-oriented systems are built on a model that is distributed, loosely coupled, and based on messages. The fact that SOC is distributed ensures that services are spread across multiple servers or geographical locations. This makes the system more scalable and resistant to changing loads and possible failures. The "loosely coupled" part means that services do not depend on each other too much. In this kind of design, services run on their own, so changes or failures in one service do not affect the others. This makes the system more stable and easier to maintain as a whole. The "message-oriented" model shows how services talk to each other. Services in a service-oriented system talk to each other by sending messages instead of calling functions directly. This method makes it easier for services to work together since they do not have to know much about each other's inner workings and can still talk to each other as long as they understand the message formats.

In the end, the architecture of service-oriented systems, which includes service providers, consumers, registries, and orchestrators, is carefully constructed to make the most of SOC. These components, which work in a distributed, loosely coupled, and message-oriented framework, make it easy for services to connect and work with each other. This makes it possible to build systems that are flexible, scalable, and reliable.

9.2.3 *Service-Oriented Computing Standards and Protocols*

Interoperability and seamless integration serve as the guiding principles for system architecture in the realm of service-oriented computing. To implement these principles, the field relies on a variety of established standards and protocols, which serve as the basis for building scalable and interoperable service-oriented systems.

The Web Services Description Language (WSDL) is one of the fundamental standards for service-oriented computing. WSDL serves as a contract between service providers and consumers, defining a service's capabilities, interfaces, and protocols (Verma & Srivastava 2014). It serves as a blueprint that informs users of the functionality, accessibility, and communication protocols of the service, allowing them to interact with the service effectively.

The Simple Object Access Protocol (SOAP) is another significant protocol within service-oriented architectures. As a messaging protocol, SOAP allows programs running on different operating systems to communicate. Its primary function is to facilitate the exchange of messages containing information between services. These SOAP messages are formatted in XML and can be transmitted over various protocols, including HTTP, SMTP, and FTP, making SOAP a versatile tool for enabling communication between services regardless of their underlying platforms or programming languages.

The Universal Description, Discovery, and Integration (UDDI) standard plays a crucial role in service-oriented computing by creating a registry of services, similar to a directory or a database of network services. UDDI uses XML as a method to independently describe and discover web services. UDDI significantly facilitates service discovery by cataloguing available services, their interfaces, and communication protocols, thereby assisting service consumers in locating and comprehending the services they require.

The Business Process Execution Language (BPEL) standard is used to orchestrate the interactions between services. BPEL permits the description of intricate business processes involving multiple service invocations. It enables service orchestrators to manage the sequence of service invocations, handle data transformations, and manage exceptions, allowing the creation of composite services or workflows from simpler individual services.

In addition to these specific standards, the operation of service-oriented systems depends on a number of general protocols and data formats. Hypertext Transfer Protocol (HTTP), a popular communication protocol, enables the transmission of hypertext across the Internet, such as web pages. HTTP is frequently used as the transport protocol for SOAP messages within service-oriented systems, ensuring their secure and reliable delivery.

Extensible Markup Language (XML) is a data format that encodes information in a format that is readable by both humans and machines. In service-oriented computing, it is widely used to create service descriptions (in WSDL), registries (in

UDDI), and messages (in SOAP). The adaptability and versatility of XML make it the ideal format for representing structured data in service-oriented environments.

In addition, JavaScript Object Notation (JSON) offers an alternative to XML as a lightweight data-exchange format. JSON is a language independent text format that follows conventions familiar to programmers of the C family of programming languages. It is frequently used to transmit data between servers and web applications, providing a compact and efficient method of data exchange.

These standards and protocols contribute to the overarching objectives of interoperability and seamless integration in service-oriented computing. By providing standardised methods for describing services, exchanging messages, discovering services, and orchestrating service interactions, they establish a common foundation for the development of scalable and interoperable service-oriented systems.

Examples of Service-Oriented Computing Applications: Service-oriented computing has been successfully implemented in numerous domains, demonstrating its efficacy and adaptability. In e-commerce, service-oriented architectures enable the seamless integration of various applications and systems, thereby facilitating the efficient processing of orders, the management of inventory, and the management of customer relationships. In the healthcare industry, service-oriented computing enables the integration of electronic health records, clinical decision support systems, and telemedicine applications, thus improving patient care and outcomes. In addition, government agencies employ service-oriented architectures to provide citizen-centric services, such as online tax filing, permit applications, and public safety initiatives. These examples illustrate the wide array of domains in which service-oriented computing has proven useful.

9.3 Opportunities: Benefits of Service-Oriented Computing

Service-oriented computing, an innovative paradigm, offers numerous advantages to organisations seeking to enhance operational processes and achieve business goals. This section explores the numerous benefits and opportunities of SOC, highlighting its impact on various aspects of enterprise systems.

The most significant contribution of SOC is its ability to improve the interoperability and integration of disparate systems. Organisations have struggled to integrate various software applications and systems that operate on disparate platforms and technologies. SOC solves this problem by proposing a standardised methodology for system integration, which enables frictionless data transfer and communication between disparate systems. Using standardised protocols and interfaces, SOC promotes interoperability, thereby fostering a higher level of system integration and collaboration within an organisation.

In addition, the ability of SOC to enhance scalability and flexibility in service delivery is a notable advantage. Due to the modular design of service-oriented systems, organisations can easily scale their services in response to fluctuations in demand. This scalability guarantees that the system will remain robust in the face of increased workloads and evolving business requirements. Furthermore, SOC allows organisations to decouple their services, allowing them to be independent of their development, deployment, and maintenance. This adaptability enables organisations to respond quickly to market demands, introduce new services, and modify existing ones without disrupting the system as a whole.

SOC's pillars, service reusability and composability, contribute significantly to its advantages. In a service-oriented architecture, services are designed as autonomous, independent units of functionality. This design promotes reusability by allowing services to be shared and used across various applications and systems. By utilising existing services rather than developing new ones, businesses can realise significant time and cost savings. In addition, services can be composed or orchestrated to produce new functionalities, enabling organisations to rapidly develop and deploy complex business processes by integrating existing services. This composability allows the rapid creation of solutions tailored to specific business requirements.

Cost-effectiveness and resource optimisation are inherent characteristics of SOC. Organisations can optimise resource allocation and reduce redundancy by adopting a service-oriented perspective. Sharing and reusing services across multiple applications eliminates redundant development efforts, saving not only time but also money on software development and maintenance. Furthermore, SOC enables organisations to maximise the use of their existing infrastructure and resources, reducing the need for additional investments.

In the current volatile business environment, SOC's dynamism and accessibility are crucial. The adaptability of service-oriented systems to fluctuating business requirements enables organisations to respond quickly to market demands. It is possible to modify, add, or replace services with minimal impact on the system as a whole. This dynamism enables organisations to remain competitive and take advantage of timely opportunities. In addition, SOC promotes high availability by employing redundant and distributed architectures, ensuring that services remain accessible despite failures or disruptions and thereby enhancing the system's overall reliability and robustness.

In addition, SOC facilitates an improved alignment between business and IT. SOC establishes a clear connection between IT capabilities and business processes by encapsulating business functionality as services. IT systems are more closely aligned with the organisation's objectives and strategies because services are modelled after real-world business functions. This alignment promotes effective communication and collaboration between business stakeholders and IT teams, fostering a shared understanding of the contribution of IT services to business value.

Therefore, service-oriented computing offers a multitude of advantages that improve enterprise systems. Key benefits of SOC include improved interoperability and integration, enhanced scalability and flexibility, increased reusability and composability, cost effectiveness and resource optimisation, improved agility and availability, and improved alignment between business and IT. By leveraging these advantages, companies can optimise their operations, encourage innovation, and achieve their business objectives more efficiently.

9.4   Challenges in Service-Oriented Computing

The adoption of service-oriented computing has gained significant attention due to its transformative potential, providing organisations with enhanced flexibility, interoperability, and scalability. However, the transition to this novel paradigm is not without hurdles. This chapter aims to explore the multifaceted challenges and limitations encountered when implementing a service-oriented approach.

9.4.1   Technical Challenges

The technical challenges in SOC cover a wide range of issues that can hinder the effective implementation and management of service-oriented systems.

First, there is the challenge of discovering and composing services. SOC relies on encapsulating discrete functionalities as services that can be reused and combined. However, identifying the most suitable services to meet specific business needs can be a complex endeavour. The distributed and diverse nature of these services can further complicate the coupling or composition process to form more intricate business processes.

In addition, managing the orchestration and choreography of the service poses another set of obstacles. Orchestration involves centrally managing multiple services to deliver a defined business process, while choreography deals with the collaborative decentralised interplay between services. Both processes require advanced coordination mechanisms and protocols to ensure seamless and reliable execution of complex business operations.

Ensuring quality-of-service (QoS) parameters, such as reliability, availability, and response time, is critical to maintaining high performance and user satisfaction. Managing these metrics effectively requires sophisticated monitoring and management mechanisms.

From a security perspective, SOC systems must address the confidentiality, integrity, and availability of data and services. Given SOC's reliance on open standards and protocols for communication, these systems can be susceptible to various security threats, necessitating robust security mechanisms and controls.

Governance and policy-related issues further compound the technical challenges in SOC. These include defining and enforcing service-level agreements, managing service versions, and controlling service usage. Scalability and performance considerations also arise when dealing with large volumes of data and high user demand, potentially impacting the efficiency and reliability of service-orientated systems.

9.4.2 Organizational and Management Challenges

Beyond the technical realm, the adoption of SOC introduces a range of organisational and managerial challenges. One of the most prominent barriers is resistance to change and the subsequent lack of adoption. Shifting to a service-oriented approach often requires significant alterations in both technical and business practises, which can meet resistance from various stakeholders.

Integrating SOC with legacy systems and infrastructure also poses a substantial challenge. Many organisations rely on established systems and infrastructures that may not align seamlessly with SOC principles. Aligning these systems with new SOC-based architectures can be a complex and costly endeavour.

Cultural and political barriers within an organisation can impede the adoption of SOC. Transitioning to a service-oriented model often necessitates changes in the organisation's culture and structure, which may face opposition from employees or departments with vested interests in maintaining the existing order.

The lack of standardisation and interoperability presents another hurdle, particularly in heterogeneous environments where different systems and technologies coexist. Despite the adoption of open standards and protocols, compatibility and inter-operability issues can still arise, complicating the process of service integration and communication.

Lastly, implementing and managing SOC requires specific skills and expertise that may not be readily available within the existing workforce. Bridging this skill gap requires substantial investment in staff training and recruitment, which can deter many organisations.

Although SOC offers numerous benefits, its adoption and implementation are not without challenges and limitations. These obstacles, which encompass technical, organisational, and managerial aspects, must be carefully considered and addressed to ensure the successful implementation and management of service-oriented systems. By comprehensively understanding these challenges, organisations can proactively take measures to mitigate them, maximising the potential benefits of SOC.

9.5 Adoption and Implementation Strategies

Service-oriented computing is a big step forward in the field of information technology, forcing companies to rethink their current IT architectures and ways of doing business. The move towards SOC is not just a change in technology; it is also a change in strategy that affects all of an organisation's operations. This chapter aims to get into the details of SOC adoption by describing effective strategies, proven practises, methods to assess readiness, and the steps needed to plan and carry out an SOC initiative. Also, it will show how to deal with any cultural or organisational problems that might arise during the adoption process.

Interoperability, reusability, and loose coupling are all built into SOC, making it a key part of modern business infrastructure. To use these features, organisations must follow established SOC standards, such as SOAP, for exchanging messages, WSDL for describing services, and UDDI for finding services. But this alignment is just one part of the larger puzzle of SOC adoption. Organisations also need to make sure that their services have the right level of granularity, which means that they are neither too broad to be reused nor too specific to be useful. The implementation of service contracts to govern interactions between service consumers and service providers, the management of service versions to handle changes over time, and the design of services to handle exceptions and failures are all just as important. Together, these practises help to build a strong and reliable SOC implementation.

But before starting the SOC journey, an organisation needs to look at itself and see if it is ready for such a change. This readiness assessment looks at the organisation's technical infrastructure, the skills and abilities of its human resources, and how well its operational processes can be changed. Key things to look at are how well legacy systems work with SOC principles, how well IT staff knows how to manage and maintain service-oriented systems, and how open the organisation's culture is to change. The readiness assessment can provide important information about potential bottlenecks and hurdles that could slow the transition, allowing organisations to deal with these problems in advance.

Thinking strategically is a must when planning and carrying out a service-oriented architecture project. Organisations need to figure out which business processes would benefit the most from service orientation and focus their first efforts on turning these processes into services. But the SOA initiative should not be seen as a separate project. Instead, it should be seen as a key part of the overall business strategy of the organisation. A phased approach to adopting SOC, starting with a pilot project, gives the organisation the opportunity to learn from early successes and problems, preparing it for future implementations that are bigger and more complicated.

The governance and management of service-oriented systems are important parts of the adoption of SOCs. Organisations must establish clear governance structures that define roles and responsibilities throughout the service lifecycle, from design and development to deployment and maintenance. Service-level agreements (SLAs) are very important because they set expectations for service performance and quality. These expectations need to be constantly monitored to make sure they are met and problems are fixed quickly. Service-oriented systems that are reliable and work well are built on a strong governance structure.

Although the technological parts of SOC adoption are important, they are only half the battle. Part of the other half is getting rid of cultural and organisational barriers. Resistance to change, which can show up in different ways such as not understanding, fear of losing one's job, or fights between departments, is a big problem for SOC adoption. To overcome these problems, organisations need to create a shared vision of SOC, encourage open communication and collaboration, and address employee concerns. Training programmes and other ways to get help can be very important in giving employees the skills they need and making the transition easier.

To sum up, moving towards SOC adoption is a complicated and multistep process. It requires meticulous planning, prudent execution, and efforts to keep improving. But if the right strategies and practises are in place, organisations can get to adoption of SOC without any problems. The switch to SOC not only opens up new operational efficiencies and opportunities, but also gives organisations the agility and flexibility they need to adapt to a business landscape that is constantly changing—changes the way organisations think about and run their information systems, making it an essential part of modern business infrastructures.

9.6 Future Trends and Directions in Service-Oriented Computing

Service-oriented computing is at the centre of innovation and change in the field of information technology, which is changing quickly. This chapter talks about the future trends and directions of SOC. It looks at emerging trends, the integration of SOC with cutting-edge technologies like AI and blockchain, advances in service-oriented architectures and platforms, and what these changes mean for research, industry, and society. It also looks at ideas like microservices architecture, serverless computing, event-driven architecture, cloud-native computing, API management and monetization, and how they will change the SOC paradigm in the coming years.

The microservices architecture shows how SOC is moving towards services that are smaller and more independent. This is a new trend. The microservice architecture is different from monolithic architectures, which build applications as a single unit. Instead, it breaks applications into smaller services that perform specific business functions. This trend not only increases the benefits of SOC, like reusability and scalability, but also improves system resilience and deployment speed, making it easier for companies to respond quickly to changes in the market.

At the same time, serverless computing has become more popular. This method removes the server layer and focusses on the execution of the service. Serverless computing fits perfectly with the SOC paradigm, so organisations can focus on service development without having to worry about managing their infrastructure. Serverless computing is cost-effective, and the pay-per-use model makes it even more so. This makes it attractive to businesses of all sizes.

Event-driven architecture, which means making services that respond to real-time business events, is another important trend. This architectural style works well with SOC because it encourages real-time responsiveness, improves system agility, and allows services to talk to each other at different times. In a world where business intelligence and decisions are made in real time, event-driven architectures give companies a big edge over their competitors.

Another important trend in SOC is the move towards cloud-native computing. Cloud-native computing uses the power of the cloud to build and run scalable applications in dynamic environments such as public, private, and hybrid clouds. This method speeds up the delivery of business value in SOC by using containerisation, orchestrating services with platforms like Kubernetes, and putting DevOps practises in place for continuous integration and delivery.

API management and monetization have also grown in popularity. In SOC, APIs are the glue that binds the different services. Effective API management ensures that APIs run smoothly, are secure, and are run by the right people. API monetization, on the other hand, lets APIs be used to make money by third-party developers.

But the future of SOC is not just about these trends; it is also about how SOC will work with other new technologies like AI and blockchain. AI can help SOC by automating service composition, improving service performance, and allowing predictive analytics. On the other hand, blockchain's immutable distributed ledger technology can make service interactions safer and more open.

Service-oriented architectures and platforms keep getting better and better, making these improvements possible. Modern SOC platforms have advanced features such as policy-based governance, real-time monitoring, and dynamic scalability. These features make service-oriented systems more efficient and reliable. We can expect these platforms to become smarter, faster and more flexible as innovation goes on.

These changes and improvements have great effects on research, business, and society as a whole. From a research point of view, they open up new areas to investigate, such as AI-powered service orchestration, blockchain-based service governance, and event-driven service modelling. They give the industry the opportunity to improve operational efficiency, make businesses more flexible, and come up with new products and services. On a larger scale, they promise to change many areas, such as healthcare, education, transportation, and e-commerce, improving lives and promoting social progress.

The combination of SOC with revolutionary technologies like artificial intelligence and blockchain is speeding up change and opening up new possibilities. AI can help SOC in many ways because it can learn, reason, and fix mistakes on its own. An important example is the composition of services, where AI algorithms can automate the process of finding, choosing, and combining services to create composite applications. This automation can reduce the time, cost, and complexity of putting together services, making them more efficient and able to grow.

Using predictive analytics, AI can also play a key role in improving service performance. By looking at how services have performed in the past, AI models can predict how they will perform in the future, find potential bottlenecks, and suggest ways to improve performance. This proactive approach can make SOC more effective and resilient by improving service reliability, responsiveness, and user satisfaction.

On the other hand, blockchain provides a strong and clear way for services to interact with each other. Its distributed ledger technology makes sure that all service transactions are recorded in a way that cannot be changed, can be tracked, and can be checked. This improves security and trust. For example, in a marketplace for services, blockchain can ensure that people can find, choose, and use services in a fair and open way, eliminating the chance of fraud or deception.

Smart contracts can also be easier to carry out with the help of the blockchain. Smart contracts are agreements that automatically execute their terms because they are written directly into the code. This can automate the enforcement of service-level agreements and the resolution of conflicts. When blockchain is combined with SOC, it can change the way service-oriented systems are governed, managed, and run.

In addition, the constant improvement of service-oriented architectures and platforms has helped make these improvements possible. With their advanced features and capabilities, modern SOC platforms make SOC stronger, more flexible, and more efficient. For example, they are adding more and more automated service deployment and scaling features. This allows organisations to quickly and easily change their service portfolio in response to changing demand patterns.

In addition, many platforms are adding advanced monitoring and analytics tools, which give real-time information about how a service is being used and how well it is performing. These insights can help organisations find and fix service problems before they occur, making services more reliable and making users happier. Other important features that are being added are policy-based governance, service version management, and security and privacy controls. All of these features make the SOC more reliable and strong.

The growing trends and new developments in SOC have a large impact on research, business and society as a whole. They are making new research paths possible, driving innovation in industry, and making it possible for society to change. They are changing the rules of competition, forcing companies to rethink their strategies, cultures, and skill sets. And they are accelerating digital transformation across all industries, changing how we work, learn, communicate, and interact with each other.

But there are big problems with these chances. They require a deep understanding of SOC and related technologies, a willingness to experiment and learn, and a commitment to ethical and responsible computing. They require us to deal with many complicated technical, organisational and social issues, such as how to make technologies work together and how to train workers and protect their privacy.

The future of service-oriented computing (SOC) holds immense potential and challenges. SOC continues to evolve, bringing about a new era of computing marked by flexibility, interoperability, and speed. This shift is transforming how software services are designed, built and delivered, enabling innovation and value creation. To fully leverage SOC's capabilities, it is crucial to understand emerging trends, seize opportunities, and address challenges. In doing so, SOC can become a powerful tool for driving innovation, growth, and social progress.

Integration of SOC with emerging technologies offers promising prospects: Researchers, practitioners, and policymakers must grasp these trends and their implications. By harnessing the power of SOC and embracing technological advancements, organisations can foster innovation, achieve operational excellence, and unlock unprecedented value for stakeholders and society.

Key trends in SOC include the adoption of microservices architecture, which breaks applications into smaller, autonomous services, enhancing reusability and scalability. Serverless computing abstracts infrastructure management, enabling organisations to focus on service development and optimise resource utilisation. Event-driven architecture enables real-time responsiveness and agility through asynchronous communication between services. Cloud native computing leverages the cloud to build and run scalable applications, driving faster-value delivery. Effective API management and monetization ensure seamless integration and governance, while the convergence of SOC with AI and blockchain enhances service performance, security, and transparency.

The continuous evolution of service-oriented architectures and platforms empowers these advances. Modern SOC platforms offer automation, policy-based governance, real-time monitoring, and scalability, improving the efficiency and robustness of service-oriented systems.

In conclusion, the future of SOC presents exciting opportunities and challenges. By understanding emerging trends and technological integration, organisations can harness SOC's potential to drive innovation and achieve operational excellence. Researchers, practitioners, and policy makers play a crucial role in navigating challenges and unlocking value. SOC has the power to shape the future of computing, leading to transformative impacts on organisations and society at large.

9.7 Conclusion

Service-oriented computing is a major milestone in the evolution of information technology, reshaping how we conceive, design, and manage software services. As detailed throughout this chapter, SOC offers numerous opportunities, while posing certain inherent challenges that demand meticulous attention. The discourse emphasises the multifaceted nature of SOC, which requires that stakeholders understand its holistic essence when formulating adoption strategies and addressing implementation complexities.

The chapter began with a discussion of the background concepts. Then we discussed the technical and organisational obstacles presented by SOC. Technical obstacles such as: service discovery, composition, orchestration, and choreography; quality of service management and assurance; and security, governance, and scalability issues. These illustrate the complexity of the SOC paradigm. Additionally, organisational obstacles such as resistance to change, integration with legacy systems, cultural barriers, lack of standardisation, and skill gaps compound the difficulty of implementing a successful SOC. Recognising these obstacles is essential to developing effective solutions and fostering an environment conducive to the adoption of SOC.

Concurrently, the chapter highlighted the strategies and best practises for the adoption and implementation of SOC. Critical aspects including organisational readiness assessment, strategic planning and execution of a service-oriented architecture initiative, robust governance mechanisms, and the management of cultural and organisational barriers were outlined. A comprehensive approach to SOC adoption, supported by best practises and strategic planning, can significantly alleviate the associated challenges and allow organisations to realise SOC's full potential.

The chapter also explored the exciting future trends and directions in SOC. We discussed emerging trends such as microservice architecture, serverless computing, event-driven architecture, cloud native computing, API management, and API monetization. In addition, the convergence of SOC with disruptive technologies such as artificial intelligence and blockchain was highlighted. These developments are not only redefining the SOC landscape, but are also opening new research frontiers, catalysing innovation in industry, and promising societal transformations.

In conclusion, SOC represents a paradigm shift, as it marks a transition from monolithic to modular, rigid to flexible, and proprietary to interoperable. It presents a plethora of opportunities, including improved business agility and operational efficiency, as well as the creation of innovative products and services. The path to these opportunities, however, is fraught with technical and organisational obstacles that require a deliberate, well-informed, and dedicated approach.

The journey of SOC adoption is comparable to navigating uncharted waters, which requires organisations to adjust their sails as they learn and mature. The dynamic nature of the SOC paradigm requires a mindset of continuous improvement and learning, fuelled by a spirit of innovation and dedication to excellence. As organisations across the globe adopt SOC, it is crucial that they build on the insights and lessons gleaned from research and practise, and contribute to the collective knowledge of the global SOC community.

The future of SOC lies at the crossroads of promise and complexity. The relentless advancement of technology, the changing dynamics of the global economy, and the changing expectations of society will continue to shape its future. As we look towards this future, it is incumbent upon us, researchers, practitioners, and policymakers, to steer the evolution of SOC in a way that maximises its benefits, mitigates its challenges, and upholds the principles of ethical and responsible computing.

In essence, the service-oriented computing paradigm presents an array of opportunities and obstacles. It requires the ability to grapple with technical complexities and cultural changes but also provides organisations with a platform to drive innovation, operational efficiency, and competitive advantage. SOC has the potential to significantly influence the future of computing and society, as we continue to investigate and comprehend this paradigm. There are numerous opportunities, the obstacles are surmountable, and the future is promising.

References

Driss, M., Aljehani, A., Boulila, W., Ghandorh, H. & Al-Sarem, M. (2020), 'Servicing your requirements: An fca and rca-driven approach for semantic web services composition', *IEEE Access* **8**, pp. 59326–59339.

El-Sheikh, E., Zimmermann, A., Jain, L. C. & Jain, L. C. (2016), 'Emerging trends in the evolution of service-oriented and enterprise architectures', *Emerging Trends in the Evolution of Service-Oriented and Enterprise Architectures.* Vol 111, 12–55.

Filippi, P. D. & Mccarthy, S. (2012), 'Cloud computing: Centralization and data sovereignty', *European Journal of Law and Technology,* information technologies (IT) and information systems (I). Vol. 3(2),1–18.

Huhns, M. N. & Singh, M. P. (2005), 'Service-oriented computing: Key concepts and principles', *IEEE Internet Computing.* Vol. 9(1), 75–81.

Li, X., Li, X., Li, X., Zheng, Z., Zheng, Z., Zheng, Z., Dai, H.-N. & Dai, H.-N. (2021), 'When services computing meets blockchain: Challenges and opportunities', *Journal of Parallel and Distributed Computing.* Vol. 150, 1–14.

Lu, Z., Delaney, D. & Lillis, D. (2023), 'A survey on microservices trust models for open systems', *IEEE Access.* 11, 28840–28855

Niknejad, N., Niknejad, N., Ismail, W., Ghani, I., Nazari, B., Bahari, M., Bahari, M., Hussin, A. R. C. & Hussin, A. R. C. (2020), 'Understanding service-oriented architecture (soa): A systematic literature review and directions for further investigation', *Information Systems.* Vol. 91, pp. 1–27.

Papazoglou, M. P. (2003), 'Service-oriented computing: Concepts, characteristics and directions', *Proceedings of the Fourth International Conference on Web Information Systems Engineering, 2003. WISE 2003,* pp. 3–12. IEEE,

Papazoglou, M. P. & Georgakopoulos, D. (2003), 'Introduction: Serviceoriented computing', *Commun. ACM* **46**(10), pp. 24–28. URL: https://doi.org/10.1145/944217.944233

Verma, R. (2020), 'Service oriented architecture for constrained environments', *Indian Institute of Technology Indore.* Available at: http://dspace.iiti.ac.in:8080/jspui/handle/123456789/2026 (Accessed on: 31 May 2023)

Verma, R., Ahmed, T. & Srivastava, A. (2014), 'Expressing workflow and workflow enactment using p systems', *The 15th International Conference on Membrane Computing (CMC), Prague,* Czech Republic, pp. 345.

Verma, R. & Srivastava, A. (2014), 'A novel web service directory framework for mobile environments', in '2014 IEEE International Conference on Web Services', pp. 614–621.

Verma, R. & Srivastava, A. (2014), Towards service description for mobile environments, *in '2015 IEEE International Conference on Services Computing'*. Vol. 1, pp. 138–145.

Wei, Y. & Blake, M. B. (2010), 'Service-oriented computing and cloud computing: Challenges and opportunities', *IEEE Internet Computing* **14**(6), pp. 72–75.

Zeng, L., Benatallah, B., Ngu, A. H. H., Dumas, M., Kalagnanam, J. R. & Chang, H. (2004), 'Qos-aware middleware for web services composition', *IEEE Transactions on Software Engineering*. Vol. *30*(5), 311–327.

Zimmermann, O. (2017), 'Microservices tenets: Agile approach to service development and deployment'. *Computer Science – Research and Development*. Vol. 32, pp. 301–310.

Chapter 10

Smart IoT System for Agricultural Production Improvement and Machine Learning-Based Prediction

Pradeep Singh Rawat,[1] Punit Gupta,[2] and Prateek Kumar Soni[3]

[1]*School of Computing, DIT University, Dehradun, India*

[2]*University College, Dublin, Ireland*

[3]*ABV-Indian Institute of Information Technology and Management, Gwalior, India*

10.1 Introduction

Smart IoT systems for agricultural production improvement are rapidly gaining popularity in the agricultural sector. These systems leverage the power of the Internet of Things (IoT) and machine learning algorithms to monitor and optimize various aspects of agricultural production. By using sensors, devices, and automation equipment, farmers can collect vast amounts of data about environmental conditions, crop growth, and yield predictions. This data is then analyzed using machine learning algorithms to make predictions and optimize production processes.

There are several factors that can affect crop productivity where traditional methods may not be effective, including:

DOI: 10.1201/9781032716718-10

- Climate change: Climate change can cause unpredictable weather patterns, which can have a significant impact on crop productivity. Traditional methods may not be able to adapt to these changes, making it challenging to maintain high crop yields.
- Soil degradation: Soil degradation is a widespread problem in many parts of the world. Traditional methods of soil management, such as fertilization and crop rotation, may not be enough to address this problem.
- Water scarcity: Water scarcity is a major issue in many regions, making it challenging to irrigate crops adequately. Traditional irrigation methods, such as flooding or sprinkler systems, may not be efficient enough to cope with water scarcity.
- Pest and disease resistance: Pests and diseases can develop resistance to traditional control methods, making it challenging to manage infestations effectively. This resistance can lead to reduced crop yields and economic losses for farmers.

To address these challenges, innovative and advanced technologies such as precision agriculture, IoT-based systems can be used. These technologies can provide more accurate and efficient ways of monitoring crops, managing soil and water resources, controlling pests and diseases, and IoT can provide farmers with more accurate and timely data, enabling them to make data-driven decisions and optimize their farming practices. This can lead to improved crop yields, reduced costs, and more sustainable agriculture practices. The use of smart IoT systems for agricultural production improvement has several benefits. First and foremost, it can significantly improve crop yields and quality. By monitoring environmental conditions including humidity, temperature, and light intensity, farmers can optimize the growing conditions for their crops. Additionally, machine learning algorithms can analyze this data to make predictions about crop growth and yield. Farmers can use these forecasts to make wise choices about when to harvest their crops, how much to irrigate, and what fertilizers to use at that particular time.

Another benefit of smart IoT systems for agricultural production improvement is reduction of waste. By monitoring crop growth and yield predictions, farmers can reduce overproduction and minimize the waste. Additionally, automation can be used to control irrigation, fertilization, and pest control, ensuring that these tasks are done consistently and at the right time. Smart IoT systems for agricultural production improvement can also increase profitability. By optimizing production processes and reducing waste, farmers can increase their profits. Additionally, these systems can help minimize the environmental impact of agricultural production by utilizing fewer fertilizers, pesticides, and water.

Despite the numerous benefits of smart IoT systems for agricultural production improvement, there are also several challenges associated with their implementation. One of the significant challenges is the cost of implementing these systems. The sensors, devices, and automation equipment required for these systems can be expensive, which may limit their adoption by small-scale farmers. Another challenge is the complexity of these systems. Farmers may require specialized training to operate and maintain these systems, which can be a barrier to adoption. Moreover, there are concerns about data privacy and security, as the data collected by these systems can be sensitive and valuable.

Now, one of the most critical components of a smart IoT system for agricultural production improvement is the use of sensors and devices. These sensors can be used to track a variety of environmental factors, including as soil moisture, temperature, and light intensity, that have an impact on crop growth. They can also monitor the health and growth of crops, as well as the presence of pests and diseases. Devices such as automated irrigation systems, fertilization systems, and pest control systems can also be integrated into these systems to automate various aspects of agricultural production. Machine learning algorithms are another essential component of smart IoT systems for agricultural production improvement. These algorithms can analyze a significant volume of data gathered through sensors and devices to make predictions about crop growth and yield. By using these predictions, farmers can make better decisions about when to harvest their crops, how much to irrigate, and what fertilizers to use. Machine learning can also help identify patterns and trends in agricultural production that may be difficult for humans to detect, allowing for more precise and efficient decision-making.

Automation is another key feature of smart IoT systems. By automating various aspects of agricultural production, farmers can reduce labor costs and increase efficiency. Automated systems can be used to control irrigation, fertilization, pest control, and other tasks. By automating these tasks, farmers can ensure that they are done consistently and precisely, leading to better crop yields and quality. Another critical feature is data analytics and visualization. These systems generate vast amounts of data, which must be analyzed and visualized to provide insights into agricultural production processes. By analyzing this data, farmers can decide how to optimize their production operations by identifying areas for improvement. Visualization tools can also help farmers understand and interpret the data more easily, allowing for better decision-making and improved outcomes. Another important aspect of smart IoT systems is the use of cloud. Farmers may store and analyse enormous volumes of data gathered from various sensors and devices in real-time by utilizing the cloud's capabilities. Cloud computing can also enable the integration of multiple smart IoT systems, allowing for more efficient data sharing and collaborations among farmers. One example of a smart IoT system for agricultural production improvement is precision agriculture. Sensors and equipment are used in precision agriculture to track a variety of environmental factors, such as soil moisture, temperature, and light intensity, that have an impact on crop growth. This data is then analyzed using machine learning algorithms to make predictions about crop growth and yield. By using these predictions, farmers can optimize their production processes, reducing waste and increasing profitability.

Another example is the smart irrigation system. Smart irrigation systems make use of sensors and devices to monitor the moisture levels of soil and weather conditions in real-time. The irrigation system is then automated using this data, ensuring that crops receive the right amount of water at the right time. By optimizing irrigation, farmers can reduce water usage, increase crop yield, and reduce the environmental impact of their agricultural production. Machine learning-based prediction models are another important aspect of smart IoT systems for agricultural production improvement [8], [11], [14], [16], [17]. These models use historical data collected from sensors and devices to make predictions about future crop growth and yield. Farmers may decide when to harvest their crops, how much to water, and what fertilizers to apply by using these forecasts. Machine learning-based prediction models can also help identify patterns and trends in agricultural production that may be difficult for humans to detect, allowing for more precise and efficient decision-making [3].

In conclusion, smart IoT systems for agricultural production improvement are rapidly transforming the agriculture industry. By leveraging the power of sensors, devices, automation, machine learning, and cloud computing, farmers can collect and analyze vast amounts of data to optimize their production processes. These systems offer numerous benefits, including increased crop yields, reduced waste, and increased profitability. However, there are a number of difficulties with their application, such as costs, complexity, and issues about the security and privacy of personal data. Despite these challenges, the benefits of smart IoT systems for agricultural production improvement make them a promising solution for the future of agriculture.

10.2   Related Works

Due to its potential to completely transform the agricultural industry, the field of Smart IoT System for Agricultural Production Improvement and Machine Learning Based Prediction has attracted a lot of interest recently. Many research projects have been carried out to investigate the various applications of this technology and its effects on crop yield, resource optimization, and environmental sustainability. We give an overview of some of the most important and recent works in this topic in this section. We concentrate on studies that enhance agricultural output and forecast crop yield using smart IoT technologies and machine learning techniques.

This study proposes an IoT-based smart farming system coupled with an effective prediction approach dubbed WPART based on machine learning techniques. Rezk, et. al. proposed an approach in 2021 in order to anticipate crop productivity and drought for effective decision support in IoT-based smart farming systems. Forecasts of crop production and drought are vital for farmers and agricultural executives since they significantly help countries all over the world that are impacted by agriculture. Drought prediction research strives to improve our understanding of the physical causes of droughts and our capacity for forecasting by utilizing all predictability sources available. In order to limit the effects of drought on agricultural productivity, drought early warning plays a crucial role in drought prediction.

An intelligent system combining a wrapper feature selection strategy with a PART classification approach is presented for forecasting crop yield and drought. Five datasets are used to estimate the suggested method. The results indicated that the projected approach is more precise, accurate, and trustworthy at classifying and forecasting crop productivity and drought when compared to the existing ones. The results show that for crops including sugarcane, soy, jowar, and bajra, the proposed method is the most accurate at predicting droughts and agricultural productivity. The WPART method outperforms the current top standard procedures in terms of accuracy, with accuracy scores of 92.51%, 96.77%, 98.04%, 96.12%, and 98.15%, respectively, for the five datasets used to classify drought and agricultural productivity [1]. The proposed solution, according to Sumathi et al. for 2021, offers an IoT network communication system's architecture to assess the soil conditions. The state of the soil affects modern agriculture, hydrological cycles, and increased productivity. The precise forecast produced by a review of the soil quality is crucial for the effective utilization of resources.

To solve these issues, an improved deep learning model for IoT network-based autonomous soil quality measuring monitors was developed. Instantaneous samples from the local sensor network are collected and analyzed here. For the purpose of predicting soil quality, a deep learning model was developed with the capacity to fit substantial volumes of data. Weight factors (W.F.) are derived for accurate measurement of soil quality. The proposed IoT network-based agriculture structure offers a versatile approach to different crop kinds and application in agricultural locations. The effectiveness and dependability of the system were demonstrated by experimental results obtained both on-site and in the lab. The results of the precision, accuracy, and processing time evaluations show that the model performs better than compared models in all three categories [2].

A method to manage heterogeneous information and data from real datasets that gather physical, biological, and sensory values was proposed by Balducci, et al. in 2018. Discovering efficient ways to use data that is constantly being collected and made available can be the best choice to achieve these goals because profitable businesses, whether they are large or small, public or private, need to increase profitability while lowering costs. By employing the Internet of Things (IoT) paradigm applied to environmental and historical information through time-series in the agriculture sector, which is only superficially resistive to digital technology, a "smart farm" model is becoming more and more popular. In order to choose where to spend efforts and resources, this study is focused on the design and implementation of practical tasks, ranging from crop harvest forecasts to the reconstruction of incomplete or erroneous sensor data. The results support the requirements and needs of enterprises wishing to hire an agricultural industrial firm that is both sustainable and optimized, showing that there is plenty of space for innovation. These companies invest in both the technology and the expertise and labor required to make the most of it [4].

Zhou et al. created the Remote Sensing Assisted Control System (RSCS) in 2022 to better serve the needs of greenhouse agriculture. Because greenhouse development is a new agricultural technique as a result of recent growth. Information systems serve as its direction. The Internet of Things (IoT) offers an intelligent system and remote access technologies, such as green infrastructure. The ability of information systems to effectively produce intelligent systems and predictive models based on artificial intelligence and machine learning in real-time within organizations (AI).

A Remote Sensing Assisted Control System (RSCS) has been created as a result to better serve the requirements of greenhouse agriculture. In order to improve the green development sector's ability to manage financial resources and promote the development of unique agricultural goods, the proposed strategy makes use of artificial intelligence and machine learning technology. So, straightforward guidelines for developing an effective marketing strategy serve as the necessary preconditions for increasing the availability of healthy food options and fostering the potential growth of local and international organic farmers. The experimental findings demonstrated that RSCS had the highest precision ratio (95.1%), performance ratio (96.35%), data transmission rate (92.3%), agriculture production ratio (94.2%), irrigation-control ratio (94.7%), lowest moisture content ratio (18.7%), and CO_2 emission ratio (21.5%) when compared to other methods [5].

During their research in 2019, Muangprathub et al. recommended developing a wireless sensor network-based system for irrigation of agricultural crops. This effort tried to build and develop a control system with data administration using a web application and smartphone app using node sensors in the agricultural field. The three components are hardware, a web application, and a mobile application. Hardware affixed to a control box that was used to collect crop data contained the first element, which was developed and put to use. Soil moisture sensors connected to the control panel are used to keep an eye on the field. The second component is a web-based application that was developed and used to modify the specifics of field and crop data. In order to forecast the appropriate temperature, humidity, and soil moisture for controlling crop development in the future, this section uses data mining to analyse the data. The last component is mostly used to control crop irrigation through a mobile app for smartphones. This makes user control possible, which can be automatic or manual. The automatic control uses data from soil moisture sensors to determine when to irrigate.

The operator has the option to manually water the crops in the functional control mode. The system has the ability to send LINE application notifications using the LINE API. The method was tested and put into practice in the Makhamtia area of Thailand's Suratthani Province. The results showed how beneficial the adoption was for agriculture. In order to grow vegetables, the soil's moisture content needed to be maintained at an appropriate level, which led to lower costs and improved agricultural productivity.

Also, this study serves as an example of how technology innovation can advance agriculture [6]. Mohamed et al. provided a method in 2021 that demonstrates data gathering, transfer, storage, analysis, and suitable solutions. This research focuses on cutting-edge SF methods from 2019 to 2021. This work also showed the versatility of robots and unmanned aerial vehicles (UAVs) for a range of tasks, such as harvesting, planting, weed detection, irrigation, spraying for agricultural pests, applications on animals, and so forth. The importance of using a 5G mobile network to build smart systems is also highlighted by this work because it enables high-speed data transfer of up to 20 Gbps and can connect many devices per square kilometer. Notwithstanding the challenges that smart agricultural applications confront in underdeveloped countries, many approaches were highlighted in this work. Moreover, Smart Decision Support Systems (SDSS) are used in developing countries to support efficient decision-making, real-time analysis, and mapping of soil characteristics [7].

The impact of the Internet of Things (IoT) on the agriculture sector is investigated by Balamurugan et al. in their paper from 2016. Modern agricultural equipment has GPS and sensors that can communicate with one another, evaluate data, and share data between themselves. The agriculture sector can use cloud-based services provided by IT. Agriculture cloud and IT companies offer farmers a service for crop cultivation, pricing, fertilizers, and the specifics of the best ways to treat illnesses. Scientists that research agriculture will present their discoveries, suggest modern farming techniques, and describe how to use fertilizers to uncover the agricultural history of the area. The study was based on the use of agriculture sensor data in the cloud. This is built on agri-cloud, which increases agricultural productivity and facilitates access to data about unsuccessful research projects. Cost and time savings will result, and communication will become easier and faster as a result. This publication would promote a lot more research on IoT use in agriculture [10].

In 2022, Bwambale et al. researched the most recent smart monitoring and irrigation management methods used for irrigation scheduling. The demand for freshwater resources has increased recently as a result of the expanding global population and rising drought indicators in agricultural regions of the world. Irrigated agriculture is almost always a wasteful user of water, taking away from other businesses' access to the scarce resource. The achievement of sustainable agricultural output hinges on irrigated agriculture's ability to use water more efficiently. Smart irrigation systems have the ability to improve water use efficiency with the development of wireless communication technologies, monitoring systems, and sophisticated management algorithms for appropriate irrigation scheduling. This research investigates the most modern smart monitoring and irrigation management methods used for irrigation scheduling. The analysis of the literature indicates that closed-loop irrigation-control strategies outperform open-loop systems that do not account for uncertainty. The efficiency of water use is said to be considerably improved by combining model predictive control with soil-based, plant-based, and weather-based monitoring systems. This assessment will help researchers and farmers choose the most efficient irrigation monitoring and management strategy in order to optimize irrigation scheduling in open field agricultural systems [12].

Hsu et al. conducted research in 2021 on how to install a wireless network in a farming field, attach a watering pipeline, and link the system to the agricultural site. For this study, a webcam and an infrared personnel sensor are put in the farm field. After the person has been recognized by the webcam and the sensor has detected their approach, the administrator will get a message telling them to sound an auditory warning. By conducting this research, they might help farmers design a smart irrigation system that would cut down on labor costs, preserve water, boost crop yields and quality, and keep farms safe [13].

In 2018, Abagissa et al. looked into ways to make it simple for farmers to combine agricultural production with the current environment. Agriculture serves as the cornerstone for the development of human civilization. In emerging and underdeveloped countries, agriculture is the main industry. There are several challenges that farmers face in agriculture, such as the necessity for professional support, crop monitoring, and manual approaches for doing crucial activities like irrigation. A few web-based farming aids have lately been developed, but due to their difficult user interfaces and farmers' lack of technological knowledge, they are not particularly useful. In this work, they proposed an IoT-based smart agricultural equipment controlling system to help farmers practice productive agriculture. They looked at how to make it simple for the farmer to integrate the current environment and agricultural productivity using the Arduino Mega and GSM module. Under the suggested approach, farmers can monitor, control, and receive advice 24 hours a day, from before farming to after farming, using a mobile device with limited features [15].

A framework for tracking and monitoring smart crops was presented by the authors Phasinam et. al. in 2022. Considering the primary issues in agricultural production are the decision-making process, crop selection, and supporting systems for boosting crop yield using fog and cloud computing. Agriculture projections are influenced by natural variables such as temperature, soil fertility, water volume, water quality, season, and crop prices. Growing advancements in agricultural technology have given rise to a myriad of tools and apps for quick knowledge acquisition. Everyone, even farmers, is utilizing mobile devices more and more. Their research covers big data analytics, Internet of Things cameras, mobile applications, and sensors. The hardware is an Arduino Uno, several sensors, and a Wi-Fi module. This method allows for the most effective use of energy while producing the least amount of agricultural waste possible [18].

The authors Ioana M. et. al. presented an IoT-based architecture to improve agricultural in 2019. Agriculture has historically been the most significant human activity for a very long time. It has undergone numerous adjustments to increase the productivity and quality of the crops. Development of new equipment and techniques using cloud computing for existing irrigation systems, harvesting machines, and farmland clearing machinery in early agriculture. The IoT-based solutions for monitoring numerous criteria, such as natural disasters and weather disasters for improved precision agriculture, must be the next revolution in this industry. It uses specialized sensors and is fueled by solar energy. Libelium for Smart Agriculture will track the factors that directly affect crops from the time they are sown until they are harvested and will offer helpful data on soil characteristics, plant health, and growth. so assisting the farmers in having productive crops [9].

For the agricultural sector, the Smart IoT System for Agricultural Production Improvement and Machine Learning Based Prediction has the potential to have a substantial positive impact.

Farmers may make knowledgeable decisions about resource management, improve crop development, and eventually boost their yields by using data from IoT devices and machine learning algorithms. Data protection, cost-effectiveness, and scalability are just a few of the issues that still need to be resolved. Future studies should concentrate on creating more complex machine learning models that can estimate crop yield more accurately as well as investigating novel approaches to incorporating IoT technologies into agricultural production systems.

10.3 System Architecture of the IoT System for Real-Time Crop Monitoring

This section shows the architecture of the IoT based system. The system architecture provides efficient crop monitoring in a real-time manner. The real-time crop monitoring system includes the three major components as shown in Figure 10.1.

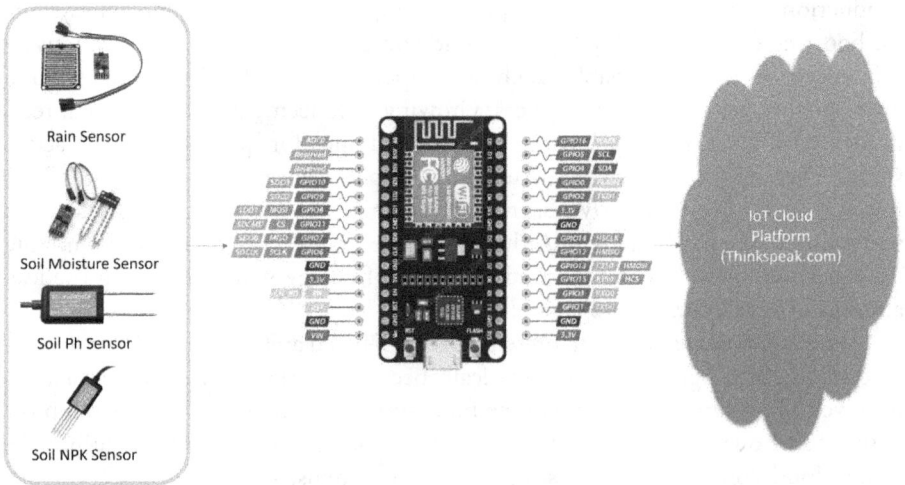

Figure 10.1 System architecture of the IoT based real-time crop monitoring.

10.3.1 Sensor Nodes

The sensor nodes sense the data from cite specific area or catchment area of the agriculture land of the farmers. The sensor nodes are broadly used for soil property sensing, soil water content sensing, Soil Nitrozen, Phasphorus and Potasium level. The sensor segment measures the samples of the soil with key parameters for crop cultivation.

Sensor nodes include the following:

10.3.1.1 Rain Sensor

Rainfall plays an important role in crop cultivation and crop production management. The soil sensor node deployed at the site provides a real-time data stream about the rainfall. It provides the indication of types of crop that will be cultivated according to the precipitation level. The precipitation level—that is averaged rain fall in the study area—helps to provide the information about classification of the types of crop. The output of the sensor node passes to the MCU unit at anlog or digital pin.

10.3.1.2 Soil Moisture Sensor

Soil moisture sensors sense the data about moisture level in the soil, which helps to improve crop production in the area. The moisture content has a threshold value, which determines crop production. The soil moisture sensor node may be capacitive or resistive, which measures the moisture in term of percentage or direct analog pin output.

10.3.1.3 Soil PH Sensor

Soil Sensor JXBS-3001-PH-I20 is used in applications for soil pH measurement. Knowing the acidity level of the soil is required to measure for healthy crop production. The farmers' income and production depends on soil quality. The soil PH is the key factor. So the sensor node provides the prior information in real time to the farmers. The acidity level will be helpful for appropriate crop cultivation.

10.3.1.4 Soil NPK Sensor

The sensor is deployed in study area of agriculture land. The NPK soil sensor provides information about the fertility level of the soil. This fertility information ensures the increase in production level. Production relies on nitrogen, phosphorus, and potassium levels in the soil.

10.3.2 MCU Unit

The microcontroller unit is an IoT device that acts as an interface between cloud platform and sensor nodes. The data of the sensor node is received at the analog/digital pin of the MCU unit (NodeMCUESP8266). The MCU unit is Wi-Fi enabled, which is directly connected with the Internet. The MCU unit writes the data inside the cloud platform thingspeak channel.

10.3.3 IoT Cloud Platform

In the present era of computing and communication real time monitoring is provided using the cloud platform with unlimited storage. The smart crop production system integrated with IoT cloud platform. The framework uses the thingspeak IoT cloud platform for real time storage of the sensor node data from study site. The data can be fetched from anywhere, anytime, across the globe.

10.4 Results and Discussions

Section 4, covers the results and discussions of the smart system and predictive analysis of the real-time data fetched from the study site. The sensor sensed data collected inside the cloud platform is analyzed using supervised machine learning approaches for predictive modeling. Figure 10.2 shows the comparative analysis of the machine learning techniques on the basis of their accuracy for IoT based system. The results show that the decision tree model provides approximately 84 percent accuracy, that is, the minimum and random forest machine learning approach provides maximum accuracy for IoT based system, for example, approximately 96.4 percent. The optimal results show that the IoT based system with predictive modeling should be our choice for crop cultivation. Future predication can be taken using various supervised machine learning models. The random forest model for prediction should be our first choice for best accuracy and study the pattern of the real-time data produced by the sensor nodes deployed in various study sites on the farmer's lands.

10.5 Conclusions

The improvement of crop production and cultivation means an appropriate soil with high fertility level. The smart IoT enabled system with cloud integration helps the farmer in smart framing. This chapter presented a framework that indicates the integration of technology, cloud, IoT, and machine learning improve the farmer's income with minimum losses. The predictive module of the framework relies on data generated by the high quality sensor nodes deployed in the study site. The

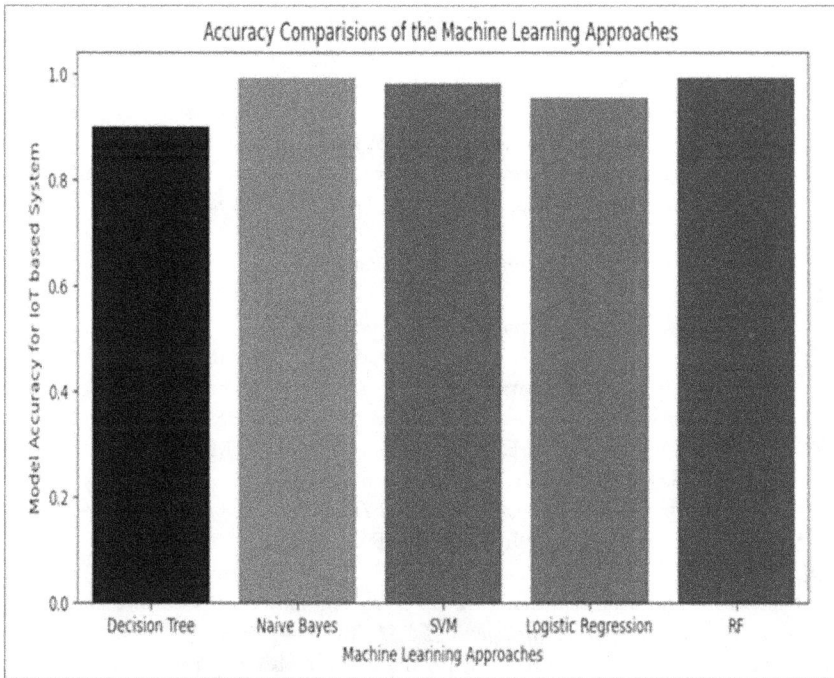

Figure 10.2   Accuracy measurement of the machine learning model for crop cultivations.

domain expert needs to support the farmer and establish a social awareness about the importance of the smart farming system. Still there is an opportunity to increase the crop production with cultivation of right crop at the right time. In the future the unmanned area visiting nodes, such as a drone can help the farmer with automatic spraying of pesticides, which will also further increase the crop productivity.

References

[1] Rezk, N. G., Hemdan, E. E. D., Attia, A. F., El-Sayed, A., & El-Rashidy, M. A. (2021). An efficient IoT based smart farming system using machine learning algorithms. *Multimedia Tools and Applications*, 80, 773–797.

[2] Sumathi, P., Subramanian, R., Karthikeyan, V. V., & Karthik, S. (2021). Retracted: Soil monitoring and evaluation system using EDL-ASQE: Enhanced deep learning model for IoT smart agriculture network. *International Journal of Communication Systems*, 34(11), e4859.

[3] Aliar, A. A. S., Yesudhasan, J., Alagarsamy, M., Anbalagan, K., Sakkarai, J., & Suriyan, K. (2022). A comprehensive analysis on IoT based smart farming solutions

using machine learning algorithms. *Bulletin of Electrical Engineering and Informatics*, 11(3), 1550–1557.

[4] Balducci, F., Impedovo, D., & Pirlo, G. (2018). Machine learning applications on agricultural datasets for smart farm enhancement. *Machines*, 6(3), 38.

[5] Zhou, Y., Xia, Q., Zhang, Z., Quan, M., & Li, H. (2022). Artificial intelligence and machine learning for the green development of agriculture in the emerging manufacturing industry in the IoT platform. *Acta Agriculturae Scandinavica, Section B—Soil & Plant Science*, 72(1), 284–299.

[6] Muangprathub, J., Boonnam, N., Kajornkasirat, S., Lekbangpong, N., Wanichsombat, A., & Nillaor, P. (2019). IoT and agriculture data analysis for smart farm. *Computers and Electronics in Agriculture*, 156, 467–474.

[7] Mohamed, E. S., Belal, A. A., Abd-Elmabod, S. K., El-Shirbeny, M. A., Gad, A., & Zahran, M. B. (2021). Smart farming for improving agricultural management. *The Egyptian Journal of Remote Sensing and Space Science*, 24(3), 971–981.

[8] Mabrouki, J., Azoulay, K., Elfanssi, S., Bouhachlaf, L., Mousli, F., Azrour, M., & El Hajjaji, S. (2022). Smart system for monitoring and controlling of agricultural production by the IoT. *In IoT and Smart Devices for Sustainable Environment* (pp. 103–115). Cham: Springer International Publishing.

[9] Marcu, I. M., Suciu, G., Balaceanu, C. M., & Banaru, A. (2019, June). IoT based system for smart agriculture. *In 2019 11th International Conference on Electronics, Computers and Artificial Intelligence (ECAI)* (pp. 1–4). IEEE.

[10] Balamurugan, S., Divyabharathi, N., Jayashruthi, K., Bowiya, M., Shermy, R. P., & Shanker, R. (2016). Internet of agriculture: Applying IoT to improve food and farming technology. *International Research Journal of Engineering and Technology (IRJET)*, 3(10), 713–719.

[11] Xu, J., Gu, B., & Tian, G. (2022). Review of agricultural IoT technology. *Artificial Intelligence in Agriculture*. 6, 10–22

[12] Bwambale, E., Abagale, F. K., & Anornu, G. K. (2022). Smart irrigation monitoring and control strategies for improving water use efficiency in precision agriculture: A review. *Agricultural Water Management*, 260, 107324.

[13] Hsu, W. L., Wang, W. K., Fan, W. H., Shiau, Y. C., Yang, M. L., & Lopez, D. J. D. (2021). Application of internet of things in smart farm watering system. *Sensors and Materials*, 33(1), 269–283.

[14] Bhagat, M., Kumar, D., & Kumar, D. (2019). Role of internet of things (IoT) in smart farming: A brief survey. *2019 Devices for Integrated Circuit (DevIC)*, vol. 1, 141–145.

[15] Abagissa, A. T., Behura, A., & Pani, S. K. (2018, April). IoT based smart agricultural device controlling system. *In 2018 Second International Conference on Inventive Communication and Computational Technologies (ICICCT)* (pp. 26–30). IEEE.

[16] Navarro, E., Costa, N., & Pereira, A. (2020). A systematic review of IoT solutions for smart farming. *Sensors*, 20(15), 4231.

[17] Srivastava, A., & Das, D. K. (2022). A comprehensive review on the application of internet of thing (IoT) in smart agriculture. *Wireless Personal Communications*, 122(2), 1807–1837.

[18] Phasinam, K., Kassanuk, T., & Shabaz, M. (2022). Applicability of internet of things in smart farming. *Journal of Food Quality*, 2022, 1–7.

Chapter 11

Service-Oriented Computing Integration with Soft Computing for Quality of Service Improvement

Pradeep Singh Rawat, Garima Verma, and Srabanti Maji

School of Computing, DIT University, Dehradun, India

11.1 Introduction

Creating modular, reusable software components known as *services* – which can be put together to form intricate, distributed applications – is the focus of the service-oriented computing (SOC) methodology for software design and development [1]. The development of intelligent systems that can reason and learn in ambiguous and imprecise contexts is the focus of the subfield of artificial intelligence known as soft computing (SC). Distributed applications' quality of service (QoS) can be significantly enhanced by the merging of SOC and SC. The level of performance, dependability, security, and other characteristics of a software system are defined by a set of non-functional standards known as QoS [2]. The QoS of SOC-based applications can be improved by dynamically applying SC techniques, including fuzzy logic, neural networks, and evolutionary algorithms.

DOI: 10.1201/9781032716718-11

A neural network may learn to forecast the response time of a service based on its past performance data, whereas a controller using fuzzy logic can modify the processing speed of a service and the workload of the system [3]. Integration of SOC and SC also makes it possible to create self-adaptive systems, which can change on their own without human involvement in response to environment, the cloud configuration and load on the datacenter changes. Self-adaptive systems are capable of monitoring service performance, identifying errors, and dynamically reconfiguring the system to maintain the required degree of QoS. All things considered, the combination of SOC and SC offers a strong framework for creating distributed applications that are scalable, dependable, and high-performance and can respond to changing cloud configuration conditions.

11.2 Related Works

The integration of Soft Computing (SC) with Service-Oriented Computing (SOC) for the enhancement of Quality of Service (QoS) has received considerable research attention. Here are some relevant publications with citations: The authors Alsheikh, Al-Nabulsi, and Baker give an overview of the integration of SOC and SC for QoS improvement in their article, "A Survey on Service-Oriented Computing and Soft Computing Integration for QoS Improvement." They go over numerous SC methods that have been utilized to boost the efficiency of SOC-based systems, including fuzzy logic, neural networks, and evolutionary algorithms. They also emphasize the difficulties and potential avenues for further study in this field [4], [5].

In "An Approach for QoS-Aware Service Composition Based on Soft Computing Techniques," authors Zeng, Zhou, and Zhang propose a QoS-aware service composition approach that uses SC techniques to optimize the QoS of the composed services [6]. They use fuzzy logic and genetic algorithms to dynamically select and compose services based on their QoS characteristics [7].

Authors Al-Jumaily and Al-Zoubi provide a self-adaptive strategy that makes use of SC techniques to monitor and enhance the QoS of SOC-based systems in their paper, "A Self-Adaptive Approach for QoS Improvement in Service-Oriented Computing." Fuzzy logic and neural networks are used to dynamically modify the system in order to maintain the required level of QoS while also detecting and diagnosing QoS issues [8].

Authors Wang and Zhu provide a hybrid fuzzy-genetic method for enhancing the QoS of service composition in SOC-based systems in their paper, "An Optimized QoS-Aware Service Composition Based on Hybrid Fuzzy-Genetic Algorithm." Fuzzy logic is used to describe the QoS specifications, and genetic algorithms are used to find the best service composition that complies with the QoS restrictions [9][10].

Authors Li, Li, and Liang provide a fuzzy logic-based method for predicting the quality of services in SOC-based systems in their paper, "A Fuzzy Logic-Based Approach for QoS Prediction in Service-Oriented Computing." They employ fuzzy inference to forecast the quality of services in various environments and use fuzzy logic to represent the QoS features and historical performance data of services. These are only a few illustrations of research on SOC and SC integration for QoS enhancement. To create more effective and efficient methods for QoS optimization in distributed systems, a lot more work needs to be done in this field [11].

11.3   Proposed Framework

A proposed framework for the integration of Service Oriented Computing (SOC) and Soft Computing (SC) techniques for Quality of Service (QoS) improvement in distributed systems can include the following components:

11.3.1   Service Discovery

The framework should provide mechanisms for discovering and selecting services according to their QoS attributes. This can include the use of fuzzy logic-based service selection algorithms that can effectively handle the uncertainty and imprecision in QoS data.

11.3.2   QoS Prediction

The framework should provide mechanisms for predicting the quality of services in different environments. This can include the use of fuzzy logic-based QoS prediction models that can learn from historical QoS data and adapt to changing environments.

11.3.3   Service Composition

The framework should provide mechanisms for composing services based on their QoS attributes. This can include the use of genetic algorithms or other optimization techniques that can search for the optimal service composition that satisfies the QoS constraints.

11.3.4   QoS Monitoring and Adaptation

The framework should provide mechanisms for monitoring the quality of services and adapting the system to maintain the desired level of QoS. This can include the use of fuzzy logic-based fault detection and diagnosis algorithms that can identify QoS faults and adapt the system accordingly.

Service Discovery	QoS Prediction	Service Composition	QoS Monitoring and Adaptation	SC-based QoS Optimization

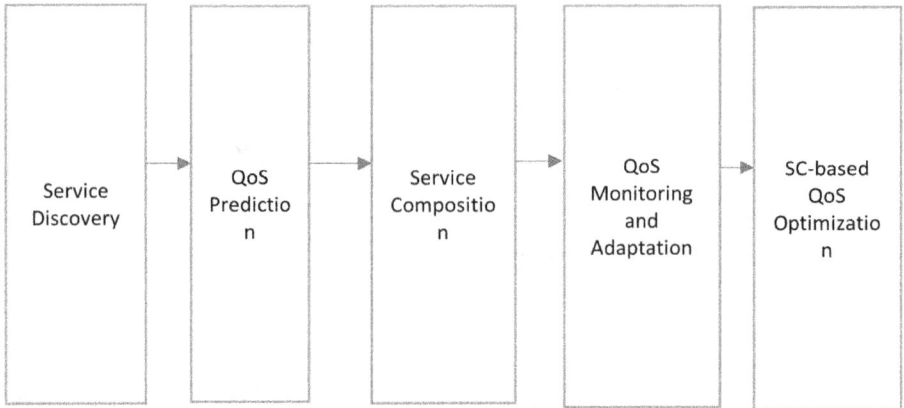

Figure 11.1   Flow of the process in integrated service and soft computing system.

11.3.5   SC–Based QoS Optimization

The framework should provide mechanisms for optimizing the quality of services using SC techniques such as fuzzy logic, neural networks, and genetic algorithms. These techniques can be used to model the QoS requirements and constraints and search for the optimal solution that satisfies the QoS requirements.

Overall, the proposed framework should provide a comprehensive and integrated approach for QoS improvement in distributed systems by leveraging the strengths of SOC and SC techniques. The framework should be scalable, efficient, and adaptable to different application domains and environments. Figure 11.1 shows the flow of the integrated framework of the soft computing technique with service oriented computing environment. The process flow starts from service discovery, QoS prediction, service composition, QoS monitoring and adaptation, and SC-based QoS optimization.

11.4   Procedure for Integrating Service Oriented Computing (SOC) and Soft Computing (SC) techniques

The following is a high-level procedure for integrating Service Oriented Computing (SOC) and Soft Computing (SC) techniques for Quality of Service (QoS) improvement in distributed systems:

11.4.1 Identify QoS Requirements

Determine the QoS requirements and constraints for the system. This includes identifying the QoS attributes such as response time, availability, reliability, and so forth, that are critical for the system's performance.

11.4.2 Select Suitable SC Techniques

Select the appropriate SC techniques based on the QoS requirements and the characteristics of the system. Common SC techniques used in QoS optimization include fuzzy logic, neural networks, genetic algorithms, and swarm intelligence.

11.4.3 Develop QoS Models

Develop SC-based models to represent the QoS attributes and requirements. This involves defining the fuzzy sets, membership functions, and inference rules for fuzzy logic models or the network architecture, activation functions, and training algorithms for neural network models.

11.4.4 Discover and Select Services

Use SOC techniques such as service discovery and selection to identify the services that best meet the QoS requirements and constraints. The selection process can be enhanced using SC techniques such as fuzzy logic-based service selection algorithms.

11.4.5 Compose Services

Compose the selected services based on their QoS attributes using SC-based service composition algorithms such as genetic algorithms or other optimization techniques.

11.4.6 Monitor QoS

Monitor the QoS of the composed services in real-time to detect QoS faults and performance issues. This can be achieved using SC-based fault detection and diagnosis algorithms.

11.4.7 Adapt System

Adapt the system to maintain the desired level of QoS using SC-based QoS adaptation algorithms. This involves dynamically adjusting the system to maintain the desired level of QoS in response to changing environmental conditions.

11.4.8 Optimize QoS

Continuously optimize the QoS of the system using SC techniques such as fuzzy logic, neural networks, and genetic algorithms. This involves modeling the QoS requirements and constraints using SC-based models and searching for the optimal solution that satisfies the QoS requirements.

Overall, this procedure provides a systematic approach for integrating SOC and SC techniques for QoS improvement in distributed systems. The approach can be customized based on the specific QoS requirements and the characteristics of the system to achieve optimal results.

11.5 Layered Architecture

The integration of Service Oriented Computing (SOC) with Soft Computing (SC) can be achieved through a layered architecture that consists of the following layers as shown in the Figure 11.2. The layers exhibit the flow from service layer to service-level agreement between service providers and consumers across the

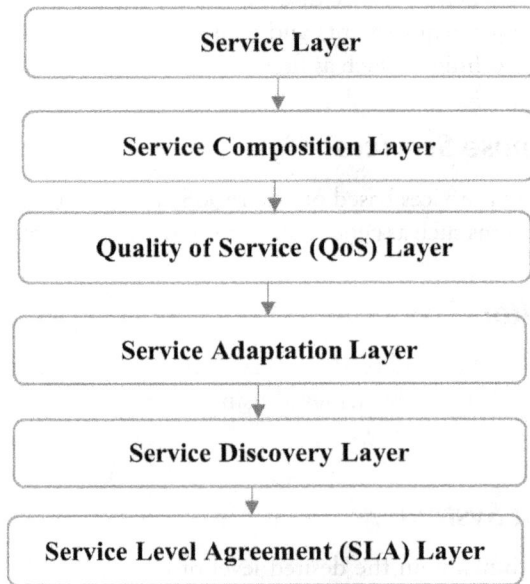

Figure 11.2 Layered architecture of the service oriented computing integration with soft computing.

globe. The detailed description about the individual layer is given in the next paragraph.

11.5.1   Service Layer

This layer includes the services that are offered by the service provider. The services can be simple or complex and can be composed of one or more sub-services.

11.5.2   Service Composition Layer

This layer is responsible for composing multiple services to create a more complex service. Soft Computing techniques can be applied to optimize the service composition process, such as selecting the best combination of services based on their QoS attributes.

11.5.3   Quality of Service (QoS) Layer

This layer is responsible for monitoring the QoS of the services and detecting any QoS violations. Soft Computing techniques can be applied to optimize the QoS monitoring process, such as predicting the QoS levels that can be achieved by the service provider and detecting any QoS violations based on historical data.

11.5.4   Service Adaptation Layer

This layer is responsible for modifying the behavior of the services to maintain or improve their QoS levels. Soft Computing techniques can be applied to optimize the service adaptation process, such as predicting the impact of different adaptation strategies on the QoS of the service.

11.5.5   Service Discovery Layer

This layer is responsible for discovering available services that can satisfy a particular request. Soft Computing techniques can be applied to optimize the service discovery process, such as predicting the availability of services based on historical data and user preferences.

11.5.6   Service-Level Agreement (SLA) Layer

This layer is responsible for negotiating the SLA between the service provider and the service consumer. Soft Computing techniques can be applied to optimize the SLA negotiation process, such as predicting the QoS levels that can be achieved by the service provider.

By using this layered architecture, SOC can be integrated with SC to optimize various processes involved in providing high-quality services to customers. The satisfaction of the customer is the first priority of the service providers. The services of the resources are ensured to the end users using service-level objectives and service-layer management to achieve the service-level agreement.

11.6 Soft Computing Techniques for Resource Optimization

Soft Computing (SC) techniques can be applied to Service-Oriented Computing (SOC) to improve the Quality of Service (QoS) of software applications. There are various nature-inspired, human-based, evolutionary, bio-based, and swarm-based techniques for quality of service improvement. The key focus of this chapter included some of the Soft Computing techniques that can be used for service-oriented computing integration:

11.6.1 Fuzzy Logic

Fuzzy Logic can be used to handle uncertain and imprecise data that is commonly encountered in QoS monitoring and service adaptation. Fuzzy logic can help predict the QoS levels that can be achieved by the service provider and detect any QoS violations.

11.6.2 Artificial Neural Networks (ANN)

ANN can be used for service discovery and service composition. ANN can be used to predict the availability of services based on historical data and user preferences and optimize the service composition process by selecting the best combination of services based on their QoS attributes.

11.6.3 Genetic Algorithms (GA)

Genetic Algorithms (GA) can be used for service adaptation. GA can help predict the impact of different adaptation strategies on the QoS of the service and optimize the service adaptation process.

11.6.4 Ant Colony Optimization (ACO)

Ant Colony Optimization (ACO) can be used for SLA negotiation. ACO can help predict the QoS levels that can be achieved by the service provider and optimize the SLA negotiation process.

11.6.5 Particle Swarm Optimization (PSO)

Particle Swarm Optimization (PSO) can be used for QoS monitoring. PSO can help predict the QoS levels that can be achieved by the service provider and detect any QoS violations based on historical data.

By using these Soft Computing techniques, SOC can be integrated with SC to optimize various processes involved in providing high-quality services to customers.

11.7 Integration of the Computing with Service-Oriented Computing

Cloud computing paradigm provides everything as a service to the end users as shown in the diagram. Figure 11.3 shows the flow of the work from services to the soft computing system for further optimization and association.

11.8 Conclusions and Future Directions

The integration of Service-Oriented Computing (SOC) and Soft Computing (SC) techniques for Quality of Service (QoS) improvement has been a topic of interest in recent years. Several research studies have proposed various approaches that utilize SC techniques such as fuzzy logic, neural networks, and genetic algorithms to optimize QoS in SOC-based systems. These approaches have shown promising results in improving the performance, reliability, and availability of distributed systems. However, there are still several challenges that need to be addressed in

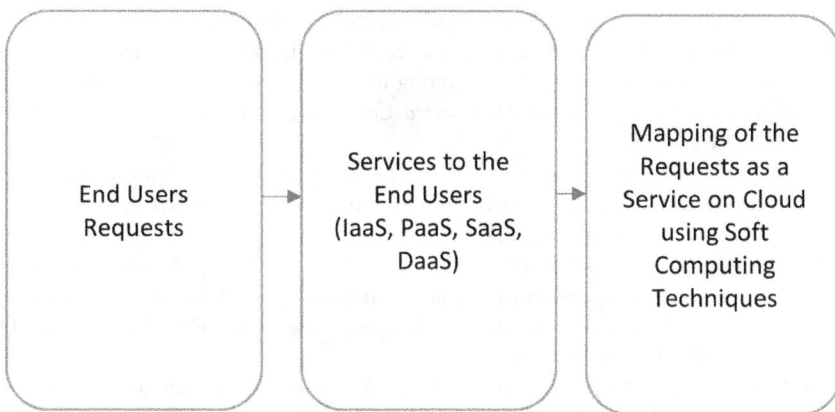

Figure 11.3 Flow of the requests and mapping using soft computing technique.

this area. One of the main challenges is the selection of appropriate SC techniques that can effectively handle the complexity and uncertainty of distributed systems. Additionally, the scalability of these approaches to handle the size of distributed computing infrastructure distributed systems is another important challenge that needs to be addressed.

Future research directions in this area should focus on developing more efficient and effective approaches that can handle the dynamic nature of distributed systems. There is also a need for more comprehensive evaluation and comparison of different approaches to identify their strengths and limitations in different application domains. Furthermore, the integration of other emerging technologies such as Blockchain and Internet of Things (IoT) with SOC and SC can also be explored for QoS improvement in distributed systems. In summary, the integration of SOC and SC techniques has shown significant potential in improving QoS in distributed systems. However, further research is required to develop more effective and scalable approaches that can handle the complexity and dynamic nature of distributed systems. The integrated system will be implemented using some soft computing techniques defined in a meta heuristic evolution library.

References

[1] Papazoglou, M. P. (2003). Service-oriented computing: Concepts, characteristics and directions. In *Proceedings of the Fourth International Conference on Web Information Systems Engineering (WISE '03)* (pp. 3–12). IEEE Computer Society.

[2] Al-Jumaily, M. A., & Al-Zoubi, A. M. (2015). A self-adaptive approach for QoS improvement in service-oriented computing. *Journal of Network and Computer Applications*, 48, 1–11. doi: 10.1016/j.jnca.2014.10.010

[3] Wang, Y., & Zhu, Q. (2014). An optimized QoS-aware service composition based on hybrid fuzzy-genetic algorithm. *Journal of Ambient Intelligence and Humanized Computing*, 5(1), 87–96. doi: 10.1007/s12652-013-0156-2

[4] Alsheikh, M. A., Al-Nabulsi, A. K., & Baker, T. (2017). A survey on service-oriented computing and soft computing integration for QoS improvement. *Journal of Ambient Intelligence and Humanized Computing*, 8(4), 631–650. doi: 10.1007/s12652-017-0476-1

[5] Zeng, S., Zhou, M., & Zhang, L. (2013). An approach for QoS-aware service composition based on soft computing techniques. *Information Sciences*, 218, 29–44. doi: 10.1016/j.ins.2012.06.027

[6] Alsheikh, M. A., Al-Nabulsi, A. K., & Baker, T. (2017). A survey on service-oriented computing and soft computing integration for QoS improvement. *Journal of Ambient Intelligence and Humanized Computing*, 8(4), 631–650. doi: 10.1007/s12652-017-0476-1

[7] Zeng, S., Zhou, M., & Zhang, L. (2013). An approach for QoS-aware service composition based on soft computing techniques. *Information Sciences*, 218, 29–44. doi: 10.1016/j.ins.2012.06.027

[8] Al-Jumaily, M. A., & Al-Zoubi, A. M. (2015). A self-adaptive approach for QoS improvement in service-oriented computing. *Journal of Network and Computer Applications*, 48, 1–11. doi: 10.1016/j.jnca.2014.10.010

[9] Wang, Y., & Zhu, Q. (2014). An optimized QoS-aware service composition based on hybrid fuzzy-genetic algorithm. *Journal of Ambient Intelligence and Humanized Computing*, 5(1), 87–96. doi: 10.1007/s12652-013-0156-2

[10] Li, J., Li, L., & Liang, Y. (2012). A fuzzy logic-based approach for QoS prediction in service-oriented computing. *IEEE Transactions on Industrial Informatics*, 8(1), 170–177. doi: 10.1109/TII.2011.2171051

[11] Li, J., Li, L., & Liang, Y. (2012). A fuzzy logic-based approach for QoS prediction in service-oriented computing. *IEEE Transactions on Industrial Informatics*, 8(1), 170–177. doi: 10.1109/TII.2011.2171051

Chapter 12

Applications of Soft Computing Integration with Cloud, Fog, and IoT-Based Computing System for Systems

Narendra Kumar

School of Computing, DIT University Dehradun, Uttarakhand, India

12.1 Introduction

Soft computing, Internet of Things, Fog Computing and Cloud Computing are all related to each other in the field of modern computing. Here is how they are connected:

Soft computing: Soft computing refers to a set of computational techniques that aim to model and solve complex problems that cannot be easily handled by traditional, rule-based methods. Genetic-algorithms (GA), neural-networks (NN), fuzzy-logic (FL) [1], and machine-learning (ML) [2] are examples of soft computing approaches [3].

Cloud computing: This is a concept that enables quick access to a use pool of computer resources (such as servers, databases, applications, and storage) over the

DOI: 10.1201/9781032716718-12

Internet. Cloud computing has several advantages, flexibility, including scalability, cost-effectiveness, and ubiquitous access.

Internet of Things (IoT): IoT is a physical device network (e.g., sensors, actuators, wearables) that they are both linked to the Internet and are able to communicate with one another. IoT enables the collection, analysis, and sharing of data in real-time, which can be used for many applications like smart homes, smart cities, and industrial automation [4].

Fog computing: This is a cloud computing extension that tries to bring resources for computing similar to the network's edge, where IoT devices reside. Fog computing enables faster data processing, lower latency, and better security by leveraging the resources for computing available at the network edge.

The relation among these technologies can be explained as follows:

Soft computing can be used in cloud computing to optimize resource allocation and workload management in Figure 12.1, as well as to develop intelligent applications that can learn and adapt to changing environments.

Cloud computing provides the infrastructure and platforms needed to support IoT applications by offering scalable, reliable, and secure computing resources that can handle large amounts of IoT device data [5].

IoT generates vast data amounts that require real-time analysis as well as processing. Fog computing allows for the arrangement of lightweight hardware and software at the network's edge, resulting in quicker data processing, reduced

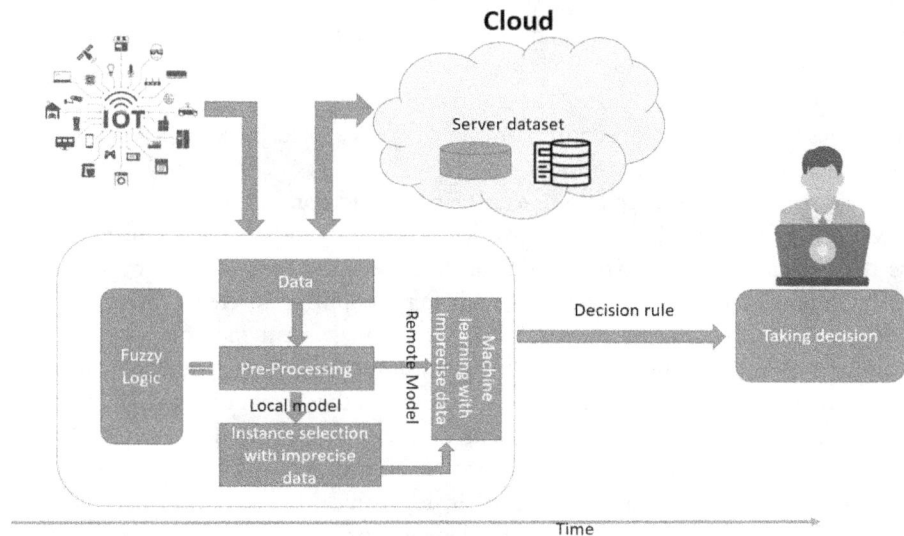

Figure 12.1   Decision rule process diagram.

latency, and improved security. Soft computing techniques can be used in fog computing to develop intelligent algorithms that can make data-based decisions that are collected from IoT devices and other sources [6]. Soft computing, IoT, fog computing, and cloud computing are interconnected technologies that work together to enable the development of intelligent, data-driven application in various domains like healthcare, transportation, manufacturing, and smart cities [7].

12.2 Related Work

A subfield of computer science known as soft computing that deals with the design and development of intelligent systems that can adapt and learn from experience. Soft computing combines a variety of AI technologies—including GA, NN, fuzzy logic, and machine learning—to construct systems that can learn and adapt over time. Soft computing has found many applications in cloud computing, fog computing, and IoT-based computing systems. This literature review aims to explore the various applications of soft computing integration with cloud, fog, and IoT-based computing systems.

Cloud computing technology enables the provision of computing services through the Internet. Soft-computing techniques such as genetic algorithms, NN, and fuzzy logic can be integrated with cloud computing to create intelligent cloud-based systems. In [8] they suggested a load balancing technique based on soft computing that may maximize resource consumption in cloud computing settings. The program employed a fuzzy logic-based technique to assign resources dynamically to distinct virtual machines depending on their resource needs. In [9] researchers introduced a virtual machine (VM) placement strategy based on soft computing that may improve resource utilization in cloud computing settings. To distribute virtual machines to real servers depending on their resource needs, the system employed a genetic algorithm-based technique.

Fog computing is a technique that brings cloud computing closer to end-user devices by extending it to the network's edge. Soft computing techniques such as fuzzy logic, neural networks, and machine learning are examples of soft computing approaches that may be used with fog computing to create intelligent fog-based systems. In [10] we present a resource management method based on soft computing that may maximize resource consumption in fog computing settings. A neural network-based technique was employed in the system to dynamically assign resources to distinct fog nodes depending on their resource needs.

In [11] is an energy-efficient resource allocation strategy based on soft computing that may optimize energy usage in fog computing settings. The technique allocated resources to distinct fog nodes depending on their energy use using a fuzzy logic-based approach.

IoT computing systems are networks of interconnected devices that can communicate with one another and with the Internet. Soft computing approaches such as NN, fuzzy logic, and machine learning may be used with IoT-based computing systems to create intelligent IoT-based systems. In [12] it is suggested that an energy-efficient routing protocol based on soft computing may optimize energy usage in IoT-based smart grids. To transport data packets via the most energy-efficient way, the protocol employed a fuzzy logic-based technique.

In [13] is presented a soft computing-based intrusion detection system capable of detecting and preventing security risks in IoT-based healthcare systems. To detect aberrant network activity and identify possible security concerns, the system employed a neural network-based technique.

Soft computing approaches are widely used in fog computing, cloud computing, and IoT-based computing systems. These methods may be used to build intelligent systems that learn and change over time. Soft computing-based algorithms and methods may improve the efficiency and effectiveness of these systems by optimizing resource use, energy consumption, and security. Soft computing is the anticipated evolution and use of these technologies as they mature.

Several works exist on the integration of soft computing with cloud, fog, and IoT-based computing systems. Research published in [14] presents a soft computing-based edge analytics architecture for IoT applications that use fuzzy logic and neural networks to increase the accuracy of data processing and decision-making at the edge. In [15] is introduced a cloud computing resource allocation system based on fuzzy logic that dynamically assigns computing resources to diverse workloads depending on their priority and needs. In [16], a survey on fog computing for smart cities includes the integration of soft computing methods such as fuzzy logic and NN to improve the efficiency and accuracy of data processing and decision-making.

In [17], a paper proposes an IoT-based soft computing approach for predicting energy consumption in smart buildings. The approach uses fuzzy logic and neural networks to model the complex relationships between various factors that affect energy consumption.

In [18], a paper proposes an intelligent resource management framework for Internet of Things devices in fog computing environments that uses soft computing techniques like fuzzy logic and NN to dynamically allocate computing resources to different devices based on their resource requirements and available resources. Computing in the fog is a categorization that overlaps with cloud computing and devices at the network's edge. In contexts characterized by fog, routers are reportedly prospective strong servers that might supply sources for fog services.

The purpose of the study in [19] is to develop an efficient algorithm that might reduce the average latency and energy consumption of real-time applications operating in a fog computing network. This is performed by deploying four distinct work scheduling algorithms in the scheduler of the fog node in order to assess their efficacy and performance.

In [20] an innovative approach to load balancing is proposed, using RTES (real-time efficient scheduling) in a fog computing setting. With this novel architecture, real-time activities may be completed on schedule while enhancing throughput and network usage, guaranteeing accurate time, and maintaining data integrity with little effort.

In [21] requests are handled not only locally by one area but also by many areas when extra resources are needed. As a result, an efficient task-scheduling approach is required to minimize the amount of time it takes to complete tasks while increasing work satisfaction. A heuristic-based technique based on their design has been developed to deal with the complexity of task scheduling. This approach was then validated by extensive simulations.

In [22], the goal of this design is to cut down on reaction time and power consumption. The idea of vehicle-to-vehicle communication has been investigated as a potential addition to cloud computing and is an important part of the architecture of the Intelligent Transportation System . Using probability and queuing theory, the authors provided a model for regulating the workload of automobiles at different levels of the VFC architecture. In [23] is a means of reducing the amount of power used by mobile devices (MD) and improving overall performance. They did this by taking into account three distinct kinds of queuing models in mobile device systems: explicit views of wireless channels, central clouds, and fog. This allowed them to generate analytical conclusions based on objective metrics. In order to process the data, they used an algorithm known as the integer programming model (IPM). At the present level, the evaluation of outcomes is greater than their plan. In spite of this, the researchers did not contemplate analyzing just fog-based scheduling approaches, despite the fact that fog was considered to be more efficient than cloud in the context of the study. In addition to this, they did not take performance parameters like the amount of time spent executing code or taking the network performance into consideration. In [24], researchers provide a first-fit, decreasing greedy technique for dealing with the challenge. This approach may be found in the referenced paper. The goal of this placement challenge is to cut down on application latency and energy usage so that fog node resources may be used more effectively. The validity of the method was tested using two different placement strategies: either applications were set up to operate in the fog-cloud interaction or they were set up to operate just in the cloud. In [25] and [26] many different scheduling methods are provided that are already in use and offer "hyper-heuristic algorithms" for assessment in fog and cloud computing. These many scheduling techniques include "First Come, First Saved," also known as "FCFS," "Particle Swarm Optimization," "Ant Colony Optimization Algorithm," "Simulated Annealing Algorithm," and "Genetic Algorithm," among others. On the other hand, not every algorithm that plays a role in FCFS has been tested and analyzed.

In the paper [27] the primary objective was to lessen the burden of labor by accelerating the processing of tasks, and it also included a subgroup-oriented attention to the resources that were readily accessible. It is claimed that costs may be reduced by increasing the operating length ratio in order to enhance user duration.

This, in turn, would minimize customer churn, which would eventually lead to an increase in operating revenue. Monitoring the incidence of failure is another crucial step in minimizing the use of computer resources that have a high failure rate. The suggested approach is trained to minimize the number of queues by properly distributing resources, which ultimately leads to the completion of user processes more quickly.

In [28], they conducted research on a variety of approaches to the management of resources for fog computing and presented their findings as a taxonomy. The writers place an emphasis on many facets of resource management, including scheduling and allocating resources, task allocation, load balancing, task offloading, and resource provisioning. The many suggested methods for resource management are contrasted by taking into consideration a variety of aspects, including case studies, the tool that was used, and quality of service measurements. Comparing these methods also involves looking at their benefits and downsides.

In [29] a practical design and methodology for supplying resources via the use of virtualization are described. When the authors put the suggested strategy into action, they discovered that the prescribed technique allowed for the most efficient assignment of available resources. When the cost of data transmission, entire response time, and use of bandwidth in the fog computing environment are taken into consideration, this technique emerges as the most appealing alternative [7].

In [30], we describe an efficient system. The notion of a virtual machine (VM) divided into fog nodes is used in this architecture to effectively process data from medical IoT devices and the body sensor network. The fog-based architecture that has been created may be used to overcome the cloud computing challenges that afflict healthcare systems. This design ensures the smooth and effective processing of patient data in a shorter amount of time while using the least amount of network bandwidth possible. In [31], we presented a modified marine predator algorithm (MMPA) for solving fog computing task scheduling in order to enhance the quality of service (QOS) that customers want.

In [6], a distributed trust mechanism was devised to safeguard the standing of fog nodes operating in the open. Smart contract technologies and the public Ethereum blockchain form the basis of the proposed trust architecture, which enables decentralized, trustworthy service provisioning between IoT devices and public fog nodes. The efficacy, efficiency, and general safety of the proposed method are evaluated.

In [32], we introduced a new bioinspired hybrid algorithm. This method is a combination of two different optimization techniques known as modified-cat-swarm optimization (MCSO) and modified-particle-swarm optimization (MPSO). Through careful planning of the activities and careful administration of the available fog resources, the purpose of this study is to make the average reaction time shorter while simultaneously increasing the efficiency with which resources are used.

12.3 Relationship among Soft Computing Integration, Cloud, Fog, and IoT

Soft computing integration, the IoT, cloud-computing, and fog-computing are all technologies that are transforming, and interact with the world around us.

Soft computing is a branch of a AI that is concerned with developing algorithms and techniques that enable machines to learn and adapt to changing environments. The smart contract technologies form the backbone of the proposed trust architecture in Figure 12.2, allowing for the decentralized, trustworthy provisioning of services between devices of IoT and public fog nodes. Cost, efficiency, and security are all considered when we try out the recommended method.

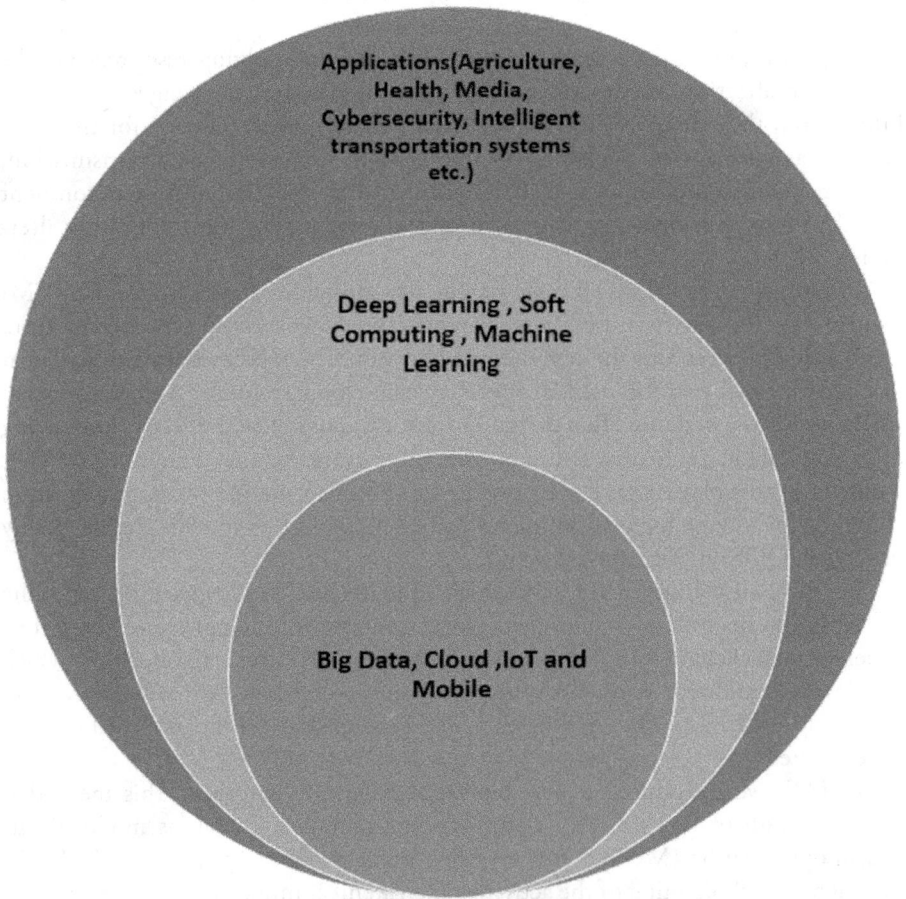

Applications(Agriculture, Health, Media, Cybersecurity, Intelligent transportation systems etc.)

Deep Learning , Soft Computing , Machine Learning

Big Data, Cloud ,IoT and Mobile

Figure 12.2 Relationship between technology and application.

Cloud computing is a methodology for offering computing services via the Internet that allows businesses to access and utilize computer resources on-demand without investing in costly gear and software. Cloud computing allows for the flexible, scalable, and cost-effective deployment of applications and services.

The term *fog computing* refers to a distributed computing system that moves computations to locations closer to the network's edge, which is where data is created and consumed. It cuts down on the amount of time needed to process data and the amount of latency experienced while uploading data to the cloud.

The Internet of Things (IoT) is a network of commonplace goods, such as vehicles and household appliances, that are outfitted with sensors, computing power, and an Internet connection. Examples of these products include smart thermostats and connected fitness trackers. The data gathered and exchanged between IoT devices makes it feasible to provide a variety of services and applications, such as smart homes, smart cities, and industrial automation.

Soft computing integration may improve IoT capabilities by allowing machines to learn from huge volumes of data produced by IoT devices. Soft computing methods like fuzzy logic and neural networks may be used to evaluate and interpret data from IoT devices, allowing businesses to make better choices and enhance their operations.

When it comes to dealing with the massive volumes of data produced by IoT devices, cloud computing offers a scalable and cost-effective platform. Organizations may immediately spot trends and abnormalities in their data with the use of real-time analytics and machine learning capabilities made available by cloud-based IoT solutions.

To reduce lag and facilitate near-real-time data processing, networks are increasingly adopting fog computing architectures. Bringing fog nodes closer to IoT devices may improve the speed and responsiveness of an organization's IoT applications by reducing the amount of data that must be sent to the cloud.

In order to provide effective and novel solutions for a wide range of applications and sectors, it may be helpful to combine technologies like soft-computing integration, cloud-computing, fog-computing, and the Internet-of-Things (IoT).

12.4 Soft Computing Integration with Cloud, Fog, and IoT based Computing System

Soft computing refers to a set of computational techniques that enable the processing of imprecise or uncertain data. These techniques can be integrated with Cloud, Fog, and IoT-based computing systems to enhance their performance and efficiency.

Cloud computing offers a scalable and adaptable data storage, processing, and analysis platform. Soft computing methods such as NN, fuzzy logic, and EA (evolutionary algorithms) may be utilized to increase data analysis accuracy and speed in cloud computing. Fuzzy logic, for example, may be used to interpret imprecise or ambiguous data, while neural networks are useful for pattern identification and prediction. Fog computing is a distributed architecture that pushes cloud computing to the network's outskirts.

In a fog computing setting, resource allocation may be optimized with the use of soft computing approaches. The location of a fog network's computing resources may be optimized using evolutionary algorithms, for instance, and the uncertainty in resource availability and demand can be managed with fuzzy logic.

IoT-based computing systems are made up of many networked devices that create massive data volumes . Soft computing techniques can be used to extract valuable insights from this data. For example, neural networks can be used to predict the behavior of IoT devices, while fuzzy logic can be used to manage the uncertainty in IoT data.

Overall, the integration of soft computing techniques with cloud, fog, and IoT-based computing systems can help improve their performance, efficiency, and accuracy.

Cloud computing is a computer approach in resources such as storage, processing power, and applications are made available to users over the Internet. In cloud computing, the user does not need to own the physical infrastructure, such as servers and data centers, to run applications and store data. Instead, they can use the resources of a third-party service provider.

Edge computing, or fog-computing, is a decentralized computing approach that moves processing and storage of data closer to the network edge—that is, where the data is generated. In fog computing, processing power, and resources such as storage are distributed across the network, including endpoints such as routers and switches, and devices such as smartphones and sensors. When compared to cloud computing, this allows for faster data processing and lower latency, which may be useful for applications that require real-time responses or deal with large amounts of data.

In Figure 12.3, IoT-based computing systems are a form of computer system that uses networked devices, sensors, and machines to gather and share data. IoT devices are often tiny, low-power devices that are meant to be linked to the Internet and utilized in a wide variety of applications, such as home automation, industrial automation, healthcare, and smart cities. In Figure 12.4, IoT-based computing systems often use cloud and fog computing technologies to handle and store the massive volumes of data produced by these devices. The integration of cloud, IoT, and fog computing may allow the development of intelligent systems capable of real-time data analysis and autonomous decision-making.

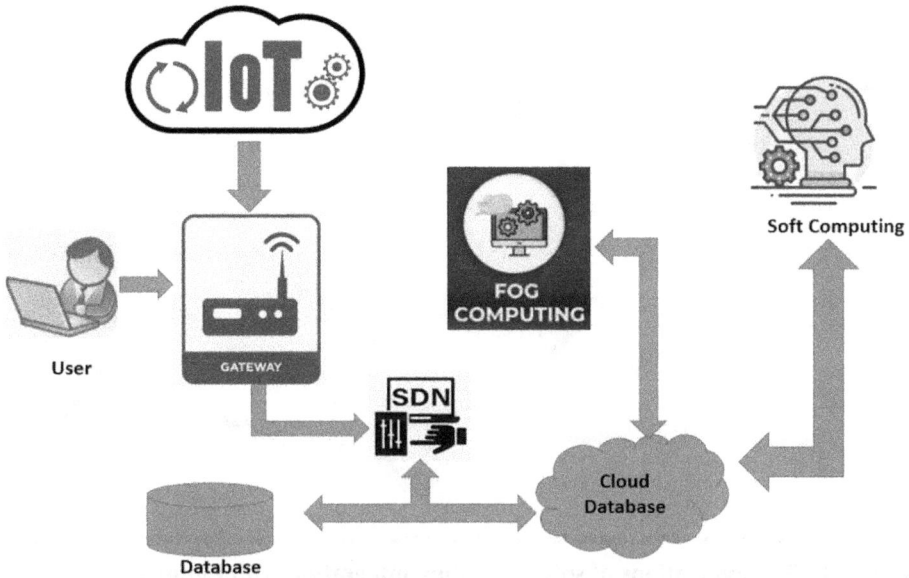

Figure 12.3   Conceptual model of cloud computing and soft computing.

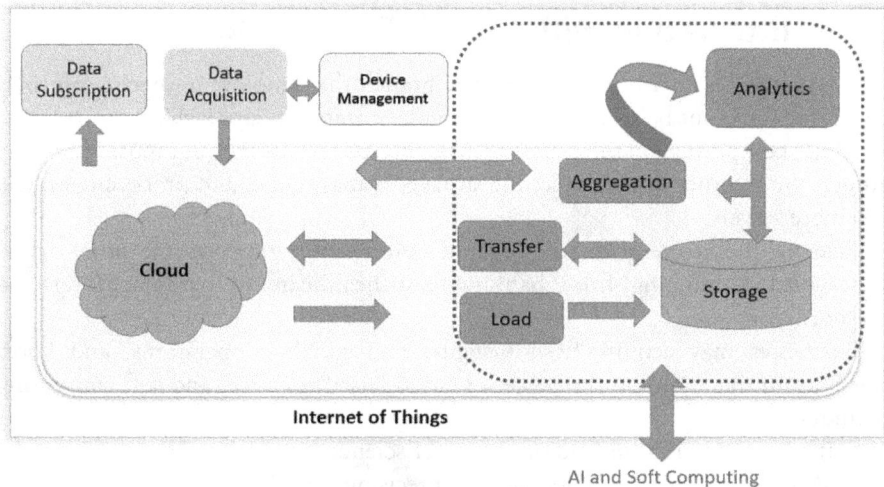

Figure 12.4   Processing between IoT and soft computing.

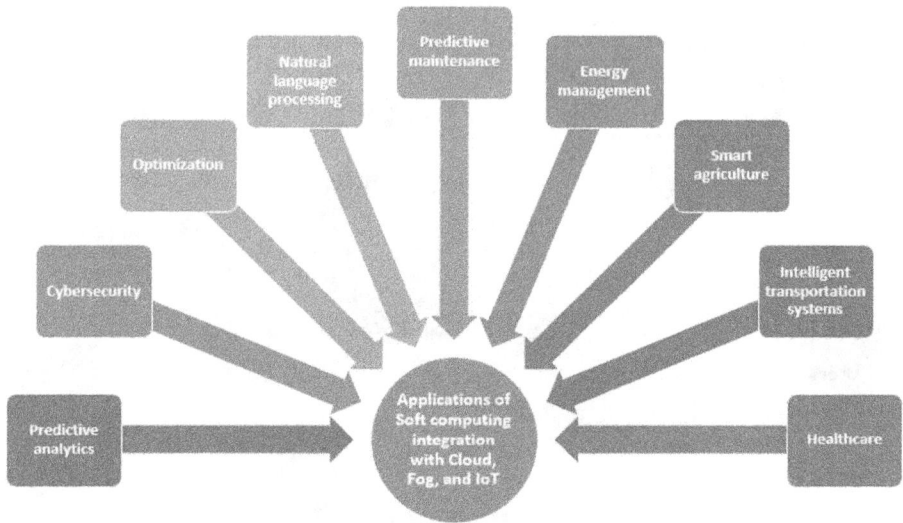

Figure 12.5 Applications of soft computing integration with Cloud, Fog, and IoT.

12.5 Applications of Soft Computing Integration with Cloud, Fog, and IoT

Soft computing is an artificial intelligence branch that employs imprecise solutions to issues that cannot be addressed using regular computer approaches.

Cloud computing, on the other hand, is a means of delivering computer resources through the Internet. It comprises the storage, management, and processing of data on remote servers.

Overall, the convergence of soft and cloud computing has the potential to alter industries ranging from banking and healthcare to manufacturing and transportation.

Businesses may acquire fresh insights, manage their operations, and boost their bottom line by using the power of cloud-based resources and soft computing techniques.

Soft computing is a subfield of computer science concerned with creating computational models that can cope with imprecision, ambiguity, and missing information. Fuzzy logic, neural networks (NN), and evolutionary computing are some of the strategies utilized to address challenging issues utilizing standard computer methods. Fog computing and IoT are two developing technologies that are being utilized to more efficiently and effectively link devices and data. Soft computing has various key uses in this area, some of which are detailed below.

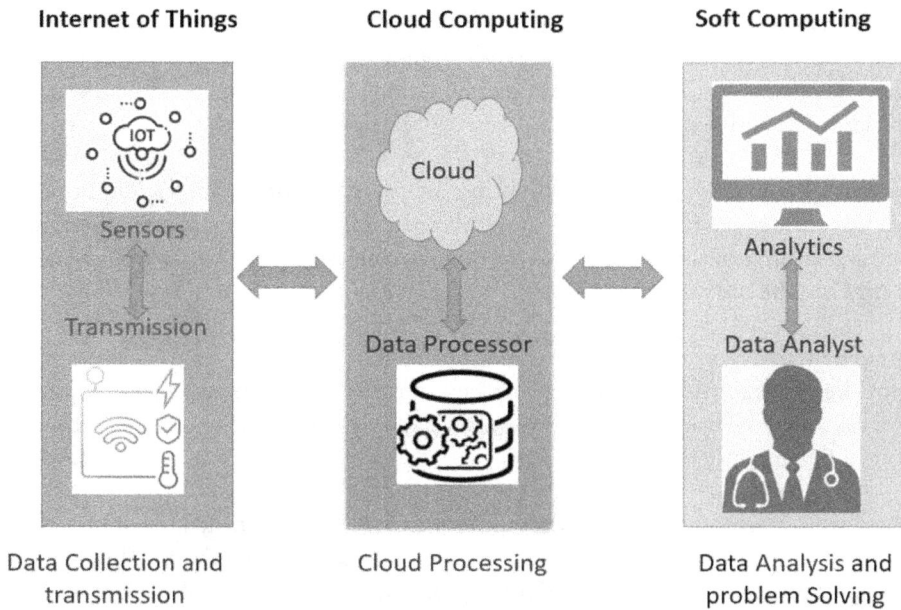

Figure 12.6 Soft computing integration with Cloud and IoT.

Predictive analytics: Soft computing approaches such as neural networks and genetic algorithms may be used to analyze huge amounts of cloud data in order to find patterns and predict future events. This is especially important in fields like banking and healthcare (see Figure 12.6).

Natural language processing: Cloud-based soft computing technologies may be used to evaluate text data in real time, allowing processes like sentiment analysis, chatbots, and language translation to be automated.

Optimization: Soft computing approaches may be used to optimize complex systems such as supply chains and logistics networks, with the computational burden handled by cloud-based computer resources.

Image and video analysis: Soft computing methods may be used to analyze cloud-stored photos and videos, allowing applications like face recognition, object identification, and video surveillance.

Cybersecurity: Soft computing approaches may be used to detect and prevent cyber assaults in real time by analyzing network traffic and identifying irregularities utilizing cloud-based resources.

Predictive maintenance: Industrial equipment, such as motors or turbines, are often monitored using IoT devices. Soft computing methods may be used to forecast when maintenance is necessary by evaluating sensor data in real-time, therefore avoiding expensive downtime.

Energy management: A fog computing architecture brings cloud computing to the network edge. To improve resource allocation in a fog computing context, soft computing approaches such as load balancing across several devices to conserve electricity may be used.

Smart agriculture: In agricultural contexts, IoT devices may be used to monitor crop health, soil moisture, and other environmental conditions. Soft computing methods may be used to evaluate this data and give farmers with advice on how to maximize agricultural output.

Intelligent transportation systems: Traffic data received from IoT devices such as cameras or sensors may be analyzed using soft computing methods. This may be used to optimize, minimize traffic congestion, and increase road safety.

Healthcare: IoT devices can monitor a patient's health in real time. Soft computing tools might be used to analyze this data and provide physicians with recommendations for improving patient care.

Overall, the convergence of soft computing, cloud computing, IoT, and fog computing has the potential to transform a broad variety of sectors, making them more efficient, effective, and sustainable.

12.6 Advantages of Using Soft Computing Integration with Cloud, Fog, and IoT-Based Computing System for System

Soft computing in conjunction with cloud, fog, and IoT-based computing systems may give numerous system advantages. Here are some of the advantages:

> **Scalability:** Cloud and fog computing systems may offer the infrastructure necessary to scale the resources required by soft computing approaches up and down. This enables the system to handle massive amounts of data and complex procedures without slowing down.
> **Real-time processing:** IoT devices that use soft computing approaches may be able to process data in real time. This is particularly important for low-latency applications like autonomous driving and healthcare.

Cost-effectiveness: Cloud and fog computing systems have the potential to reduce the hardware and maintenance costs associated with soft computing technologies. This is because the infrastructure is provided as a service, eliminating the need for expensive hardware and maintenance.

Improved accuracy: Soft computing methods can examine enormous volumes of data and uncover patterns that standard computer systems find difficult to recognize. This may result in more accurate forecasting and improved decision-making.

Improved security: Cloud and fog computing systems may enable safe data storage and processing. Soft computing methods may also be used to identify irregularities and possible attacks, hence improving system security.

Flexibility: The usage of cloud and fog computing systems may allow for the deployment of soft computing techniques on a variety of devices and platforms. As a result, the system may adapt to various surroundings and hardware specs.

Energy efficiency: Soft computing combined with cloud, fog, and IoT-based computing systems may result in more energy-efficient operations. This is because data processing and storage may be dispersed across several devices, lowering each device's energy usage.

Better Decision-Making: Soft computing algorithms can evaluate large amounts of data and provide insights and forecasts that may be utilized to make decisions. Individuals and companies may make educated choices based on accurate and timely information by employing IoT devices to gather data and cloud computing to process and analyze it.

Soft computing integration with cloud, fog, and IoT-based computing systems may provide various benefits, including scalability, real-time processing, cost-effectiveness, better accuracy, enhanced security, flexibility, and energy efficiency. These benefits may result in improved performance and cost savings for enterprises and organizations.

While there are numerous benefits to using soft computing, IoT, and cloud computing, there are some drawbacks to consider. Below are some of the potential drawbacks.

Complexity: Integrating soft computing, IoT, and cloud computing may be difficult and time-consuming, requiring particular skills and understanding. This might make implementation harder for smaller firms or groups.

Dependence on the Internet: Cloud computing needs a stable Internet connection, and Internet of Things devices depend on network access to operate. This implies that any problems with the Internet connection might result in downtime and data loss.

Security Risks: The integration of several technologies might expand the system's attack surface, posing security vulnerabilities. Cloud computing may potentially raise the likelihood of data breaches and cyber attacks.

Cost: The utilization of cloud computing and IoT devices may incur ongoing expenditures, such as subscription and maintenance fees. The expense of establishing and maintaining soft computing methods might be too expensive.

Data privacy concerns: Cloud computing includes storing data on third-party servers, which might create issues about data privacy. The adoption of IoT devices might also raise privacy issues since they capture sensitive data that hackers can use.

Compatibility issues: When integrating different technologies, compatibility issues can arise, especially when integrating legacy systems with newer technologies.

While the use of soft computing, IoT, and cloud computing can provide numerous advantages, it is critical to be aware of the potential drawbacks. Complexity, reliance on the Internet, security threats, expense, data privacy concerns, and compatibility challenges are among the drawbacks. Businesses and organizations may take actions to reduce these problems and maximize the advantages of these technologies by understanding them.

12.7 Conclusions

Soft computing refers to a group of computer techniques aiming at emulating the human brain's ability to reason and make decisions in an uncertain and imprecise environment. With the growing popularity of cloud, fog, and IoT-based computing systems, there has been a spike in interest in employing soft computing methodologies to improve these systems' performance and efficiency.

Soft computing combined with cloud computing may result in improved resource allocation, load balancing, and fault tolerance. Soft computing approaches like fuzzy logic and neural networks may be used to enhance computer resource allocation based on workload, as well as identify and avoid system faults.

Similarly, merging soft and fog computing may improve data processing and decision-making abilities. Soft computing approaches such as genetic algorithms and swarm intelligence may be used to improve data processing and decision-making in fog computing settings because of their dynamic and varied character. Finally, combining soft computing with IoT-based computing systems may improve data analytics through the use of tools and decision-making skills. Machine learning and deep learning are two soft computing technologies that may be used to analyze massive amounts of data produced by IoT devices and make accurate predictions and decisions based on that data. Soft computing integration with cloud, fog, and IoT-based computing systems has the potential to significantly improve the performance, efficiency, and reliability of these systems. As these technologies grow and mature, we might expect to see more new applications of soft computing in the world of computer systems.

References

[1] Kumar, N., Shukla, H., & Tripathi, R. (2017). Image restoration in noisy free images using fuzzy based median filtering and adaptive particle swarm optimization – richardson-lucy algorithm. *International Journal of Intelligent Engineering and Systems*, 10(4), 50–59. https://doi.org/10.22266/ijies2017.0831.06

[2] Kumar, K., Kumar, N., Kumar, A., Mohammed, M. A., Al-Waisy, A. S., Jaber, M. M., Pandey, N. K., Shah, R., Saini, G., Eid, F., & Al-Andoli, M. N. (2022). Identification of cardiac patients based on the medical conditions using machine learning models. *Computational Intelligence and Neuroscience*, 2022, 1–15. https://doi.org/10.1155/2022/5882144

[3] Laghari, R. A., Li, J., Laghari, A. A., & Wang, S. Q. (2020). A review on application of soft computing techniques in machining of particle reinforcement metal matrix composites. *Archives of Computational Methods in Engineering*, 27, 1363–1377

[4] Kumar, K., Saini, G., Shah, R., Kumar, N., & Gupta, M. (2023). IOT-based dam and barrage monitoring system. *Enabling Methodologies for Renewable and Sustainable Energy*, 151–161. https://doi.org/10.1201/9781003272717-9

[5] Suneja, B., Negi, A., Kumar, N., & Bhardwaj, R. (2022). Cloud-based tomato plant growth and health monitoring system using IOT. *2022 3rd International Conference on Intelligent Engineering and Management (ICIEM)*. https://doi.org/10.1109/iciem54221.2022.9853170

[6] Debe, M., Salah, K., Rehman, M. H. U., & Svetinovic, D. (2019). IoT public fog nodes reputation system: A decentralized solution using Ethereum blockchain. *IEEE Access*, 7, 178082–178093.

[7] Kumar, N. (2022). Future challenges in fog and edge computing applications. *Bio-Inspired Optimization in Fog and Edge Computing Environments*, 39–54. https://doi.org/10.1201/9781003322931-3

[8] Joshi, G., &; K. Verma, S. (2015). Load balancing approach in cloud computing using improvised genetic algorithm: A soft computing approach. *International Journal of Computer Applications*, 122(9), 24–28. https://doi.org/10.5120/21729-4894

[9] Xu, B., Peng, Z., Xiao, F., Gates, A. M., & Yu, J. P. (2015). Dynamic deployment of virtual machines in cloud computing using multi-objective optimization. *Soft computing*, 19, 2265–2273.

[10] Zhang, X., & Nazari, H. (2022). An efficient resource management mechanism based on developed political optimizer in fog computing. *Cybernetics and Systems*. Vol. 54, 1–15.

[11] Apat, H. K., Bhaisare, K., Sahoo, B., & Maiti, P. (2020, March). Energy efficient resource management in fog computing supported medical cyber-physical system.

In 2020 International conference on computer science, Engineering and Applications (ICCSEA), 13–14 March 2020, IEEE Explorer, pp. 1–6.

[12] Ilyas, M., Ullah, Z., Khan, F. A., Chaudary, M. H., Malik, M. S. A., Zaheer, Z., & Durrani, H. U. R. (2020). Trust-based energy-efficient routing protocol for Internet of things-based sensor networks. *International Journal of Distributed Sensor Networks,* 16(10, 1–20).

[13] Bhatti, D. G., & Virparia, P. V. (2020). Soft computing-based intrusion detection system with reduced false positive rate. *Design and Analysis of Security Protocol for Communication,* 109–139.

[14] Hassan, M. M., Hassan, M. R., de Albuquerque, V. H. C., & Pedrycz, W. (2022). Soft computing for intelligent edge computing. *Applied Soft Computing,* 128, 1–4.

[15] Zavvar, M. (2016). Fuzzy logic-based algorithm resource scheduling for improving the reliability of cloud computing. *Asia-Pacific Journal of Information Technology and Multimedia,* 5(01), 39–48. https://doi.org/10.17576/apjitm-2016-0501-04

[16] Perera, C., Qin, Y., Estrella, J. C., Reiff-Marganiec, S., & amp; Vasilakos, A. V. (2017). Fog computing for sustainable smart cities. *ACM Computing Surveys,* 50(3), 1–43. https://doi.org/10.1145/3057266

[17] Floris, A., Porcu, S., Girau, R., & Atzori, L. (2021). An iot-based smart building solution for indoor environment management and occupants prediction. *Energies,* 14(10), 2959.

[18] Tran-Dang, H., Bhardwaj, S., Rahim, T., Musaddiq, A., & Kim, D. S. (2022). Reinforcement learning based resource management for fog computing environment: Literature review, challenges, and open issues. *Journal of Communications and Networks,* 24(1), 83–98

[19] Mtshali, M., Kobo, H., Dlamini, S., Adigun, M., & Mudali, P. (2019). Multi-objective optimization approach for task scheduling in fog computing. *2019 International Conference on Advances in Big Data, Computing and Data Communication Systems (IcABCD).* https://doi.org/10.1109/icabcd.2019.8851038

[20] Verma, M., Bhardwaj, N., & Yadav, A. K. (2016). Real time efficient scheduling algorithm for load balancing in fog computing environment. *International Journal of Information Technology and Computer Science,* 8(4), 1–10. https://doi.org/10.5815/ijitcs.2016.04.01

[21] Hoang, D., & amp; Dang, T. D. (2017). FBRC: Optimization of task scheduling in FOG-based region and cloud. *2017 IEEE Trustcom/BigDataSE/ICESS.* https://doi.org/10.1109/trustcom/bigdatase/icess.2017.360

[22] Hussain, M., SaadAlam, M., Sufyan Beg, M. M., & Akhtar, N. (2020). Towards minimizing delay and energy consumption in vehicular fog computing (VFC). *Journal of Intelligent & Fuzzy Systems,* 38(5), 6549–6560.

[23] Liu, L., Chang, Z., Guo, X., Mao, S., & Ristaniemi, T. (2017). Multiobjective optimization for computation offloading in fog computing. *IEEE Internet of Things Journal,* 5(1), 283–294.

[24] Natesha, B. V. & Guddeti, R. M. (2018). Heuristic-based IOT application modules placement in the fog-cloud computing environment. *2018 IEEE/ACM International Conference on Utility and Cloud Computing Companion (UCC Companion).* https://doi.org/10.1109/ucc-companion.2018.00027

[25] Kabirzadeh, S., Rahbari, D., & Nickray, M. (2017). A hyper heuristic algorithm for scheduling of fog networks. *2017 21st Conference of Open Innovations Association (FRUCT)*. https://doi.org/10.23919/fruct.2017.8250177

[26] Gibet Tani, H., & El Amrani, C. (2018). Smarter round robin scheduling algorithm for cloud computing and big data. *Journal of Data Mining & Digital Humanities, Special Issue on Scientific...* https://doi.org/10.46298/jdmdh.3104

[27] Singh, S.P., Nayyar, A., Kaur, H., &Singla, A. (2019). Dynamic task scheduling using balanced VM allocation policy for fog computing platforms. *Scalable Computing Practice and Experience*, 20, 433–456.

[28] Ghobaei-Arani, M., Souri, A., & Rahmanian, A. A. (2020). Resource management approaches in fog computing: A comprehensive review. *Journal of Grid Computing*, 18(1), 1–42.

[29] Agarwal, S., Yadav, S., & Yadav, A. K. (2016). An efficient architecture and algorithm for resource provisioning in fog computing. *International Journal of Information Engineering and Electronic Business*, 8(1), 48.

[30] Awaisi, K. S., Hussain, S., Ahmed, M., Khan, A. A., & Ahmed, G. (2020). Leveraging IoT and fog computing in healthcare systems. *IEEE Internet of Things Magazine*, 3(2), 52–56.

[31] Abdel-Basset, M., Mohamed, R., Elhoseny, M., Bashir, A. K., Jolfaei, A., & Kumar, N. (2020). Energy-aware marine predators algorithm for task scheduling in IoT-based fog computing applications. *IEEE Transactions on Industrial Informatics*, 17(7), 5068–5076.

[32] Rafique, H., Shah, M. A., Islam, S. U., Maqsood, T., Khan, S., & Maple, C. (2019). A novel bio-inspired hybrid algorithm (NBIHA) for efficient resource management in fog computing. *IEEE Access*, 7, 115760–115773.

Chapter 13

Metaheuristic Methodologies in Service-Oriented Computing

Srabanti Maji, Pooja Gupta, Maanas Singal, and Pradeep Singh Rawat

School of Computing, DIT University, Dehradun, India

13.1 Introduction

The emergence of integration technology starts with a point-to-point connection between applications that are simple but tightly coupled with the convergence of several real-time data analytics, Big Data (BD), Advanced Technologies (AT), Cloud Computing (CC), Machine Learning (ML), Internet of Things (IoT), Artificial Intelligence (AI), and embedded systems that support one or more widely adopted but intricate systems and are made up of commodity sensors and actuators. This is made available through an Enterprise Application Integration (EAI) hub, which offers a number of apps to integrate through a virtual hub that is conveniently positioned in the centre and much easier to manage. EAI is not a methodology, unlike Enterprise Service Bus (ESB) or Service-Oriented Architecture (SOA). On the contrary, EAI refers to the internal usage of systems and services that enables the fusion of hardware and software. It deals with more integration links than middleware, along with distributed technologies combined. SOA has been identified as

DOI: 10.1201/9781032716718-13

the framework of the future for creating adaptable distributed applications over the Internet. Applications are provided as Web services, which may be discovered and constructed into hybrid solutions, which are coarser-grained services (Canfora et al., 2004).

In order to develop a new service with the greatest QoS possible while still meeting user or service designer requirements, the best combination of services must be found. In reality, when a single online service is often inadequate to finish a particular business process, complex demands may be satisfied by a composite of numerous Web services. As a result, there may be the magic solution that businesses have been searching for, and it has garnered the attention of several studies (Bertino & Chu, 2009; Jaeger et al., 2004; M. Li et al., 2013; Sherchan et al., 2008; Q. Yu & Bouguettaya, 2010; T. Yu & Lin, 2005; L.-J. Zhang, 2009). Web services, which represent a particular business activity or feature, are the essential building block for creating such systems. When services are exposed and made accessible to other Web-based resources and services, they can create more complex structures and interactions that bring additional value to aggregation services (Zhao et al., 2019). To fully support the extremely unexpected nature of such systems, services must be considered flexible, composite, and adaptable elements that can be easily changed, transformed, or even integrated with other services (Valle et al., 2019).

The foundational elements of SOA and service orientation have paved the way for a variety of emerging service innovations in technology, including AT, encompassing IoT, CC, and BD. At the same time, the primary building sections of SOA and service orientation continue to evolve through the incorporation of fundamental service innovations, procedures, and concepts, as well as supporting legacy systems (Aziz et al., 2020). SOA is defined by the World Wide Web Consortium (W3C) as a set of components having accessible and identifiable interface standards that may be called upon. Service orientation is a method of thinking about service-based development and the outcomes of services, according to the Open SOA Working Group (Group, 2009; Josey, 2011). SOA is described as an approach to architecture that supports this way of thinking. The SOA is a type of software architecture that, according to the Object Management Group (OMG), categorizes functionality around business procedures and packages it as interoperable services. It is vital to remember that application programming interface (API) development may also be used to create SOA applications. It is a set of resources that developers may use to facilitate the development of software. Developers will not have to continually create everything from the start since a decent API will provide simple instructions that they can use once and then reuse.

It is vital to keep in mind that application programming interface software may also be created using the SOA methodology. It is a set of resources that programmers may use to help in software development. A way of communication is provided via API and Web services. The sole distinction is that a Web service enables two machines to communicate with each other across a communication network. In order for two separate programmes to interact with each other, an API serves as a connection between them. Web services need a communication network, whereas APIs may be used either online or offline (Thompson et al., 2010). While XML-RPC, UDDI, and REST are options for Web services that frequently utilize SOAP, APIs can use any kind of protocol or architectural style (Bamhdi, 2021). APIs do not care about protocols. In June 2012, Gartner published its Magic Quadrant for Service Architecture for Comprehensive SOA Infrastructure Projects as an overview of the current SOA adoption trends. The research included 17 vendors, including Fujitsu, Red Hat, Microsoft, Oracle, IBM, Tibco Software, SAP, Software AG, Seebuger, MuleSoft, Magic Software Enterprise, iWay Software, Talend, Axway, WSO2, Fiorano, InterSystems without recommending any particular vendor.

Gartner named MuleSoft the industry leader in their 2019 "Magic Quadrant for Enterprise Integration Platform as a Service (PaaS)" research (Malinverno et al., 2016). The two primary criteria by which Gartner analyses each vendor in these studies are the ability to execute and the comprehensiveness of vision. The technical attributes and skills evaluated for the product's performance include technical and business maturity, technical extensibility, and functionality. The requirement for modularisation and standardisation, as well as the issues brought on by heterogeneity and inadequate latency, led to the invention, study, and development of SOC and SOC systems. Research, development, and deployment of SOC systems have expanded due to the widespread use of SOC – practically across all human endeavours—the interconnectedness afforded by wireless networks, enormous volumes and diversity of data, increased frequency of security assaults, and dependability expectations. Only the next generation of SOC systems could handle these conditions and demands. The state suggests that quick, high-quality research and widespread, effective distribution of the obtained novel outcomes are required. Therefore, it is necessary to emphasise advanced results sufficiently to address open research issues and significantly progress the field of SOC (Yangui et al., 2021).

13.2 Literature Review

Table 13.1 consists of 28 primary studies from renowned publishers such as Elsevier, IEEE, MDPI, and Taylor and Francis. The detailed summary and methodology used has also been described in detail.

13.3 Limitations and Future Scopes

The Software as a Service (SaaS) project is SOA's next generation. It is a cutting-edge approach to using Web services to access centrally hosted software applications. Because it frees consumers from hardware and software setup and management,

Table 13.1 Summaries and Methodology Used in Primary Studies

Reference	Journal	Year	Summary	Technique/Methodology
(Mesmoudi et al., 2020)	Elsevier	2018	A strategy capable of addressing the heterogeneity challenges was created using middleware based on service-oriented architecture. The technique was carried out in three stages, beginning with using REST API to gather data from various heterogeneous sensor devices, then implementing disparate networking user interfaces, and finishing with testing the produced middleware on gateways running multiple operating systems.	The establishment of middleware with a service-oriented design that can find connected devices using various networking interfaces and make its services available through Web services using REST API, as well as the existing methods of IoT middleware, were discussed. Different use cases for managing and processing data generated from heterogeneous IoT devices linked in a Bluetooth or Wi-Fi network were used to evaluate the methodology.
(Traore et al., 2019)	Taylor and Francis	2018	Remarkably, the management of the maintenance procedure for train component components is the focus of this study's enterprise information system servicization effort. Servicization is possible because of the SOA architectural approach, which provides a flexible set of design concepts used throughout modelling practises (realization and abstraction). Given the complex problems the corporate information system is experiencing, combining these two techniques may be beneficial.	The selected technique assists the regarded information modelling structure for handling maintenance. A formal description of connections that provides a clearer picture of model features distinguishes it. Furthermore, the monitoring/control model requirements make it simpler to understand the functioning state of the target systems.

(Continued)

Table 13.1 (Continued)

Reference	Journal	Year	Summary	Technique/Methodology
(Mohamed et al., 2021)	Elsevier	2019	The present federated identity systems' security weaknesses and vulnerabilities have been investigated. An adaptable security model leveraging critical public infrastructure and complying with SOA secure standards and specifications was proposed for identification federation at the inter- and intra-organizational levels to solve the observed deficiencies. A massive federated identity enterprise system for computing was used to test and implement the recommended architecture to reap the benefits promised.	The Intelligent Security Engine (ISE), founded on the Predict-Prevent-Learn layout, was created to defend SOA from security breaches. Utilizing a flexible forward solution that provides simple cross-organizational service-oriented application integration, developing a complete security architectural model based on the ISE principle with a proof-of-concept for federated identity management protection was feasible.
(H. Zhou et al., 2020)	Elsevier	2019	A Circular Area Search (CAS) method was devised to challenge multi-robot service scheduling in varied locations. The results demonstrated that the multi-robot app cloud platform given in this study's CAS methods is more valuable than the global search. Additionally, the service's search duration is reduced by almost 58% compared to the Greedy technique trial, proving the efficiency of the CAS approach.	Django is the Web framework for building a cloud-based SOA multi-robot services infrastructure. Then, based on the already-registered service information in MySQL and the Gaode Map, latitude and longitude, the service type as well as the service's scoring criteria, are selected as the service search metrics to design the CAS algorithm for evaluating the most suitable service and providing the support applicant with the best service.

(Almarimi et al., 2019)	Elsevier	2019	The study directed the search process towards identifying an appropriate compromise among the three optimisation objectives. SerFinder, a unique automated technique to suggest service sets for automatic mashup development, was presented for this purpose. The non-dominated sorting genetic algorithm (NSGA-II) was used as a search strategy in the set service recommendation problem, phrased as a multi-objective combinatorial problem. The goal was to find the best collection of services to combine into a particular mashup.	The non-dominated sorting genetic algorithm (NSGA-II) is used in the new multiple-purpose search-based approach for service set recommendation to find the best trade-off between service historical co-usage, working corresponding with the requirement of a mashup, and the available variety of the suggested offerings. In addition, the study offered a lower-granularity semantic similarity model to improve available matching based on specified parameters.
(Nivethitha et al., 2019)	Springer	2019	The precision of the confidence-based resource selection algorithms and the CSP's trust score depends on how well the TMP subset was chosen concerning the kind of service. The study attempt provided an efficient rough set theory-based hypergraph-binary fruit fly optimization (RST-HGBFFO) to determine the optimal service-specific TMPs. RST-HGBFFO beat the most sophisticated feature selection algorithms, according to tests on the QWS dataset, Cloud Armour, and the CISH—SASTRA trust feedback dataset.	The hyper-clique characteristic of hypergraphs was used to generate starting populations, which improved the efficiency of the binary fruit fly optimization method by reducing time complexity and preventing premature convergence. Determining the best TMP with the least amount of time complexity also involved integrating HGBFFO with rough set theory, in which each HGBFFO particle's fitness was assessed using a fitness function unique to RST.

(Continued)

Table 13.1 (Continued)

Reference	Journal	Year	Summary	Technique/Methodology
(Badawy et al., 2020)	Springer	2019	The paper presented a dynamic QoS provisioning framework (QoPF) for service-oriented IoT based on the backtracking search optimisation algorithm (BSOA). The QoPF framework suggested maximising the composite service quality at the IoT application layer by balancing service dependability and an acceptable computing time cost. The QoPF framework's success is measured using a variety of performance indicators such as productivity, latency time, and jitter.	Cloud computing and IoT convergence are common communications platforms enabling seamless, intelligent contact among physical and virtual things. The suggested framework intended to maximise the composite service quality in the IoT application layer by striking a compromise between service dependability and an acceptable cost of computing time.
(Dang et al., 2019)	IEEE	2019	The presented work acknowledged the difficulties and suggested a service-oriented architecture for orchestrating a fully application-aware mobile network. An orchestration platform for virtualized mobile networks was built as a prototype realization of the proposed architecture. A 5G enhanced mobility management application is used to evaluate the framework on our software-defined mobile network testbed.	The researchers used event calculus to describe the network layers and abductive reasoning for independent policy translation and provisioning of services in a 2-phase method to overcome the difficulties of multi-stakeholder and multi-layer wireless network design. For valuable insights into the suggested framework, preliminary performance metrics were examined.

| (Cakır et al., 2019) | IEEE | 2019 | In addition to a multi-protocol stack that supports the different types of communication as determined by a thorough requirements analysis, the research also offered a framework for dynamic QoS negotiation. For future autos, they produced a service-oriented gateway for QoS-sensitive communication. The recommended approach's efficacy was evaluated using a simulation model of an existing in-car network, and its practicality was established through a case study. | The suggested method may meet a variety of purposes by utilizing an adaptable procedure framework and a QoS mediation mechanism which allows services to negotiate any demands made dynamically. Clients can then receive QoS assurances depending on their QoS class in this manner. The presented idea was evaluated after a case study utilizing simulations constructed on a realistic vehicle infrastructure. |
| (Du et al., 2019) | IEEE | 2019 | The ability to determine a personalised reputation for each user at runtime still poses a significant challenge since the QoS data changes over time due to changes in user reputation. To effectively deliver a personalised reputation for each user, the study presented an online reputation calculating system, the OPRC. Many Web services are available in SOC setups enabling users to create SOSs. Compared to other techniques, the findings demonstrate that OPRC has excellent accuracy and efficacy. | Customers are selected for a Web service according to quality-of-service (QoS) feedback from customers with similar demands. The functionality of the same Web service differs depending on the viewpoints of various users. The OPRC uses MF and online learning techniques to generate personalized reputations based on the users' observed QoS data. Large-scale tests are conducted with 142 dependable users and 15 inconsistent users utilizing two QoS criteria to validate the approach. |

(Continued)

Table 13.1 (Continued)

Reference	Journal	Year	Summary	Technique/Methodology
(Saluja & Batra, 2019)	Taylor and Francis	2019	The elimination of antipatterns through refactoring operations has a detrimental influence on how software systems behave regarding power and energy consumption. Even if there are many defined antipatterns, their correctness is still a matter of opinion. Several factors are to consider, including boundary definition, uncertainty, rule conversion, and metric combination. The study focused on using optimized algorithms for antipattern identification to get beyond these constraints.	The research work that has been done integrates the current antipattern identification methods and a new, improved algorithm that not only uses static measurements but also factors into account dynamic metrics when it comes to execution. Additionally, the findings are improved using a genetic algorithm, and the existing and suggested models are compared. The results showed unequivocally that the recommended strategy had greater accuracy and a recall rate of almost 90%.
(Azzedin & Ghaleb, 2019)	IJACSA	2019	Organisations should use various vendors' top-tier technologies and tools when constructing big data solutions. The authors postulated that an SOA strategy might be used to overcome the shortcomings of the big data architectures for the offered oil and gas sectors. The research effort, therefore, put out the concept of decomposing complicated systems into specific discrete yet dependable	The framework consists of sophisticated systems built from a mixture of essential components. Therefore, as long as the requirements are satisfied, services may be offered. Because service providers are loosely tied, oil and gas businesses can pick the service that best suits their needs. Since every organisation is different, by offering the architecture as services, solutions may be customised for each one.

				A real-world application from the autonomous driving domain validated the proposed architectural candidate. Based on the matching simulation findings, the study learned more about the viability of implementing this candidate inside the presently under consideration future E/E architecture generation. The results show that early run-time evaluations are critical to deploying service-oriented architectures.
(Kugele et al., 2021)	IEEE/ACM	2019	distributed services. With the help of the suggested architecture, the petroleum industry may choose the essential SOA-based ecosystem services and build workable big data solutions. To assess and synthesise the hardware resources of automobile service-oriented architectures, the research's authors set out to develop a model-based design technique. To put the strategy into practice, the researchers used the ideas of design space exploration and simulation to examine and synthesise deployment variants early in the development process. Modelling and model transformations provide logical paths by also considering development speed and quality.	
(Masood et al., 2021)	Springer	2020	Using the study's findings, it was decided to create a semantic performance-oriented decision support system (SPODSS) for SOA. As services evolve, SPODSS provides recommendations for service reuse. Five structural components support SPODSS. These foundational elements include judgement,	SPODSS delivers provisioning recommendations for atomic services, composite services, and resource allocation. Handling new business requirements, dynamicity challenges, and assuring performance ensure the sustainability and adaptability of service-based systems. Performance criteria include functional appropriateness, time management, resource use, and dependability regarding accessibility, development, and hazard.

(Continued)

Table 13.1 (Continued)

Reference	Journal	Year	Summary	Technique/Methodology
			traces, machine learning, data, and semantics. Data is classified by SPODSS, which also validates it (via semantic enrichment, fractions, and analytical assessment) at various time intervals. Based on the combined results, consumption and prediction are then improved.	
(H. Li et al., 2020)	Elsevier	2020	The suggested model assessed the partners based on economic, environmental, and social considerations, all interrelated and contradictory. Then, using ranking algorithms, we must choose the best choice among all analysed couples. As a result, the hybrid model is a viable supplier selection strategy. As a result, the given technique is relevant for future supplier selection and assessment, and successful collaboration with suppliers adds to the supply chain's sustainability attainment.	With the help of the fuzzy decision-making trial and evaluation laboratory (FDEMATEL) and entropy weighting (EW), the offered method combines subjective and objective weights with a complete weight strategy. A later defuzzification VIKOR (LDVIKOR) is proposed to rank the optional options. An actual case study confirms the viability of the suggested approach.

(Chen et al., 2020)	Elsevier	2020	(BBO-EL), a unique Biogeography-based Optimization (BBO) approach for multimodal medical image registration, was introduced in the study report. The population had the chance to expand the search area, and each person was allowed to carry out the migration operation thanks to creating a combination of a complete migration operator. This made it possible to enhance the BBO technique's search power and better adapt it to multimodal medical image registration characteristics.	The Biogeography-based Optimization Technique with Elite Learning. The goal of the work was to develop and use the BBO-EL algorithm, a unique approach inspired by nature, to the multimodal biomedical image registration issue. Improvements have been made to the method BBO-EL, which relies on the principle of biological migration. The authors developed three operators expressly for this function: the combination of the undo operator, the elite learning, and the full migration operator.
(Dehraj & Sharma, 2020)	Elsevier	2020	The paper's authors have examined several elements of the upgraded ISO 9126 quality model's proposed quality measures for autonomous computing. Measuring a system's autonomic to establish if it is autonomic would be a generally accepted method of ensuring quality for autonomic computing systems. Autonomicity is a great way to guarantee the quality of autonomous software and to suggest new measures for quality traits to gauge the overall effectiveness of such applications.	The approach to evaluating the subjective quality of autonomy uses fuzzy theory, which combines Analytic Hierarchy Process (AHP). Fuzzy techniques are the most incredible option for quantifying human assessments because they are qualitative. Three different query optimizers were looked at to determine autonomic for empirical study. The outcomes of these research projects that had already been offered served as validation for the findings of the empirical analysis.

(Continued)

Table 13.1 (Continued)

Reference	Journal	Year	Summary	Technique/Methodology
(Georgievski et al., 2020)	ACM	2020	If micro grids are to fulfil their potential, the researchers hypothesised that energy systems must integrate structural and operational viewpoints. As a result, the authors suggested a unique design for an energy management system that considers both views and is based on service-orientation concepts. We tested the viability of the proposed architecture by running simulations using actual data from the study's prototype service-oriented energy management system.	In a unique service-oriented design for EMSs that takes the functioning of different types of micro grids into account, a collection of micro grid services was designed and placed within it. The implementation of the prototype illustrates the viability of our concept and methodology by modelling several individual components of a micro grid and the micro grid in its entirety.
(Mishra & Sarkar, 2022)	Elsevier	2021	A large-scale SOA (IoT-LSS) ontology that supports flexibility, interoperability, manageability, heterogeneity, scalability, and extendibility has been recommended. The large-scale SOA (LSS) concept is linked with using the semantic sensor network (SSN) ontology. A case study using the proposed clinical decision support system (CDSS) ontology has been considered. A thorough comparison between the proposed system and several already-existing IoT-based service ontologies was also carried out based on several criteria.	IoT-LSS, a unique ontology-based technique, was used to address a variety of IoT service restrictions. IoT-LSS uses the status property to identify any device's availability and unavailability. The SSN ontology idea is expanded by IoT-LSS, which may be used to determine the findings' geographic coordinates, dates, and times. IoTLSS may be coupled with other ontologies and allows service clustering, discovery, and large-scale service composition procedures.

(Wang et al., 2020)	IEEE	2021	The study concentrated on online start task identification in video interpretation and analysis, essential to multimedia security in smart cities. To address this issue, we put forth a brand-new model that produces cutting-edge outcomes when applied to the benchmark THUMOS14 data set. Regarding the requirements of the ODAS task, the model demonstrated efficiency and effectiveness using the most well-liked soft computing technology, deep learning.	The suggested model produced state-of-the-art results on all criteria on the benchmark THUMOS14 data set, thanks to a unique "looking back" method created by the researchers in the conducted study that improved the performance of the current models. The suggested approach might be spread over the entire city, operating as an intelligent city with edge and cloud computing.
(Calderón-Gómez et al., 2021)	MDPI	2021	Since present and developing methods employing digital clinical histories increasingly demonstrate their ability to maintain the standard of improvements in health care services, especially for CACD in the area of infectious diseases and due to the deteriorating persistent illnesses, the research conducted proposed an utterly novel structure for a Cloud-based eHealth platform concept that is concentrated on Cloud computing environments.	The SPIDEP system, which focuses on distant telemonitoring of older people, was designed, implemented, and deployed as part of the study. It is built on the SOA and MSA architectural patterns. Therefore, leveraging current ICT breakthroughs and AI algorithms, a repeatable framework was presented to help identify infectious illnesses and their derivatives early.

(Continued)

Table 13.1 (Continued)

Reference	Journal	Year	Summary	Technique/Methodology
(Lahmar & Mezni, 2021)	Springer	2021	The research provided a security-aware multi-cloud computing service composition technique using fuzzy formal concept analysis (fuzzy FCA) and rough set theory (RS), two methods with a solid mathematical foundation. We use the fuzzy correlations of fuzzy FCA and the approximation of RS to provide a high level of security for the hosting clouds and the chosen services. These techniques narrowed the search space by eliminating unreliable services and irrelevant shadows.	The suggested method involved choosing and assembling services in a multi-cloud environment. The first approach (fuzzy FCA) created fuzzy links between clouds/services and security regulations to assure accuracy. The second method (rough set theory) was used to estimate the individual's inquiry, which reduced the quantity of travelling notions and, consequently, the composing time.
(Liu et al., 2021)	Elsevier	2021	The study suggested combining the BWM with D numbers and D numbers BWM (D-BWM) weighting model to apply the BWM approach to specific scenarios. Following a discussion of the D numbers extended fuzzy preference relations (DNFPRs), an algorithm was designed to choose the best and worst criteria based on the DNFPRs. This was accomplished by computing the out- and in-degrees. The weights of the benchmark were also determined using a linear programming approach.	To deal with the conflicting perspectives of information provided by experts, the study's authors suggested a strategy that may select the best and worst criterion among n criteria based on subjective evaluation information from experts. The D-number evaluation matrix was tested for coherence using a measure of the consistency ratio, which was also provided.

(Kugele et al., 2021)	Springer	2021	One of its main limitations is the extensive integration of current designs into the internal communication network based on pre-set dependencies at design time. The authors of the work aimed to develop a technique for assessing hardware resources and synthesizing automobile SOAs based on service models independent of platforms. The researchers next concentrated on converting these models into an AUTOSAR Adaptive model-based platform-specific architecture realization approach.	The platform-independent component of the approach utilizes the concepts of design space exploration and simulation to evaluate and synthesize deployment options, that is, to map services onto hardware assets at the beginning of the development stage. These variables are refined further into AUTOSTAR Adaptive software frameworks, which serve as a critical input for the subsequent platform-specific portion implementation process.
(Wang et al., 2021)	Elsevier	2021	Recent years have seen a significant increase in interest in the cloud manufacturing service selection and scheduling (CMSS) issue. However, most current approaches refer to this as single, dual, or tri-objective models. This issue is only briefly addressed in work that concurrently addresses four or more objectives. To adequately address the CMSSS issue, it was necessary to consider the requirements of cloud platforms, consumers, and providers of services.	A multi-objective evolutionary algorithm with adaptive environment selection (MaOEA-AES) and an eight-objective CMSSS model was developed to solve the stated issue. The population was divided into several subregions using diversity-based population partition technology, and an APBI distance is intended to choose elitist solutions at various phases of the evolutionary process.

(Continued)

Table 13.1 (Continued)

Reference	Journal	Year	Summary	Technique/Methodology
(Sahin & Akay, 2021)	Elsevier	2021	RESTful API speed varies depending on the kind of issue being solved. The study is completed and implements the core Artificial Bee Colony (ABC) approach for autonomously testing RESTful Web services to address several problems with RESTful test creation. The Discrete Dynamic Artificial Bee Colony handles these issues with Hyper-Scout (DABC-HS) approach developed by the researchers as an approach to the service-oriented challenge.	The proposed observer bee phase generates a pool of all solutions and mutations and selects high-quality solutions relevant to found targets using a dominance-based selection method. The trial results demonstrate that, despite performing wonderfully in other problems, the DABC-HS performed best in four of the seven tasks.
(Vasanthi et al., 2021)	Springer	2022	The ubiquitous computing environment (UCE) is becoming more dependent on component-based middleware for USCE-FACS that can fully utilise interactive service characteristics and allow user-centric services in UCE. End users must locate the correct services to fulfil their different expectations because of the multitude of available services without ontologies and Metadata repositories (MR). The study focuses on how users connect with gadgets to facilitate extensive and quick accessibility to the UCE's offerings.	According to a user-centric methodology, the suggested effort tried to satisfy the user's demand by finding, recognising, and presenting the best service. The authors carried out unique testing where a user persisted in the USCE-FACS. The FACS's disconnected and online displays illustrated how, by learning about the user's behaviours, it could update its regulations online to the user's interests when the surroundings had entirely changed.

| (Beisel et al., 2023) | Springer | 2023 | Monolithic applications are frequently used to implement hybrid quantum-classical applications. Thus, in the performed presentation, the authors developed "Quokka," a service ecosystem that offers specialised services for executing each job in variational quantum algorithms to ease workflow-based creation and execution of quantum applications. The paper also demonstrates how workflows may be utilised to orchestrate an example quantum application. | The Quokka Hub and five micro services tailored specifically for quantum tasks comprise Quokka's system architecture. The fact that all Quokka micro services are written in Python makes it simple to integrate the two most popular Python-based quantum SDKs at the moment, Qiskit and Bracket. They also have a modular architecture that makes it simple for developers to add features to them. |

it improves the essential qualities of SOA, such as loose coupling flexibility and cheaper costs. Unlike SOA, which distributes specific business operations as services, SaaS shares the complete application with its clients as a service. Security is, yet again, the main issue with SaaS.

The study in Mohammed et al.'s 2021 work will take into consideration (i) enforcing the Zero Trust model on FIM, whereby every component, including IdPs, should be viewed as having the same degree of security for authenticating; (ii) developing an Identity as a Service (IDaaS) framework instead of treating identity management as an API, and (iii) enhance the security aspects of the ISE enabling Identity Governance and Administration (IGA) models, the latter of which is the most current trend.

The study conducted in Mishra and Sarkar (2022) includes extending the proposed ontology with assistance with autonomous, flexible service generation, which would be the primary focus of the subsequent research path. A suitable semantic reasoner will be developed using the proposed method to automate the design of large-scale services. This reasoner will allow us to assess system performance at the implementation level. A framework will be developed using an IoT service-based ontology to bridge the gap between Internet of Things (IoT) systems and context-aware management of business processes.

The researchers Almarimi et al. (2019) want to develop SerFinder as a crucial component of further work by adding a time dimension to capture the complex patterns of service composition better. When new services are introduced and older ones are retired, service ecosystems alter constantly. Additionally, we intend to involve the developer in the search process by recommending interactive services.

Future research in the gaps in the works of Badawy et al. (2020) will examine how the suggested structure may be altered to consider minimising the amount of power consumed by IoT composite services. More complex topologies and real-time software will be used to assess the efficacy of the suggested structure to accommodate new QoS situations.

The research done by Masood et al. (2021) still needs to be improved in a few areas for future study. For now, experts recommend continuing to use existing services and procedures. However, there may be times when introducing an innovative service with a fresh SLA, or an entirely novel business procedure is critical. It is crucial to determine the additional value from the application's economic perspective by utilising real-time cost analytics data.

There are further scopes that the study might need to cover in the works of H. Li et al. (2020). First, the selection of machine tools may be studied using hybrid methodologies (BWM, FUCOM, and TOPSIS) and more compressive assessment criteria (economic, environmental, and social factors). The MCDM (Multiple Criteria Decision Making) paradigm will be enhanced by developing a friendlier human-computer interaction based on artificial intelligence. The suggested strategy may also be applied to other industries, including service, supply chains, and markets.

The works of Cakır et al. (2019) are to calculate runtime delays in the actual world and to study the many interactions inside such a system. It will involve the construction of a demonstration using genuine automobile components in subsequent work.

Although the model proposed by Wang et al. (2020) performed better than expected, there is still potential for improvement in the detection precision in the high-recall zones. To improve the feature representation, we will include new video modalities in future studies, such as the motion field, and fuse them. To get better detection outcomes while using several cameras, we will further reinforce the model reasoning using strategies like the convolution of graphs.

Furthermore, researchers are looking at the potential for expanding our framework to additional eHealth domains (Takeda et al., 2020), such as early COVID-19 prediction (Casiraghi et al., 2020; Han et al., 2020; Rimsan et al., 2020; Zhong et al., 2020), patient monitoring systems for haemodialysis (Zainol et al., 2019), and the identification of heart and kidney concerns in diabetic patients (Ananthi & Bhuvaneswari, 2017; Patil & Malpe, 2019; Qiao et al., 2020).

Another potential area for future research is the application of this suggestion to other 4.0 industry areas, such as tourism or smart buildings (Saputra et al., 2019); however, additional studies are necessary to produce sufficient results to demonstrate the frameworks' resilience in terms of the modifications of its characteristics for these types of industries (Bigheti et al., 2019; Mendoza-Pitti et al., 2021; Prasetyo, 2018).

The works of Chen et al. (2020) involved subsequent research, which will expand the BBO-EL to address increasingly challenging optimisation issues and practical applications. First, as multi-core GPU is a popular acceleration platform for scientific computation, we may use concurrent computing resources to speed up the BBO-EL's execution (Kim et al., 2018; Y. Zhou et al., 2017, 2018).

The work of Dehraj and Sharma (2020), one of our following projects will be to estimate the weight of trustworthiness. The computation index, agent activation time, and failure tolerance rate have the lowest weightage among all possibilities.

The method employed in Lahmar and Mezni (2021) only examined if existing clouds implemented a particular set of security policies; it did not investigate whether they also validated it. Because of this, researchers will employ the history of vulnerabilities present in the US National Vulnerability Database (NVD), which provides data on standards-based vulnerability management. Future work will focus on fusing relevant cloud computing security ideas to create the safety-aware MCSC (multi-cloud service composition) in the vertical and horizontal composition setting.

The work of Liu et al. (2021) suggested as a paradigm in this study and needed more information on dynamically adjusting pairwise comparisons in light of expert viewpoints, which might restrict interactive dialogue with experts. The subsequent work is focused on merging specific intelligence algorithms with the D-BWM model to overcome this issue(Vescoukis et al., 2012; Z. Zhang et al., 2006). The D-BWM model's application to environmental monitoring will also be a vital component of the subsequent study.

The following issues need to be considered in future endeavours for the study that was done by Kugele et al. (2021):

1. The enhancement of communication channels among professionals and software developers in order to handle incremental advancement, which is not commonly utilised today.
2. The execution as well as evaluation of our structure design approach within a more comprehensive vehicle creation method.
3. The further development of motor vehicle service-oriented architecture.
4. The next challenge to handling versions and variants.

The suggested idea in the works of Vasanthi et al. (2021) is limited by the absence of an integrated architecture for the numerous services, such as flexibility, scalability, dynamicity, reusability, and fault tolerance, as well as a single global framework for handling the diverse user demands. Future development concentrated on creating such a complete architecture. We suggested an automated procedure for creating FACS sets straight from data for further work.

First of all, the work of Wang et al. (2021), despite the suggested algorithm's more fantastic performance compared to previous methods, has to be further investigated and enhanced in other CMfg modes to increase its applicability. Second, the considerable goal space of the proposed algorithm makes the search process time-consuming, and decision-makers often seek solutions they are interested in. As a result, additional work will be done to study and incorporate decision-maker's preference information into the algorithm architecture.

In the works Sahin and Akay (2021), future research might look at an improved algorithm that includes the proper methods to address the challenges' distinctive structure. Future versions may support the GraphQL query language, a well-liked method for structuring intricate RESTful API architectures.

13.4 Conclusion

By leveraging service interfaces that employ a standard communication language over a network, SOA is a style of software design that makes software components reusable. A service is a standalone piece of software capability, or group of functions, created to carry out a particular purpose, such as accessing a specific piece of information or performing an action. It may be accessed remotely, interacted with, or updated independently, and it has the code and data integrations required to carry out a full, independent business function. In other words, SOA unifies software components that have been independently deployed and maintained and enables them to cooperate and construct software applications for various systems. SOA saves developers from performing integration from scratch by exposing services using standard network protocols (such as SOAP, JSON, ActiveMQ, or Apache Thrift) to transmit requests or retrieve data. Instead, businesses can use enterprise service bus (ESB) patterns, which integrate centralised components with backend systems and make them accessible as service interfaces. As a result, developers may reuse current functions rather than having to create them from scratch.

The cornerstone of the SOA comprises three pillars: the service provider, who produces Web services and makes them available to a service registry. The service provider is in charge of the service's terms of use. The service broker or service registry is next, and they give a requester information on the service. There are public and private brokers. The architecture also uses a service requester, a service consumer, who searches for services in service registries or service brokers and then connects with the service provider to obtain those services. Services communicate using a "loose coupling" system in an SOA design. To convey information or coordinate a business process while minimising their reliance on one another, a system or network's components (sometimes referred to as "elements") are connected in this fashion. The software parts work independently as loosely connected entities. These devices are independent of vendors or proprietary technological systems because they deliver services or data over a network protocol. Consider these services the building blocks of a large consumer service, where each feature comprises numerous small services that can be developed, managed, changed, and replaced independently of other components (and services). These services can be independent, repeatable, and self-contained tasks of global system functionality. Thus, compared to its monolithic equivalents, SOA has significant advantages in applications connected to soft computing. Scalability, the ability to leverage legacy infrastructure in new markets, increased dependability, simplicity in maintenance, cost savings through increased development efficiency and agility, quicker time to market, and better flexibility may be summed up as these benefits. The SOA, however, is not without flaws and has several limitations. Some drawbacks include security concerns, speed ramifications, complexity queries, and data management challenges. The lack of consensus about SOA and its dual character as a business and technical strategy results in incorrect interpretation of the information that is currently accessible. However, the outlook of SOA is overall positive, and hence its applications in computing services are disposable, offering unparalleled advantages.

References

Almarimi, N., Ouni, A., Bouktif, S., Mkaouer, M. W., Kula, R. G., & Saied, M. A. (2019). Web service API recommendation for automated mashup creation using multi-objective evolutionary search. *Applied Soft Computing, 85*, 105830.

Ananthi, S., & Bhuvaneswari, V. (2017). Prediction of heart and kidney risks in diabetic prone population using fuzzy classification. *2017 International Conference on Computer Communication and Informatics (ICCCI)* 5–7 Jan. 2017, IEEE, 1–6.

Aziz, O., Farooq, M. S., Abid, A., Saher, R., & Aslam, N. (2020). Research trends in enterprise service bus (ESB) applications: A systematic mapping study. *IEEE Access, 8,* 31180–31197.

Azzedin, F., & Ghaleb, M. (2019). Towards an architecture for handling big data in oil and gas industries: Service-oriented approach. *International Journal of Advanced Computer Science and Applications, 10*(2), 554–562.

Badawy, M. M., Ali, Z. H., & Ali, H. A. (2020). QoS provisioning framework for service-oriented internet of things (IoT). *Cluster Computing, 23,* 575–591.

Bamhdi, A. (2021). Requirements capture and comparative analysis of open source versus proprietary service oriented architecture. *Computer Standards & Interfaces, 74,* 103468.

Beisel, M., Barzen, J., Garhofer, S., Leymann, F., Truger, F., Weder, B., & Yussupov, V. (2023). Quokka: A service ecosystem for workflow-based execution of variational quantum algorithms. *Service-Oriented Computing–ICSOC 2022 Workshops: ASOCA, AI-PA, FMCIoT, WESOACS 2022, Sevilla, Spain, November 29–December 2, 2022 Proceedings,* IEEE proceedings, 369–373.

Bertino, E., & Chu, W. C.-C. (2009). Guest editorial: Special section on service-oriented distributed computing systems. *IEEE Transactions on Services Computing, 2*(03), 245–246.

Bigheti, J. A., Fernandes, M. M., & Godoy, E. P. (2019). Control as a service: A microservice approach to Industry 4.0. *2019 II Workshop on Metrology for Industry 4.0 and IoT (MetroInd4. 0&IoT),* vol. 1, 438–443.

Cakır, M., Häckel, T., Reider, S., Meyer, P., Korf, F., & Schmidt, T. C. (2019). A QoS aware approach to service-oriented communication in future automotive networks. *2019 IEEE Vehicular Networking Conference (VNC),* vol. 1, 1–8.

Calderón-Gómez, H., Mendoza-Pittí, L., Vargas-Lombardo, M., Gómez-Pulido, J. M., Rodríguez-Puyol, D., Sención, G., & Polo-Luque, M.-L. (2021). Evaluating service-oriented and microservice architecture patterns to deploy ehealth applications in cloud computing environment. *Applied Sciences, 11*(10), 4350.

Canfora, G., Di Penta, M., Esposito, R., & Villani, M. L. (2004). A lightweight approach for QoS-aware service composition. *Proc. 2nd International Conference on Service Oriented Computing (ICSOC'04)-Short Papers.*

Casiraghi, E., Malchiodi, D., Trucco, G., Frasca, M., Cappelletti, L., Fontana, T., Esposito, A. A., Avola, E., Jachetti, A., & Reese, J. (2020). Explainable machine learning for early assessment of COVID-19 risk prediction in emergency departments. *Ieee Access, 8,* 196299–196325.

Chen, Y., He, F., Li, H., Zhang, D., & Wu, Y. (2020). A full migration BBO algorithm with enhanced population quality bounds for multimodal biomedical image registration. *Applied Soft Computing, 93,* 106335.

Dang, X.-T., Khan, M. A., & Sivrikaya, F. (2019). An autonomous service-oriented orchestration framework for software defined mobile networks. *2019 22nd Conference on Innovation in Clouds, Internet and Networks and Workshops (ICIN),* 277–284.

Dehraj, P., & Sharma, A. (2020). An empirical assessment of autonomicity for autonomic query optimizers using fuzzy-AHP technique. *Applied Soft Computing, 90,* 106137.

Du, X., Xu, J., Cai, W., Zhu, C., & Chen, Y. (2019). Oprc: An online personalized reputation calculation model in service-oriented computing environments. *IEEE Access*, 7, 87760–87768.

Georgievski, I., Fiorini, L., & Aiello, M. (2020). Towards service-oriented and intelligent microgrids. *Proceedings of the 3rd International Conference on Applications of Intelligent Systems*, 1–6.

Group, T. O. (2009). *Soa Source Book*. Van Haren Publishing.

Han, R., Liu, Z., Philip Chen, C. L., Xu, L., & Peng, G. (2020). Mortality prediction for COVID-19 patients via Broad Learning System. *2020 7th International Conference on Information, Cybernetics, and Computational Social Systems (ICCSS)*, 837–842.

Jaeger, M. C., Rojec-Goldmann, G., & Muhl, G. (2004). Qos aggregation for web service composition using workflow patterns. *Proceedings. Eighth IEEE International Enterprise Distributed Object Computing Conference, 2004. EDOC 2004*, 149–159.

Josey, A. (2011). *TOGAF® Version 9.1 A Pocket Guide*. Van Haren.

Kim, M., Liu, L., & Choi, W. (2018). A GPU-aware parallel index for processing high-dimensional big data. *IEEE Transactions on Computers*, 67(10), 1388–1402.

Kugele, S., Obergfell, P., & Sax, E. (2021). Model-based resource analysis and synthesis of service-oriented automotive software architectures. *Software and Systems Modeling*, 20, 1945–1975.

Lahmar, F., & Mezni, H. (2021). Security-aware multi-cloud service composition by exploiting rough sets and fuzzy FCA. *Soft Computing*, 25(7), 5173–5197.

Li, H., Wang, W., Fan, L., Li, Q., & Chen, X. (2020). A novel hybrid MCDM model for machine tool selection using fuzzy DEMATEL, entropy weighting and later defuzzification VIKOR. *Applied Soft Computing*, 91, 106207.

Li, M., Zhu, D., Deng, T., Sun, H., Guo, H., & Liu, X. (2013). GOS: A global optimal selection strategies for QoS-aware web services composition. *Service Oriented Computing and Applications*, 7, 181–197.

Liu, P., Zhu, B., & Wang, P. (2021). A weighting model based on best–worst method and its application for environmental performance evaluation. *Applied Soft Computing*, 103, 107168.

Malinverno, P., O'Neill, M., Gupta, A., & Iijima, K. (2016). Magic quadrant for full life cycle API management. *The Gartner Group. Document ID G*, 277632.

Masood, T., Cherifi, C. B., & Moalla, N. (2021). A machine learning approach for performance-oriented decision support in service-oriented architectures. *Journal of Intelligent Information Systems*, 56, 255–277.

Mendoza-Pitti, L., Calderón-Gómez, H., Vargas-Lombardo, M., Gómez-Pulido, J. M., & Castillo-Sequera, J. L. (2021). Towards a service-oriented architecture for the energy efficiency of buildings: A systematic review. *IEEE Access*, 9, 26119–26137.

Mesmoudi, Y., Lamnaour, M., El Khamlichi, Y., Tahiri, A., Touhafi, A., & Braeken, A. (2020). A middleware based on service oriented architecture for heterogeneity issues within the internet of things (MSOAH-IoT). *Journal of King Saud University-Computer and Information Sciences*, 32(10), 1108–1116.

Mishra, S. K., & Sarkar, A. (2022). Service-oriented architecture for internet of things: A semantic approach. *Journal of King Saud University-Computer and Information Sciences*, 34(10), 8765–8776.

Mohamed, M. I. B., Hassan, M. F., Safdar, S., & Saleem, M. Q. (2021). Adaptive security architectural model for protecting identity federation in service oriented computing. *Journal of King Saud University-Computer and Information Sciences, 33*(5), 580–592.

Nivethitha, S., Gauthama Raman, M. R., Gireesha, O., Kannan, K., & Shankar Sriram, V. S. (2019). An improved rough set approach for optimal trust measure parameter selection in cloud environments. *Soft Computing, 23*, 11979–11999.

Patil, S. S., & Malpe, K. (2019). Implementation of diabetic retinopathy prediction system using data mining. *2019 3rd International Conference on Computing Methodologies and Communication (ICCMC)*, 1206–1210.

Prasetyo, Y. A. (2018). Microservice platform for smart city: Concepts, services and technology. *2018 International Conference on Information Technology Systems and Innovation (ICITSI)*, 358–363.

Qiao, L., Zhu, Y., & Zhou, H. (2020). Diabetic retinopathy detection using prognosis of microaneurysm and early diagnosis system for non-proliferative diabetic retinopathy based on deep learning algorithms. *IEEE Access, 8*, 104292–104302.

Rimsan, M., Mahmood, A. K., Umair, M., & Hassan, F. (2020). COVID-19: A novel framework to globally track coronavirus infected patients using blockchain. *2020 International Conference on Computational Intelligence (ICCI)*, 70–74.

Sahin, O., & Akay, B. (2021). A discrete dynamic artificial bee colony with hyper-scout for RESTful web service API test suite generation. *Applied Soft Computing, 104*, 107246.

Saluja, S., & Batra, U. (2019). Optimized approach for antipattern detection in service computing architecture. *Journal of Information and Optimization Sciences, 40*(5), 1069–1080.

Saputra, R. Y., Nugroho, L. E., & Kusumawardani, S. S. (2019). Collecting the tourism contextual information data to support the tourism recommendation system. *2019 International Conference on Information and Communications Technology (ICOIACT)*, 79–84.

Sherchan, W., Loke, S. W., & Krishnaswamy, S. (2008). Explanation-aware service selection: rationale and reputation. *Service Oriented Computing and Applications, 2*, 203–218.

Takeda, Y., Yokoyama, D., Nakamichi, N., Inaba, R., Watanabe, K., & Yamada, T. (2020). Visualization of remote touch panel for dialysis patient on prototype bed. *2020 IEEE 2nd Global Conference on Life Sciences and Technologies (LifeTech)*, 54–58.

Thompson, J., Natis, Y. V, Pezzini, M., Sholler, D., Altman, R., & Iijima, K. (2010). Magic quadrant for application infrastructure for systematic application integration projects. Gartner, June 2012.

Traore, B. B., Kamsu Foguem, B., Tangara, F., & Desforges, X. (2019). Service-Oriented computing for intelligent train maintenance. *Enterprise Information Systems, 13*(1), 63–86.

Valle, P. H. D., Garcés, L., & Nakagawa, E. Y. (2019). A typology of architectural strategies for interoperability. *Proceedings of the XIII Brazilian Symposium on Software Components, Architectures, and Reuse*, 3–12.

Vasanthi, R., Jayavadivel, R., Prasadh, K., Vellingiri, J., Akilarasu, G., Sudhakar, S., & Balasubramaniam, P. M. (2021). A novel user interaction middleware component system for ubiquitous soft computing environment by using fuzzy agent computing system. *Journal of Ambient Intelligence and Humanized Computing, 12*, 4827–4840.

Vescoukis, V., Doulamis, N., & Karagiorgou, S. (2012). A service oriented architecture for decision support systems in environmental crisis management. *Future Generation Computer Systems, 28*(3), 593–604.

Wang, T., Chen, Y., Lv, H., Teng, J., Snoussi, H., & Tao, F. (2020). Online detection of action start via soft computing for smart city. *IEEE Transactions on Industrial Informatics, 17*(1), 524–533.

Wang, T., Zhang, P., Liu, J., & Zhang, M. (2021). Many-objective cloud manufacturing service selection and scheduling with an evolutionary algorithm based on adaptive environment selection strategy. *Applied Soft Computing, 112*, 107737.

Yangui, S., Goscinski, A., Drira, K., Tari, Z., & Benslimane, D. (2021). Future generation of service-oriented computing systems. In *Future Generation Computer Systems, 118*, pp. 252–256. Elsevier.

Yu, Q., & Bouguettaya, A. (2010). Guest editorial: Special section on query models and efficient selection of web services. *IEEE Transactions on Services Computing, 3*(3), 161–162.

Yu, T., & Lin, K.-J. (2005). A broker-based framework for qos-aware web service composition. *2005 IEEE International Conference on E-Technology, e-Commerce and e-Service*, 22–29.

Zainol, M. F., Farook, R. S. M., Hassan, R., Halim, A. H. A., Rejab, M. R. A., & Husin, Z. (2019). A new IoT patient monitoring system for hemodialysis treatment. *2019 IEEE Conference on Open Systems (ICOS)*, 46–50.

Zhang, L.-J. (2009). Modern services engineering. *IEEE Transactions on Services Computing, 2*(4), 276.

Zhang, Z., Wu, X., Yang, X., & Zhu, Y. (2006). BEPAS—a life cycle building environmental performance assessment model. *Building and Environment, 41*(5), 669–675.

Zhao, X., Li, R., & Zuo, X. (2019). Advances on QoS-aware web service selection and composition with nature-inspired computing. *CAAI Transactions on Intelligence Technology, 4*(3), 159–174.

Zhong, L., Mu, L., Li, J., Wang, J., Yin, Z., & Liu, D. (2020). Early prediction of the 2019 novel coronavirus outbreak in the mainland China based on simple mathematical model. *Ieee Access, 8*, 51761–51769.

Zhou, H., Zhang, J., Liu, Z., Nie, D., Wu, W., & de Albuquerque, V. H. C. (2020). Research on Circular Area Search algorithm of multi-robot service based on SOA cloud platform. *Applied Soft Computing, 88*, 105816.

Zhou, Y., He, F., & Qiu, Y. (2017). Dynamic strategy based parallel ant colony optimization on GPUs for TSPs. *Science China Information Sciences, 60*, 1–3.

Zhou, Y., He, F., Hou, N., & Qiu, Y. (2018). Parallel ant colony optimization on multi-core SIMD CPUs. *Future Generation Computer Systems, 79*, 473–487.

Index

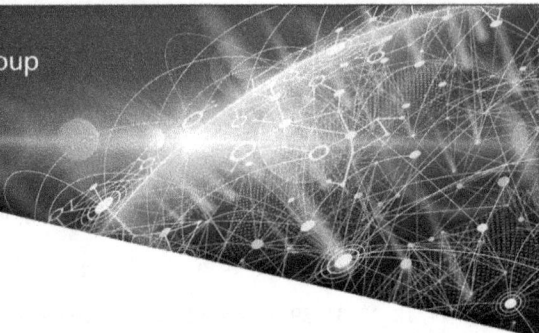

For Product Safety Concerns and Information please contact our EU
representative GPSR@taylorandfrancis.com
Taylor & Francis Verlag GmbH, Kaufingerstraße 24, 80331 München, Germany